Functional Programming in Java

From Basics to Expert Proficiency

Contents

Introduction

Functional Programming has risen to prominence in recent years as a paradigm that emphasizes immutability, statelessness, and the use of functions as first-class citizens. Java, predominantly an object-oriented language, has adapted to this trend by introducing robust support for functional programming concepts since version 8. This book, "Functional Programming in Java: From Basics to Expert Proficiency," aims to equip the reader with a deep understanding of functional programming principles and their application in Java.

At its essence, functional programming is a declarative approach to writing software. It focuses on the use of pure functions—functions that always produce the same output given the same input and have no side effects. This contrasts with imperative programming, where state changes and mutable data are more common. Functional programming's focus on immutability and statelessness makes reasoning about programs simpler and enhances concurrency and parallelism capabilities.

In Java, functional programming concepts are primarily implemented through lambda expressions, method references, and the Stream API. These features allow developers to write more concise and expressive code. The introduction of functional interfaces in the java.util.function package provides the necessary infrastructure for integrating functional programming techniques into Java applications.

This book is methodically structured to guide the reader from foundational principles to advanced techniques. It starts with a comprehensive introduction to functional programming, its history, evolution, and comparison with object-oriented programming. The initial chapters lay down the core principles, such as pure functions, immutability, and higher-order functions.

Subsequently, the book delves into Java-specific implementations, covering functional interfaces, lambda expressions, and the Stream API. These chapters include practical examples, patterns, and best practices for leveraging Java's functional programming capabilities effectively. The discussion extends to popular functional programming libraries in Java, including Guava, Apache Commons, and Vavr, demonstrating how they can be used to simplify complex problems.

Understanding immutability and persistent data structures is a critical aspect of functional programming. Dedicated chapters examine techniques for creating immutable objects and implementing persistent data structures in Java. Practical considerations, performance trade-offs, and common patterns are addressed to ensure a well-rounded understanding of these concepts.

Advanced chapters explore sophisticated functional programming techniques such as currying, memoization, monads, and function composition. These sections are designed to push the reader's understanding to an expert level, providing the tools needed to implement complex functional programming solutions in real-world scenarios.

Error handling is another area where functional programming offers refined approaches. The book covers functional error handling techniques using constructs like Optional, Try, and Either, contrasting these with traditional Java error handling mechanisms. Best practices and patterns for robust error handling in a functional style are thoroughly discussed.

Concurrency and parallelism are fields where functional programming's immutability and statelessness prove particularly advantageous. The book addresses concurrency and parallelism from a functional programming perspective, exploring Java's concurrency utilities, the CompletableFuture class, reactive programming, and the actor model.

Finally, the book culminates in a chapter on practical applications of functional programming in Java. Real-world case studies, domain-specific languages (DSLs), event-driven systems, and other practical applications are explored to demonstrate the tangible benefits and applicability of functional programming techniques.

"Functional Programming in Java: From Basics to Expert Proficiency" is a comprehensive resource designed to provide a deep and practical understanding of functional programming in the Java ecosystem. Whether you are a beginner seeking to grasp the basics or an experienced developer aiming to refine your functional programming skills, this book is crafted to support your learning journey and enhance your expertise.

Chapter 1

Introduction to Functional Programming

This chapter provides a fundamental understanding of functional programming, tracing its history and evolution. It distinguishes functional programming from object-oriented programming and highlights its benefits. Key concepts like pure functions, higher-order functions, and first-class citizens are introduced. The chapter also explores Java's support for functional programming, setting up the development environment, basic syntax, and common terminology to establish a solid foundation for further learning.

1.1 What is Functional Programming?

Functional programming is a programming paradigm that treats computation as the evaluation of mathematical functions and avoids changing-state and mutable data. This paradigm contrasts sharply with imperative programming, where the computation is performed via statements that change a program's state. Functional programming emphasizes the application of functions, in a manner akin to mathematical functions that consistently produce the same output for the same input without side effects.

In a functional programming paradigm, functions are first-class citizens. This means that functions can be passed as arguments to other functions, returned as values from other functions, and assigned to variables. The focus is on the 'what' rather than the 'how' in problem-solving.

Pure Functions are a core concept in functional programming. A pure function is a function where the return value is only determined by its input values, without observable side effects. Pure functions ensure referential transparency, which implies that a function, given the same inputs, will always return the same outputs. As a result, pure functions make the reasoning about program behavior more straightforward and predictable.

```
public int add(int a, int b) {
    return a + b;
}
```

In the example above, the function add is pure because it consistently returns the same result given the same inputs and does not have side effects such as changing global variables or modifying input parameters.

Contrary to pure functions, impure functions may involve side effects such as modifying a global state, changing the contents of data structures, or I/O operations. Functional programming minimizes and controls these side effects to maintain function purity and declarative code styles.

Higher-Order Functions take other functions as parameters or return a function as a result. These functions allow the construction of more abstract, reusable, and composable code structures. Common higher-order functions include map, filter, and reduce, which operate on collections of data.

```
import java.util.function.Function;

public class HigherOrderFunction {

    public static Function<Integer, Integer> add(int x) {
        return y -> x + y;
    }

    public static void main(String[] args) {
        Function<Integer, Integer> addFive = add(5);
        System.out.println(addFive.apply(3)); // Output: 8
    }
}
```

In the above example, the add method is a higher-order function because it returns a function that adds a given integer to its input. This demonstrates function composition, where simple functions are combined to build more complex functionality.

The concept of **First-Class Citizens** in functional programming indicates that functions are treated as first-class entities. This implies that functions can be stored in data structures, passed as arguments, or returned from other functions. This property enhances function reusability and composability, leading to cleaner and more modular code design.

```
import java.util.function.Function;

public class FirstClassFunctions {

    public static void main(String[] args) {
        Function<Integer, Integer> square = x -> x * x;
        Function<Integer, Integer> doubleIt = x -> x * 2;

        applyAndPrint(square, 5); // Output: 25
        applyAndPrint(doubleIt, 5); // Output: 10
    }

    public static void applyAndPrint(Function<Integer, Integer> func, int value) {
        System.out.println(func.apply(value));
    }
}
```

Here, square and doubleIt are functions assigned to variables and passed as arguments to the applyAndPrint method, demonstrating the first-class citizen property.

In essence, functional programming in Java is facilitated by functional interfaces like Function<T,R>, Predicate<T>, Consumer<T>, and Supplier<T>, which are part of the java.util.function package. These interfaces enable the creation and manipulation of functions as first-class entities.

- **Function<T,R>**: Represents a function that accepts one argument and produces a result.
- **Predicate<T>**: Represents a function that accepts one argument and returns a boolean-valued result.
- **Consumer<T>**: Represents a function that accepts one argument and performs some operation without returning a result.
- **Supplier<T>**: Represents a function that does not accept any arguments and produces a result.

A functional programming approach can make code easier to test and maintain by promoting immutability and avoiding side effects. Functions can be composed to build more complex operations, leading to a concise and expressive codebase.

1.2 History and Evolution of Functional Programming

Functional programming's roots trace back to the formal foundations of computation theory and mathematical logic. It was heavily influenced by lambda calculus, a formal system devised by Alonzo Church in the 1930s. Lambda calculus provided a framework for defining functions and deriving their outputs, using function abstraction and application as primary tools. The notation and operations defined within lambda calculus remain crucial to understanding functional programming principles.

The programming paradigm emerged more distinctly during the 1950s and 1960s alongside the development of modern computing. John McCarthy's invention of Lisp in 1958 marked one of the initial practical implementations of functional ideas. Lisp (short for List Processing) introduced many concepts fundamental to functional programming, including recursive functions, conditionals, and a dynamic type system.

The evolution of functional programming continued through the 1970s and 1980s, with significant academic contributions. Two other notable languages from this era, ML (MetaLanguage) and Scheme, further solidified functional programming's place in the computational landscape.

ML was developed in the 1970s as part of a theorem-proving project at the University of Edinburgh. It introduced important features such as a strong static type system and pattern matching, both of which have influenced many functional languages and paradigms in subsequent years.

Scheme, an offshoot of Lisp created by Guy L. Steele Jr. and Gerald Jay Sussman, synthesized lexical scoping, first-class procedures, and a minimalist design philosophy. Scheme's simplicity and power significantly impacted programming language design, promoting functional concepts widely.

The 1980s and 1990s saw even more growth and diversity in functional programming languages. Haskell, first released in 1990, became a prominent language that embraced purely functional programming. Developed by a committee of researchers and named after logician

Haskell Curry, Haskell provided a platform for exploring lazy evaluation, type inference, and monads, which have become essential concepts in advanced functional programming.

Here is an example of a function written in Haskell, demonstrating lazy evaluation:

```
-- Haskell code demonstrating lazy evaluation
fibonacci :: Int -> Int
fibonacci 0 = 0
fibonacci 1 = 1
fibonacci n = fibonacci (n - 1) + fibonacci (n - 2)
```

Functional programming's influence expanded into other paradigms, impacting the design and features of multi-paradigm languages. By the 2000s, languages such as Python, JavaScript, and Ruby began incorporating functional programming constructs like first-class functions, closures, and higher-order functions.

Java, traditionally an object-oriented language, integrated functional programming features more extensively with the release of Java 8 in 2014. This release included the addition of lambda expressions, the Stream API, and functional interfaces, allowing developers to utilize functional programming paradigms within the Java ecosystem.

Example of a lambda expression in Java:

```
// Java code demonstrating lambda expression
import java.util.Arrays;
import java.util.List;

public class LambdaExample {
    public static void main(String[] args) {
        List<String> names = Arrays.asList("Alice", "Bob", "Charlie");
        names.forEach(name -> System.out.println(name));
    }
}
```

The embrace of functional programming paradigms extended beyond language features and into development environments and communities. Projects like Apache Spark, a unified analytics engine for large-scale data processing, relied heavily on functional paradigms, further cementing functional programming's utility and popularity in modern software development.

Presently, functional programming stands as a robust paradigm well-suited for concurrent and parallel processing. Its focus on immutability, stateless functions, and higher-order functions positions it advantageously for tackling challenges posed by modern, complex, and distributed systems. The synthesis of fundamental theoretical concepts from lambda calculus with pragmatic language features and optimization techniques ensures that functional programming continues to play a pivotal role in computer science and software engineering.

1.3 Functional Programming vs Object-Oriented Programming

Functional programming (FP) and object-oriented programming (OOP) are two paradigms that fundamentally differ in their approach to problem-solving and system design. Understanding these differences is pivotal in leveraging Java's functional programming capabilities to complement its object-oriented features.

OOP is built around the concept of "objects," which are instances of classes encompassing both data (attributes) and behavior (methods). The primary focus is on encapsulating state and behavior within objects and managing interactions between them through methods. In contrast, FP emphasizes the use of pure functions and immutable data, aiming to minimize side-effects and facilitate reasoning about code. The key characteristics of each paradigm are essential for gaining a deeper understanding:

1. Data and State Management In OOP, objects maintain state within their internal fields and provide methods to manipulate this state. State changes are intrinsic to object behavior, enabling modeling of real-world entities. Here is an illustrative example in Java:

```
public class BankAccount {
    private double balance;

    public BankAccount(double initialBalance) {
        this.balance = initialBalance;
    }

    public void deposit(double amount) {
        balance += amount;
    }

    public void withdraw(double amount) {
        if (amount <= balance) {
            balance -= amount;
        } else {
            System.out.println("Insufficient funds");
        }
    }

    public double getBalance() {
        return balance;
    }
```

```
}
```

In FP, the emphasis is on immutable data and pure functions, which do not alter state but return new data derived from the input. Here is how the same bank account example is handled in a functional style using Java:

```
import java.util.function.Function;

public class BankAccount {
    private final double balance;

    public BankAccount(double initialBalance) {
        this.balance = initialBalance;
    }

    public BankAccount deposit(double amount) {
        return new BankAccount(this.balance + amount);
    }

    public BankAccount withdraw(double amount) {
        if (amount <= balance) {
            return new BankAccount(this.balance - amount);
        } else {
            System.out.println("Insufficient funds");
            return this;
        }
    }

    public double getBalance() {
        return balance;
    }
}
```

2. Methods vs. Functions In OOP, methods are functions associated with an object/class, and they often operate by modifying the object's internal state. Consider the method withdraw in the BankAccount class:

```
public void withdraw(double amount) {
    if (amount <= balance) {
        balance -= amount;
    } else {
        System.out.println("Insufficient funds");
    }
}
```

FP promotes the use of pure functions, which have no side-effects and always produce the same output given the same input. This deterministic behavior simplifies testing and reasoning about code:

```
public class BankFunctions {
    public static double withdraw(double balance, double amount) {
        if (amount <= balance) {
            return balance - amount;
        } else {
            System.out.println("Insufficient funds");
```

```
            return balance;
        }
    }
}
```

Invocation of the function:

```
double newBalance = BankFunctions.withdraw(currentBalance, withdrawalAmount);
```

3. Reusability and Extensibility OOP encourages reusability and extensibility through mechanisms like inheritance and polymorphism. New behaviors can be added by extending existing classes or implementing interfaces. Here's a simple example:

```
public class SavingsAccount extends BankAccount {
    private double interestRate;

    public SavingsAccount(double initialBalance, double interestRate) {
        super(initialBalance);
        this.interestRate = interestRate;
    }

    public void applyInterest() {
        double interest = getBalance() * interestRate / 100;
        deposit(interest);
    }
}
```

Here, SavingsAccount extends BankAccount to add interest-related functionality.

FP achieves reusability by composing small, reusable functions. Higher-order functions (functions that take other functions as arguments or return them as results) and function composition are common techniques:

```
import java.util.function.Function;

public class AccountOperations {
    public static Function<Double, Double> deposit(double amount) {
        return balance -> balance + amount;
    }

    public static Function<Double, Double> withdraw(double amount) {
        return balance -> (amount <= balance) ? balance - amount : balance;
    }
}
```

Functions can be composed to build complex operations:

```
Function<Double, Double> transaction = AccountOperations.deposit(100).andThen(
    AccountOperations.withdraw(50));
double finalBalance = transaction.apply(initialBalance);
```

4. Concurrency and Parallelism OOP approaches to concurrency often rely on synchronization mechanisms to manage concurrent access to shared state. This can lead to complex, error-prone code. For instance:

```
public class ConcurrentBankAccount {
    private double balance;

    public synchronized void deposit(double amount) {
        balance += amount;
    }

    public synchronized void withdraw(double amount) {
        if (amount <= balance) {
            balance -= amount;
        } else {
            System.out.println("Insufficient funds");
        }
    }

    public double getBalance() {
        return balance;
    }
}
```

FP, with its emphasis on immutability and stateless computations, naturally fits into parallel computation models. Pure functions can be executed in parallel without the risk of state corruption:

```
import java.util.Arrays;

public class ParallelProcessing {
    public static double[] processBalances(double[] balances, Function<Double, Double>
            operation) {
        return Arrays.stream(balances).parallel().map(operation::apply).toArray();
    }
}
```

5. Error Handling In OOP, error handling is typically done using exceptions. Methods throw exceptions that are caught and handled within try-catch blocks:

```
public class BankAccount {
    private double balance;

    public void withdraw(double amount) throws Exception {
        if (amount <= balance) {
            balance -= amount;
        } else {
            throw new Exception("Insufficient funds");
        }
    }
}
```

In FP, errors can be handled through constructs like Option, Either, or Try, allowing for safer and more predictable error management:

```
import java.util.Optional;

public class BankFunctions {
    public static Optional<Double> withdraw(double balance, double amount) {
        if (amount <= balance) {
            return Optional.of(balance - amount);
        } else {
            return Optional.empty();
        }
    }
}
```

Handling the result:

```
Optional<Double> newBalance = BankFunctions.withdraw(currentBalance,
    withdrawalAmount);
newBalance.ifPresentOrElse(
    balance -> System.out.println("New balance: " + balance),
    () -> System.out.println("Insufficient funds")
);
```

Both paradigms offer distinct advantages, and modern Java allows for a hybrid approach, leveraging the strengths of both OOP and FP. Understanding these differences empowers developers to choose the most appropriate tools and techniques for their specific use cases.

1.4 Benefits of Functional Programming

Functional programming (FP) offers numerous advantages, especially in modern software development, where applications demand higher scalability, maintainability, and robustness. Exploring these benefits provides deeper insights into why FP is becoming increasingly prominent in software engineering.

Immutability and State Management

One of the foundational aspects of FP is immutability. In FP, data structures are immutable, meaning once they are created, they cannot be modified. This immutability leads to easier reasoning about code as functions do not produce side effects by altering the state. Consider the following Java example:

```
import java.util.List;
import java.util.ArrayList;
import java.util.Collections;

public class ImmutableExample {
    public static void main(String[] args) {
        List<String> strings = new ArrayList<>();
        strings.add("Functional");
```

```
        strings.add("Programming");

        List<String> immutableStrings = Collections.unmodifiableList(strings);
        try {
            immutableStrings.add("in Java"); // This will throw
                UnsupportedOperationException
        } catch (UnsupportedOperationException e) {
            System.out.println("Cannot modify immutable list");
        }
    }
}
```

The use of immutable objects helps avoid unintended side effects, making the code more predictable and easier to debug.

Pure Functions

Pure functions, another critical concept in FP, produce the same output for the same input and have no side effects. This predictability enables various benefits:

- **Referential Transparency**: Pure functions uphold the property of referential transparency, where a function call can be replaced with its result without changing the application's behavior.
- **Easy Testing and Debugging**: Since pure functions depend only on their inputs and not on any external state, they are inherently easier to test and debug.

```
public class PureFunctions {
    public static int add(int a, int b) {
        return a + b;
    }

    public static void main(String[] args) {
        System.out.println(add(2, 3)); // Outputs 5
        System.out.println(add(2, 3)); // Always outputs 5
    }
}
```

Concurrency and Parallelism

FP excels in concurrent and parallel execution environments. Because pure functions do not alter shared state, problems associated with state synchronization and race conditions are mitigated.

```
import java.util.Arrays;
import java.util.concurrent.ForkJoinPool;

public class ParallelProcessing {
    public static void main(String[] args) {
        int[] array = {1, 2, 3, 4, 5, 6, 7, 8, 9, 10};
        ForkJoinPool forkJoinPool = new ForkJoinPool(4);
```

```
        int sum = forkJoinPool.submit(() ->
            Arrays.stream(array).parallel().sum()).join();

        System.out.println("Sum is " + sum); // Outputs Sum is 55
    }
}
```

Algorithm 1: Parallel Sum Calculation

Result: Parallel Sum Calculation
Initialize an array of integers;
Divide the array into smaller chunks;
foreach *chunk in chunks* **do**
    Compute the sum of elements in the chunk in parallel;
end
Combine the results from each chunk;

Higher-Order Functions

Higher-order functions (HOFs) take other functions as parameters or return them as results. This capability encourages a declarative approach to problems, enhancing code modularity and reusability.

```
import java.util.function.Function;

public class HigherOrderFunctions {
    public static Function<Integer, Integer> doubler() {
        return x -> x * 2;
    }

    public static void main(String[] args) {
        Function<Integer, Integer> doubleFunction = doubler();
        System.out.println(doubleFunction.apply(5)); // Outputs 10
    }
}
```

Enhanced Development Productivity

FP often leads to more concise and expressive code. By leveraging functions like map, filter, and reduce, complex operations can be succinctly expressed, reducing boilerplate code.

```
import java.util.Arrays;
import java.util.List;

public class MapReduceExample {
    public static void main(String[] args) {
        List<Integer> numbers = Arrays.asList(1, 2, 3, 4, 5);

        int sum = numbers.stream()
                         .map(x -> x * x)
                         .reduce(0, Integer::sum);
```

```
        System.out.println("Sum of squares: " + sum); // Outputs Sum of squares: 55
    }
}
```

Improved Code Maintainability

FP simplifies code maintenance by isolating side effects and minimizing mutable state. Updating or extending FP-based systems is typically more manageable since changes in one part of the system are less likely to produce unexpected behaviors in other parts.

Advantages of functional programming are increasingly relevant in today's software industry, emphasizing immutability, purity, concurrency, modularity, productivity, and maintainability. Understanding these benefits enables developers to write more robust and expressive code.

1.5 Key Concepts: Pure Functions, Higher-Order Functions, and First-Class Citizens

Understanding the foundational concepts of functional programming is crucial for leveraging its full potential. This section will delve into three pivotal concepts: pure functions, higher-order functions, and first-class citizens. Mastering these will enable you to write more efficient, readable, and maintainable code.

A pure function is a function where the output value is determined only by its input values, without observable side effects. This implies that given the same inputs, a pure function will always yield the same output. A pure function should not modify any external state or depend on mutable states. This characteristic allows for easier reasoning about code behavior and facilitates debugging and testing.

Here is a straightforward example of a pure function in Java:

```
// Pure Function Example
public int add(int a, int b) {
    return a + b;
}
```

In the example above, the function add consistently returns the sum of a and b without altering any external state or relying on any external variable.

Consider an impure function for contrast:

```
// Impure Function Example
public int addToGlobal(int a) {
    globalVar += a;
    return globalVar;
}
```

Here, addToGlobal modifies the external variable globalVar. This modification constitutes a side effect, making the function impure.

Higher-order functions are functions that can take other functions as arguments or return them as results. These functions elevate the expressiveness and flexibility of code, enabling abstract and modular solutions.

An example of a higher-order function in Java using the Function interface is shown below:

```
import java.util.function.Function;

// Higher-Order Function Example
public <T, R> R higherOrderFunction(T input, Function<T, R> func) {
    return func.apply(input);
}
```

In this example, higherOrderFunction accepts a function func as a parameter and applies it to input. Higher-order functions are integral to many functional programming concepts, such as map, reduce, and filter operations.

First-class citizens in functional programming are entities that can be passed as arguments to functions, returned from functions, and assigned to variables. In Java, functions can be treated as first-class citizens through the use of functional interfaces, lambda expressions, and method references.

Consider the following demonstration of functions as first-class citizens:

```
import java.util.function.Function;

public class FirstClassExample {
    public static void main(String[] args) {
        Function<Integer, Integer> square = x -> x * x;

        // Passing function as an argument
        int result = higherOrderFunction(5, square);
        System.out.println("Square of 5 is: " + result);

        // Assigning function to a variable
        Function<Integer, Integer> adder = add(10);
        System.out.println("Add 10 to 5: " + adder.apply(5));
    }

    // Higher-Order Function Example
```

```
    public static <T, R> R higherOrderFunction(T input, Function<T, R> func) {
        return func.apply(input);
    }

    // Returning a function
    public static Function<Integer, Integer> add(int toAdd) {
        return x -> x + toAdd;
    }
}
```

The higherOrderFunction is called with a lambda expression square, and add returns a function that adds a specified value. This illustrates how Java treats functions as first-class citizens, promoting reusable and concise code structures.

Understanding these key concepts of functional programming forms the basis for constructing efficient and maintainable programs. By leveraging pure functions, higher-order functions, and first-class citizens, developers can write code that is not only elegant but also easier to reason about and test. This section has provided concrete examples and explanations to illustrate the utility and implementation of these concepts in Java.

1.6 Introduction to Java's Functional Programming Features

Java, traditionally known as an object-oriented programming language, introduced significant features to support functional programming with the release of Java 8. These additions include lambda expressions, functional interfaces, the Stream API, and enhanced support for higher-order functions. The inclusion of these features facilitates a functional style of programming while maintaining Java's existing object-oriented paradigms.

Lambda Expressions: Lambda expressions provide a clear and concise way to represent instances of single-method interfaces (also known as functional interfaces). Lambda expressions enable you to treat functionality as a method argument or to create small function implementations.

```
(int x, int y) -> x + y
```

In this example, (int x, int y) represents the parameters, and x + y is the expression for the body of the lambda, which adds two integers.

Functional Interfaces: A functional interface in Java is an interface that contains exactly one abstract method. They are also called Single Abstract Method (SAM) interfaces. The @FunctionalInterface annotation in Java is used to indicate that the interface is intended to be a functional interface.

```
@FunctionalInterface
public interface Calculator {
    int calculate(int x, int y);
}
```

This interface can now be instantiated using a lambda expression as shown below:

```
Calculator addition = (a, b) -> a + b;
System.out.println("Addition: " + addition.calculate(10, 5));
```

Output:

```
Addition: 15
```

The Stream API: Streams in Java provide a powerful way to work with collections of data. The Stream API supports operations like filtering, mapping, and reducing data in a declarative manner. It allows for the execution of a sequence of operations on data, leveraging the lambda expressions.

```
List<String> names = Arrays.asList("Alice", "Bob", "Charlie");
List<String> filteredNames = names.stream()
                                  .filter(name -> name.startsWith("A"))
                                  .collect(Collectors.toList());
System.out.println(filteredNames);
```

Output:

```
[Alice]
```

Higher-Order Functions: Java's functional programming features also include the support for higher-order functions. These are functions that take other functions as arguments or return functions as results. This is particularly useful for functional composition and function chaining.

For example, consider a function that applies another function to each element in a list:

```
public static List<Integer> applyFunction(List<Integer> list, Function<Integer,
      Integer> func) {
   return list.stream()
              .map(func)
              .collect(Collectors.toList());
}
```

```
List<Integer> numbers = Arrays.asList(1, 2, 3, 4, 5);
Function<Integer, Integer> squareFunction = x -> x * x;

List<Integer> squares = applyFunction(numbers, squareFunction);
System.out.println(squares);
```

Output:

```
[1, 4, 9, 16, 25]
```

Java also includes default methods in interfaces to allow methods with implementations in interfaces. This enables multiple inheritance of behavior (i.e., implementations). Additionally, the Optional class is introduced, providing a means to handle potentially absent values in a more functional and expressive manner, reducing the likelihood of NullPointerException.

Usage of Optional Class:

```
Optional<String> optional = Optional.of("Hello");
optional.ifPresent(System.out::println); // Output: Hello

Optional<String> emptyOptional = Optional.empty();
String orElseValue = emptyOptional.orElse("Default Value");
System.out.println(orElseValue); // Output: Default Value
```

Enhancements in functional programming support also include method references, which provide a shorthand notation for calling methods. These can be utilized wherever lambda expressions are used when they are performing simple methods invocations.

Example of Method References:

```
List<String> strs = Arrays.asList("a", "b", "c");
strs.forEach(System.out::println);
```

Output:

```
a
b
c
```

These features facilitate a more expressive and succinct code, enhancing the readability and maintainability of Java programs. The incorporation of lambda expressions, the Stream API, functional interfaces, higher-order functions, and the Optional class fundamentally augment Java's capabilities, making it well-suited to both object-oriented and functional programming paradigms. The introduction of these functional programming features signifies a shift towards a more versatile and modern approach to Java development.

1.7 Setting up Your Development Environment

Functional programming in Java requires a proper development environment to facilitate seamless coding and execution of programs. This section will guide you through the steps to set up an effective development environment, including the necessary software installations, configuration settings, and tools to streamline your programming tasks.

- Java Development Kit (JDK)
- Integrated Development Environment (IDE) or Text Editor
- Build Tools
- Version Control System (VCS)

First, ensure that you have the latest version of the Java Development Kit (JDK) installed on your system. The JDK provides the essential components to develop and run Java applications, including the Java Runtime Environment (JRE) and command-line development tools.

```
$ java -version
```

The above command checks the installed Java version. You should see an output similar to the following:

```
java version "17.0.1" 2021-10-19 LTS
Java(TM) SE Runtime Environment (build 17.0.1+12-LTS-39)
Java HotSpot(TM) 64-Bit Server VM (build 17.0.1+12-LTS-39, mixed mode, sharing)
```

If Java is not installed or you need to upgrade, download the latest JDK from the official Oracle website or use a package manager suitable for your operating system.

Installing JDK on Different Operating Systems

- Windows: Download the JDK installer from the Oracle JDK downloads page. Run the installer and follow the on-screen instructions to complete the installation. Finally, set the JAVA_HOME environment variable and update the PATH variable to include the bin directory of your JDK installation.
- macOS: Use Homebrew to install JDK by running:

```
$ brew install --cask adoptopenjdk
```

Configure the JAVA_HOME environment variable in your shell profile, such as .bash_profile or .zshrc.

- Linux: Use your distribution's package manager. For example, on Ubuntu, you can install the JDK with:

```
$ sudo apt update
$ sudo apt install openjdk-17-jdk
```

Set the JAVA_HOME environment variable in your .bashrc or equivalent shell profile file.

Choosing an Integrated Development Environment or Text Editor

An IDE or text editor that supports Java development significantly enhances productivity by providing features such as syntax highlighting, code completion, debugging, and project management. Popular choices include:

- IntelliJ IDEA: A powerful IDE for Java, offering extensive support for functional programming and a comprehensive set of tools for coding, debugging, and testing.
- Eclipse IDE: A widely-used, open-source IDE that offers Java development support and can be extended with plugins to incorporate functional programming tools.
- Visual Studio Code: A lightweight, versatile text editor that can be configured for Java development through extensions such as Language Support for Java(TM) by Red Hat, Debugger for Java, and Java Test Runner.
- NetBeans: Another robust IDE that provides an integrated development environment for Java with support for varied plugins and tools to enhance functional programming tasks.

Setting up Build Tools

Using build tools like Maven or Gradle is essential for managing project dependencies, building projects, and automating tasks such as testing and packaging.

Maven

To install Maven, follow these steps based on your operating system:

- Windows: Download the Maven binary zip archive from the official Maven website. Extract the archive and configure the MAVEN_HOME environment variable, and add the bin directory to the PATH variable.
- macOS & Linux: Use a package manager to install Maven. For macOS, use:

```
$ brew install maven
```

  For Ubuntu and other Debian-based distributions, run:

```
$ sudo apt update
$ sudo apt install maven
```

Verify the installation by running:

```
$ mvn -version
```

The expected output should display information about the installed Maven version and your Java version.

Gradle

Similar steps apply to Gradle installation:

- Windows: Download the Gradle binary zip file from the Gradle releases page, extract it, and set the GRADLE_HOME environment variable. Add the bin directory to your PATH variable.
- macOS & Linux: For macOS, use:

```
$ brew install gradle
```

  For Ubuntu and similar distributions:

```
$ sudo apt update
$ sudo apt install gradle
```

Verify the installation by running:

```
$ gradle -version
```

You should see output confirming the installed Gradle version and Java environment details.

Version Control System

Using a version control system (VCS) like Git is crucial for managing source code versions, collaboration, and tracking changes. For Git installation:

- Windows: Download Git from the official Git website and follow the installer instructions. Ensure Git is added to your system's PATH.
- macOS: Install Git through Homebrew with the command:

```
$ brew install git
```

- Linux: For Ubuntu and similar distributions, use:

```
$ sudo apt update
$ sudo apt install git
```

Configure Git with your user identity by running:

```
$ git config --global user.name "Your Name"
$ git config --global user.email "your.email@example.com"
```

Setting up these tools and configurations establishes a solid foundation for developing and executing functional programs in Java, ensuring a smooth workflow and enhanced productivity.

1.8 Basic Syntax of Functional Programming in Java

The basic syntax of functional programming in Java revolves around lambda expressions, functional interfaces, method references, and the Stream API. These constructs facilitate a functional paradigm by promoting immutability, first-class functions, and operations over sequences of data without explicit iteration.

Lambda expressions are a shorthand notation for anonymous classes with a single abstract method (SAM). They enable treating functions as first-class citizens. A lambda expression in Java is defined using the following syntax:

```
// Basic structure of a lambda expression
(parameters) -> expression

// With multiple statements in the body
(parameters) -> { statement1; statement2; }
```

```
// Example of a simple lambda expression
(int x) -> x + 1;

// Example of a lambda expression with inferred types
x -> x * 2;
```

A lambda expression can have zero or more parameters. If a lambda body contains a single expression, curly braces are optional. However, if the body contains multiple statements, curly braces are required.

Functional interfaces play a crucial role in Java's functional programming paradigm. A functional interface contains exactly one abstract method, and thus, it can serve as the target for lambda expressions. The @FunctionalInterface annotation is used to declare an interface as a functional interface, although it is optional. Examples of common functional interfaces in Java's java.util.function package include Function, Predicate, Consumer, and Supplier.

```
// Example of a functional interface
@FunctionalInterface
interface MyFunction {
    int apply(int x);
}

// Using a lambda expression with the functional interface
MyFunction f = (int x) -> x + 10;
System.out.println(f.apply(5)); // Output: 15
```

Java provides method references as a shorthand for more readable and succinct lambda expressions. A method reference uses the :: operator to call methods by their names. There are four types of method references:

- Reference to a static method ClassName::staticMethodName
- Reference to an instance method of a particular object instance::instanceMethodName
- Reference to an instance method of an arbitrary object of a particular type ClassName::instanceMethodName
- Reference to a constructor ClassName::new

```
// Example of a static method reference
Function<String, Integer> parseInt = Integer::parseInt;
System.out.println(parseInt.apply("123")); // Output: 123

// Example of an instance method reference of a particular object
String str = "Hello";
```

```
Supplier<Integer> length = str::length;
System.out.println(length.get()); // Output: 5

// Example of an instance method reference of an arbitrary object
Function<String, String> toUpperCase = String::toUpperCase;
System.out.println(toUpperCase.apply("functional")); // Output: FUNCTIONAL

// Example of a constructor reference
Supplier<ArrayList<String>> arrayListSupplier = ArrayList::new;
ArrayList<String> list = arrayListSupplier.get();
```

The Stream API is a fundamental part of functional programming in Java, providing a fluent interface for sequence manipulation. Streams allow processing sequences of elements through declarative operations, supporting lazy evaluation. The three main stages of working with streams are obtaining a stream, performing intermediate operations, and executing a terminal operation. Intermediate operations are lazy and return a new stream, while terminal operations process and close the stream.

```
// Example of a Stream pipeline
List<String> words = Arrays.asList("functional", "programming", "in", "java");
List<String> result = words.stream()
    .filter(word -> word.length() > 3) // Intermediate operation
    .map(String::toUpperCase) // Intermediate operation
    .sorted() // Intermediate operation
    .collect(Collectors.toList()); // Terminal operation

System.out.println(result); // Output: [FUNCTIONAL, JAVY, PROGRAMMING]
```

Intermediate operations like filter, map, and sorted return a stream, allowing method chaining. Terminal operations like collect, forEach, reduce, and count trigger the processing of the stream.

```
// Example of collecting elements into a List
List<Integer> numbers = Arrays.asList(1, 2, 3, 4, 5);
List<Integer> squares = numbers.stream()
    .map(n -> n * n) // Intermediate operation
    .collect(Collectors.toList()); // Terminal operation

System.out.println(squares); // Output: [1, 4, 9, 16, 25]

// Example of reduction operation
int sum = numbers.stream()
    .reduce(0, (a, b) -> a + b); // Terminal operation

System.out.println(sum); // Output: 15
```

The Stream API supports parallel processing to leverage multicore architectures. Using parallelStream() enables parallel execution of stream operations, which can significantly improve performance for large datasets.

```
// Example of parallel processing with streams
```

```
long count = numbers.parallelStream()
    .filter(n -> n > 2) // Intermediate operation
    .count(); // Terminal operation

System.out.println(count); // Output: 3
```

Comprehension of these syntactic elements is essential, as they form the foundation for writing functional-style Java code. Through lambda expressions, functional interfaces, method references, and streams, Java provides robust support for adopting functional programming paradigms within a primarily object-oriented environment.

1.9 Common Functional Programming Terminology

Functional programming introduces a range of terminology essential for understanding and effectively applying its paradigms. This section explains these terms, ensuring clarity and precision for accurate comprehension.

- **Pure Function:** A pure function is a function where the return value is determined solely by its input values, without observable side effects. In other words, the same input will always return the same output, maintaining referential transparency. Consider the following example:

  ```
  public int add(int a, int b) {
      return a + b;
  }
  ```

  This function add is pure because it consistently produces the same output for the same input values and performs no side effects like modifying variables or I/O operations.

- **First-Class Citizen:** In functional programming, functions are first-class citizens, meaning they can be assigned to variables, passed as arguments, and returned from other functions. Java supports first-class functions through functional interfaces and lambda expressions. For example:

  ```
  Function<Integer, Integer> square = x -> x * x;
  ```

  Here, square is a function assigned to a variable, illustrating the first-class citizen principle.

- **Higher-Order Function:** A higher-order function is a function that takes one or more functions as arguments or returns a function as its result. Higher-order functions enable function composition and other powerful programming techniques. An example in Java is the map function:

```
List<Integer> numbers = Arrays.asList(1, 2, 3, 4);
List<Integer> squaredNumbers = numbers.stream()
                                  .map(x -> x * x)
                                  .collect(Collectors.toList());
```

  Here, the map function is a higher-order function that applies a given function to each item in a list and returns a new list with the results.

- **Immutability:** Immutability refers to the concept that data once created cannot be modified. Instead of altering values, new values are created. This leads to predictability and easier debugging. In Java, the String class is immutable; once a String object is created, it cannot be changed. For instance:

```
String hello = "Hello";
String world = hello.concat(" World");
```

  When concat is called, a new String is created rather than modifying the original hello.

- **Lambda Expression:** A lambda expression is a concise way to create anonymous functions in Java. It allows the implementation of functional interfaces with a single method in a more readable and compact form. An example of a lambda expression:

```
(int x, int y) -> x + y
```

  This lambda expression takes two integers and returns their sum.

- **Functional Interface:** A functional interface is an interface with a single abstract method, which can be implemented using lambda expressions. Java 8 introduced several built-in functional interfaces in the java.util.function package, including Function, Predicate, and Supplier. For example:

```
@FunctionalInterface
public interface Function<T, R> {
    R apply(T t);
}
```

- **Side Effect:** A side effect occurs when a function modifies some state or interacts with the outside world (I/O operations, modifying variables, etc.) beyond returning a value. Functional programming aims to minimize side effects to achieve referential transparency and predictability.

- **Functor:** A functor is a type that implements a map function, typically found in categories like lists. It allows the application of a function to a wrapped value or collection of values. In Java, the Stream API can be viewed as an implementation of the functor concept, where map applies a function to each element in a stream.

- **Monoid:** A monoid is an algebraic structure with a single associative binary operation and an identity element. Monoids are useful in functional programming for building scalable and parallelizable algorithms. In Java, the Collectors utility can take advantage of monoidal properties for efficient data processing:

```
List<String> words = Arrays.asList("functional", "programming", "in", "
    java");
String sentence = words.stream()
                      .collect(Collectors.joining(" "));
```

  Here, joining uses a monoidal operation to concatenate strings with a space separator.

- **Monad:** A monad is a design pattern used to handle program-wide concerns like state and I/O within a functional framework. It provides a standard way to chain operations together. In Java, the Optional class is a monad used to represent optional values. An example is:

```
Optional<String> name = Optional.of("Alice");
Optional<String> upperName = name.map(String::toUpperCase);
```

  Here, map lifts the toUpperCase function to operate within the Optional monad.

- **Referential Transparency:** A property of expressions in functional programming means an expression can be replaced with its corresponding value without changing the program's behavior. Referential transparency ensures that functions yield consistent results without side effects. For instance, the expression $2 + 3$ is referentially transparent because it always evaluates to 5.

- **Currying:** Currying is the process of converting a function that takes multiple arguments into a series of functions that take single arguments. This technique is useful for partial function application. In Java, currying can be simulated with lambda expressions:

```
Function<Integer, Function<Integer, Integer>> curriedAdd = x -> y -> x +
    y;
```

Here, curriedAdd transforms a binary function into a curried form.

- **Memoization:** An optimization technique to speed up programs by storing the result of function calls and returning the cached result when the same inputs occur again. Memoization ensures functions are called with identical arguments only once, improving performance in applications like dynamic programming.

- **Lazy Evaluation:** Lazy evaluation delays the evaluation of an expression until its value is actually needed, potentially improving performance by avoiding unnecessary calculations. Java's Stream API supports lazy evaluation:

```
List<String> names = Arrays.asList("Alice", "Bob", "Charlie", "David");
Stream<String> filteredNames = names.stream()
                                    .filter(name -> name.startsWith("A"));
```

  The filter operation is not performed until a terminal operation like collect is executed.

Understanding these terms is fundamental to grasping the functional programming paradigm in Java. Proper application of these concepts can lead to more predictable, maintainable, and concise code.

Chapter 2

Core Principles of Functional Programming

This chapter delves into the essential principles that underpin functional programming. It covers pure functions, immutability, first-class and higher-order functions, function composition, closures, and the distinctions between recursion and iteration. The chapter also explains concepts like lazy evaluation, referential transparency, and declarative programming, while addressing strategies to avoid side effects, providing a comprehensive understanding of core functional programming principles.

2.1 Introduction to Core Principles

Functional programming (FP) is grounded in a range of core principles that emphasize the application of mathematical functions to process data. These principles are fundamental to understanding and effectively employing functional programming paradigms in Java and other languages.

Functional programming centers around the concept of pure functions. Pure functions are characterized by their deterministic outputs for any given set of inputs, devoid of any side effects. This determinism significantly simplifies reasoning about the behavior of programs. Given the importance of pure functions, their definition forms the foundation of functional programming.

Another vital principle is immutability. In functional programming, the state of data remains unchanged once created. Instead of modifying existing data structures, new versions are generated when changes are required. This property leads to more maintainable and predictable code, as it precludes the complications associated with mutable shared state.

First-class and higher-order functions enhance the expressiveness of FP. A first-class function is treated as a value, allowing it to be passed as an argument, returned from other functions, and assigned to variables. Higher-order functions, which either take other functions as arguments or return them as results, facilitate functional composition and abstraction, enriching the language's ability to express intricate computational logic succinctly.

Function composition enables the creation of complex functionality by building new functions from existing ones. This compositionality allows smaller, well-defined functions to be reused and combined in various ways, fostering modularity and clarity.

Closures extend function capabilities by capturing the lexical scope in which they are defined. This means that functions can retain access to variables present in their enclosing scope even when executed outside that context. Closures are crucial for maintaining a function's state without relying on mutable variables, aligning with the immutability principle.

In contrast to the imperative paradigm's preference for iteration, recursion is a core principle in FP. Recursive functions invoke themselves to divide problems into simpler sub-problems, often mirroring the problem's inherent structure. This approach is particularly suitable for problems that can be naturally expressed in terms of smaller instances of the same problem.

Lazy evaluation, another fundamental concept, delays computations until their results are required. This deferral leads to potential performance optimizations and resource savings, particularly in scenarios involving large or infinite data structures.

Referential transparency is a consequence of pure functions and immutability. An expression is referentially transparent if it can be replaced with its corresponding value without altering the program's behavior. This property is pivotal for program proving and parallel execution, as it guarantees consistent outcomes independent of evaluation order.

Declarative programming is emphasized in FP, contrasting with the imperative style. Instead of specifying explicit steps to achieve a result, declarative programming focuses on what the outcome should be. This high-level approach abstracts the underlying control flow, making the code more succinct and readable.

Avoidance of side effects is integral to FP principles. Side effects, such as changing the state of variables or I/O operations, complicate debugging and testing because they introduce dependencies between different parts of the code. By minimizing side effects, functional programming promotes more predictable and reliable programs.

Understanding these core principles is critical for mastering functional programming in Java. The principles not only set the stage for subsequent discussions but also serve as a guiding framework for writing robust and efficient functional code. The application of these principles ensures that programs are maintainable, concurrent-ready, and scalable, aligning with the goals of modern software development practices.

2.2 Pure Functions

A pure function is a fundamental concept in functional programming, grounding the approach in mathematical function theory. A pure function is defined by two key properties: the function always produces the same output given the same input, and it has no side effects, meaning it does not alter any state or interact with the outside world (e.g., by performing I/O operations).

Consider the following example of a pure function add in Java, which simply adds two numbers:

```
public int add(int a, int b) {
    return a + b;
}
```

Given the same inputs, a and b, the add function will always produce the same result. Furthermore, the function does not modify any external state or perform operations such as writing to a file or printing to a console, making it side-effect-free.

Predictability and Testability

Pure functions are predictable due to their deterministic nature. This predictability simplifies debugging and testing since the evaluation depends solely on the input parameters. Consider writing a unit test for the add function:

```
@Test
public void testAdd() {
    assertEquals(4, add(2, 2));
    assertEquals(0, add(-1, 1));
    assertEquals(-3, add(-1, -2));
}
```

Every assertion checks the add function with specific inputs and compares the result with the expected output. Each test case will always pass or fail consistently, eliminating nondeterminism from factors such as internal state changes or external dependencies.

No Side Effects

The absence of side effects in pure functions means they do not alter any state outside the scope of the function. For example:

```
public List<Integer> append(List<Integer> list, int value) {
    List<Integer> newList = new ArrayList<>(list);
    newList.add(value);
    return newList;
}
```

This append function creates a new list and appends a value without modifying the original list. This immutability aligns with functional programming, enhancing reliability in concurrent and parallel computations by avoiding race conditions.

In contrast, consider an impure version that mutates the input list:

```
public void impureAppend(List<Integer> list, int value) {
    list.add(value);
}
```

This function changes the original list, introducing side effects. Such side effects can lead to unpredictable behavior in complex systems, especially when functions have shared mutable state.

Referential Transparency

Pure functions exhibit referential transparency, allowing any expression involving a pure function call to be replaced with its resulting value without changing the overall program behavior. Referential transparency simplifies reasoning about programs and enables advanced optimization techniques such as memoization and lazy evaluation. For instance:

```
int sum = add(2, 3) + add(2, 3);
```

Since add(2, 3) is referentially transparent, its repeated evaluation can be replaced by its computed value:

```
int sum = 5 + 5;
```

Memoization

Memoization is an optimization technique where the results of costly function calls are cached based on their inputs, improving performance. This technique works seamlessly with pure functions due to their deterministic nature. Consider a Fibonacci function:

```
public int fibonacci(int n) {
    if (n <= 1) {
        return n;
    }
    return fibonacci(n - 1) + fibonacci(n - 2);
}
```

A memoized version stores previously computed results:

```
private Map<Integer, Integer> cache = new HashMap<>();

public int memoizedFibonacci(int n) {
    if (n <= 1) {
        return n;
    }
    if (cache.containsKey(n)) {
        return cache.get(n);
    }
    int result = memoizedFibonacci(n - 1) + memoizedFibonacci(n - 2);
    cache.put(n, result);
    return result;
}
```

This enhanced version avoids redundant computations by caching results, significantly improving the function's efficiency.

Pure functions are central to functional programming, offering predictability, ease of testing, referential transparency, and enabling advanced optimization techniques. Implementing pure functions fosters code that is more maintainable, reliable, and efficient.

2.3 Immutability

In functional programming, immutability is a fundamental principle that plays a crucial role in ensuring the predictability and reliability of code.

When an object is immutable, its state cannot be modified after it is created. This characteristic contrasts with mutable objects, whose state can be changed.

Immutability is favored in functional programming due to several reasons:

- **Predictability**: Since immutable objects do not change state, they are inherently easier to understand and reason about. Functions that return immutable objects are guaranteed to produce the same output given the same input.
- **Thread-safety**: In multi-threaded programming, immutable objects can be shared across threads without requiring synchronization mechanisms, thus avoiding the typical pitfalls associated with mutable shared state.
- **Simplified Testing**: Testing is more straightforward because state changes do not occur, reducing the number of scenarios and allowing more deterministic test outcomes.

In Java, immutability can be enforced in several ways. Here's an example of an immutable class:

```
// An example of an immutable class in Java
public final class Point {
  private final int x;
  private final int y;

  public Point(int x, int y) {
    this.x = x;
    this.y = y;
  }

  public int getX() {
    return x;
  }

  public int getY() {
    return y;
  }
}
```

In this Point class:

- The class is declared as final, which prevents it from being subclassed.
- The fields x and y are declared final, ensuring they remain constant once assigned.

- There are no methods provided that modify the state of the object.

Modifying State with Immutability: Instead of modifying the state directly, new instances are created with altered state:

```
// Creating a new Point with modified state
Point p1 = new Point(1, 2);
Point p2 = new Point(p1.getX() + 1, p1.getY());
```

p2 is a new instance with updated coordinates, ensuring p1 remains unchanged.

Collections: Implementing immutability in collections requires using immutable collections or making defensive copies. Java provides Collections.unmodifiableList() and other similar methods to create immutable views of collections:

```
List<String> originalList = new ArrayList<>(Arrays.asList("A", "B", "C"));
List<String> immutableList = Collections.unmodifiableList(originalList);

// Attempting to modify the immutable collection results in an
    UnsupportedOperationException
immutableList.add("D"); // Throws UnsupportedOperationException
```

Advantages in Functional Programming: Immutability boosts the power of functional programming by ensuring functions have no hidden side effects. As a result, functions become pure, making the overall system more robust and easier to maintain. Here's an example demonstrating immutability and pure functions:

```
import java.util.List;
import java.util.stream.Collectors;

public class OrderProcessor {

    public List<Double> applyDiscount(List<Double> prices, double discountRate) {
        return prices.stream()
                     .map(price -> price * (1 - discountRate))
                     .collect(Collectors.toList());
    }
}
```

Here, the applyDiscount method processes a list of prices and returns a new list with the discount applied. The original list remains unaltered.

Deep Immutability: Achieving deep immutability involves ensuring that not only the object but also objects referenced by it are immutable. This is commonly achieved by:

- Using immutable types for fields.
- Returning copies of mutable collections or data structures.

- Ensuring accessor methods do not expose internal references.

In large-scale systems, deep immutability is crucial for ensuring global state consistency and avoiding unintended side-effects.

Immutability is an essential aspect of functional programming, enabling developers to write more predictable, reliable, and maintainable code. By embracing immutability, functional programs achieve enhanced simplicity and concurrency, underpinning the core principles of functional programming.

2.4 First-Class and Higher-Order Functions

First-class functions are a cornerstone of functional programming languages, including Java. A function is considered first-class if it can be passed as an argument to other functions, returned from other functions, and assigned to a variable. This capability enables high modularity and code reuse by treating functions as first-class citizens.

In Java, first-class functions are achieved using lambda expressions and method references introduced in Java 8. A lambda expression is essentially an anonymous function that can be used wherever a functional interface is expected. A functional interface is an interface with a single abstract method, also known as a SAM interface.

Consider the functional interface Function<T, R> from the java.util.function package:

```
@FunctionalInterface
public interface Function<T, R> {
    R apply(T t);
}
```

A lambda expression can implement this interface in the following way:

```
Function<Integer, Integer> square = x -> x * x;
int result = square.apply(5); // result is 25
```

Here, the lambda expression x -> x * x is assigned to the variable square, demonstrating that functions in Java can be first-class citizens.

Higher-order functions are functions that can either take other functions as arguments or return them as results, or both. Higher-order functions facilitate function composition and functional patterns such as map, filter, and reduce.

Consider a higher-order function that takes a function as its parameter:

```
public class HigherOrderFunctionExample {
    public static <R> R applyFunction(Function<Integer, R> func, int value) {
        return func.apply(value);
    }

    public static void main(String[] args) {
        Function<Integer, String> intToStr = i -> "Number: " + i;
        String result = applyFunction(intToStr, 10);
        System.out.println(result); // Output: Number: 10
    }
}
```

In this example, the method applyFunction demonstrates higher-order functionality as it takes a function func and an integer value as parameters, applying func to value.

Higher-order functions can also return other functions. This property is highly useful for creating factory functions or curried functions.

Consider a function that returns another function:

```
public class FunctionFactory {
    public static Function<Integer, Integer> makeAdder(int addend) {
        return x -> x + addend;
    }

    public static void main(String[] args) {
        Function<Integer, Integer> addFive = makeAdder(5);
        int result = addFive.apply(10); // result is 15
        System.out.println(result);
    }
}
```

In this example, makeAdder creates and returns a lambda expression that adds a specified addend to its input. The function addFive is a customized adder created using makeAdder.

The use of higher-order functions often involves composing functions. Function composition allows the creation of new functions by combining simpler ones. This is useful for pipelines or processing sequences of operations.

In Java, function composition can be achieved using the andThen and compose methods provided by the Function interface:

```
Function<Integer, Integer> multiplyByTwo = x -> x * 2;
Function<Integer, Integer> subtractThree = x -> x - 3;

// Compose two functions: subtractThree(multiplyByTwo(x))
Function<Integer, Integer> composedFunction = subtractThree.compose(
    multiplyByTwo);
int result = composedFunction.apply(5); // result is 7

System.out.println(result);
```

In this case, subtractThree.compose(multiplyByTwo) results in a new function which first executes multiplyByTwo and then subtractThree, adhering to the combination of multiple function logic into a single operation.

Java's support for first-class and higher-order functions enriches its functional programming capabilities, promoting modularity, reusability, and elegant solutions for complex problems.

2.5 Function Composition

Function composition is a powerful feature in functional programming that allows the creation of complex functions by combining simpler ones. This principle hinges on the mathematical concept of compositionality, where the output of one function becomes the input for another function. It enables a modular and declarative approach to problem-solving, fostering reusability and readability of the code.

Let f and g be two functions, where $f : B \to C$ and $g : A \to B$. The composition of f and g, denoted as $f \circ g$, is a function that maps A to C. Mathematically, it can be expressed as:

$$(f \circ g)(x) = f(g(x))$$

In Java, function composition can be effectively managed using functions from the java.util.function package. The primary functional interfaces involved in function composition are Function<T, R> and BiFunction<T, U, R>. These interfaces can be composed using default methods such as andThen and compose.

```
import java.util.function.Function;

public class FunctionCompositionExample {
    public static void main(String[] args) {
        Function<Integer, Integer> multiplyByTwo = x -> x * 2;
        Function<Integer, Integer> addThree = x -> x + 3;

        Function<Integer, Integer> combinedFunction = multiplyByTwo.andThen(
            addThree);

        int result = combinedFunction.apply(5); // First multiply by 2, then add 3
        System.out.println(result); // Output: 13
    }
}
```

In this example, the function multiplyByTwo multiplies the input by 2, and the function addThree adds 3 to the input. These functions are composed using the andThen method, which first applies multiplyByTwo and then applies addThree to the result. The output of this composition when applied to the input 5 is 13.

Alternatively, the compose method can be used, which applies functions in the reverse order:

```
Function<Integer, Integer> combinedFunction2 = multiplyByTwo.compose(addThree);

int result2 = combinedFunction2.apply(5); // First add 3, then multiply by 2
System.out.println(result2); // Output: 16
```

Here, combinedFunction2 first applies addThree and then applies multiplyByTwo. The resulting output when applied to the input 5 is 16, demonstrating the significance of the order of function application in composition.

Function composition is not limited to unary functions. It can also be extended to binary functions using the BiFunction interface.

```
import java.util.function.BiFunction;

public class BiFunctionCompositionExample {
    public static void main(String[] args) {
        BiFunction<Integer, Integer, Integer> add = (x, y) -> x + y;
        Function<Integer, Integer> square = x -> x * x;

        BiFunction<Integer, Integer, Integer> addAndSquare = add.andThen(square);

        int result = addAndSquare.apply(3, 4); // First add (3 + 4), then square the
            result
        System.out.println(result); // Output: 49
    }
}
```

In the above code, add is a BiFunction that adds two integers, and square is a Function that squares an integer. The andThen method creates a composed function addAndSquare, which adds two integers first and then squares the result. Applying it to the inputs 3 and 4 yields 49, as expected.

The power of function composition lies in building pipelines of transformations. By chaining functions together, one can succinctly express complex transformations without the need to write imperative code cluttered with temporary variables and explicit loops. This approach not only enhances code readability but also promotes the reusability of individual functions across different compositions.

A practical example encompassing function composition can be illustrated through data processing tasks. Consider a scenario where we need to process a list of integers by incrementing each value, then squaring the result, and finally converting it to a string:

```
import java.util.List;
import java.util.stream.Collectors;
import java.util.function.Function;

public class DataProcessingExample {
    public static void main(String[] args) {
        List<Integer> numbers = List.of(1, 2, 3, 4, 5);

        Function<Integer, Integer> increment = x -> x + 1;
        Function<Integer, Integer> square = x -> x * x;
        Function<Integer, String> convertToString = x -> "Number: " + x;

        Function<Integer, String> processPipeline = increment.andThen(square).
            andThen(convertToString);

        List<String> result = numbers.stream()
                                     .map(processPipeline)
                                     .collect(Collectors.toList());

        result.forEach(System.out::println);
    }
}
```

This example showcases how function composition simplifies the transformation of a list of integers. The composed function processPipeline increments each number, squares the incremented number, and converts the result to a string with a prefix "Number: ". The entire list of integers undergoes this transformation through the stream API, resulting in a printed list of strings with each computation neatly encapsulated within composed functions.

Utilizing function composition in such data processing tasks epitomizes the declarative nature of functional programming, allowing the programmer to state what needs to be done rather than how to do it procedurally. This approach not only reduces cognitive load but also ensures that the individual transformations remain pure and free from side effects, adhering to core functional programming principles.

2.6 Closures

Closures constitute a crucial concept in functional programming, allowing functions to have access to variables from their lexical scope even after the context in which they were created has finished executing. Understanding closures is vital for mastering functional programming as they enable the creation of more adaptable and reusable code structures.

A closure is essentially a function that captures the bindings of free variables in its lexical context. A free variable is one that is not bound within the function itself nor passed as a parameter. Closures open up a range of possibilities, such as enabling functions to retain state, simulating private variables, and creating functions with customized behavior.

Consider the following example in Java to demonstrate closures:

```
import java.util.function.Function;

public class ClosureExample {
    public static void main(String[] args) {
        Function<Integer, Function<Integer, Integer>> adder = createAdder();
        Function<Integer, Integer> add5 = adder.apply(5);
        System.out.println(add5.apply(10)); // Output: 15
        System.out.println(add5.apply(20)); // Output: 25
    }

    public static Function<Integer, Function<Integer, Integer>> createAdder() {
        return (Integer x) -> (Integer y) -> x + y;
    }
}
```

In the code above, createAdder() produces a function that takes an integer x and returns another function that adds x to its argument y. This demonstrates how a closure retains access to the variable x, even after createAdder() has completed execution. When createAdder() is called, it returns a new function with x bound to the value passed in, and this nested function can still access x when it is later invoked with a new argument.

Closure allows for the creation of higher-order functions that are both powerful and expressive. It provides a way to encapsulate environmental context along with operational logic, thereby promoting code encapsulation and modularity.

A more complex use of closures involves their application in maintaining state. Closures can emulate private variables and internal state management within a functional paradigm:

```
import java.util.function.Supplier;

public class Counter {
    public static void main(String[] args) {
        Supplier<Integer> counter = createCounter();
        System.out.println(counter.get()); // Output: 1
        System.out.println(counter.get()); // Output: 2
        System.out.println(counter.get()); // Output: 3
    }

    public static Supplier<Integer> createCounter() {
        final int[] count = {0};
```

```
        return () -> ++count[0];
    }
}
```

In this example, createCounter() returns a Supplier that increments and returns an internal count each time it's called. The array count is effectively private; it is only accessible within the closure formed by the lambda expression. This technique allows state to be managed without the need for mutable variable declarations within the function's outer scope.

Closures also facilitate the creation of more configurable and reusable functions. Leveraging closures, it's possible to produce functions that are highly specific yet derived from more generalized forms, as this enhances both code readability and maintainability:

```
import java.util.function.Function;

public class ConfigurableMultiplier {
    public static void main(String[] args) {
        Function<Integer, Integer> doubler = createMultiplier(2);
        Function<Integer, Integer> tripler = createMultiplier(3);

        System.out.println(doubler.apply(5)); // Output: 10
        System.out.println(tripler.apply(5)); // Output: 15
    }

    public static Function<Integer, Integer> createMultiplier(int factor) {
        return (Integer x) -> x * factor;
    }
}
```

Here, createMultiplier(int factor) returns a function that multiplies its input by a specified factor. The function used internally retains access to factor through closure, thus enabling the creation of customized multiplication functions such as doubler and tripler.

Revisiting core principles, a closure demonstrates the power of combining higher-order functions with the encapsulation of state in a purely functional manner. By defining functions that inherently capture and retain context, closures help in building robust and extensible functional constructs.

Understanding and effectively utilizing closures enables programmers to write code that is not only more expressive but also adheres to the core tenets of functional programming such as immutability and statelessness. This seamless blending of functions and environment provides a powerful tool for tackling complex programming challenges with elegance and efficiency.

2.7 Recursion vs Iteration

One of the fundamental concepts in both functional and imperative programming is the mechanism through which repetitive processes are implemented. Two primary methods for accomplishing this are **recursion** and **iteration**. Both techniques have their own benefits and trade-offs, and understanding their differences is crucial in mastering functional programming in Java.

Recursion is defined as a function calling itself to solve a problem. This self-referential capability allows problems to be broken down into smaller, more manageable sub-problems. Recursive solutions are closely aligned with the principles of functional programming due to their declarative nature and inherent ability to express computations as mathematical functions.

Consider the example of computing the factorial of a number using recursion:

```
public class Factorial {
    public static int factorial(int n) {
        if (n == 0) {
            return 1;
        } else {
            return n * factorial(n - 1);
        }
    }
}
```

The code defines a simple factorial function that uses a base case $n == 0$ to terminate the recursion and returns 1 as $0! = 1$. For values of $n > 0$, the function calls itself with $n - 1$ and multiplies the result by n, thus breaking the problem down into smaller subproblems until the base case is reached.

Iteration, on the other hand, involves the use of loop constructs (such as for, while, or do-while loops) to repeat an operation until a condition is met. Iterative solutions are typically more familiar to those with an imperative programming background and often provide straightforward implementation.

Here is the factorial function implemented using iteration:

```
public class Factorial {
    public static int factorial(int n) {
        int result = 1;
        for (int i = 1; i <= n; i++) {
            result *= i;
        }
        return result;
```

```
    }
}
```

Using a for loop, the function initializes result to 1 and then iteratively multiplies it by each integer up to n. Upon loop termination, the accumulated product is returned.

Beyond these basic definitions, there are several key differences and considerations when deciding between recursion and iteration:

- **Readability and Maintainability**: Recursive solutions often align more closely with the mathematical definition of the problem, making them easier to understand and reason about. However, for those unfamiliar with recursion, iterative approaches can appear more intuitive.
- **Termination Conditions**: Recursive functions must have well-defined base cases to terminate, whereas iterative loops require carefully designed exit conditions. Missing or improper termination can lead to infinite recursions or endless loops.
- **Performance and Stack Usage**: Recursive calls generate new stack frames, which can lead to stack overflow errors for deep recursions, especially in languages with limited stack size. Iterative solutions, typically using constant stack space, avoid this issue. Tail call optimization (TCO) can mitigate this in some languages, although standard Java does not natively support TCO.
- **State Management**: Functional programming emphasizes immutability and statelessness, which recursive solutions naturally embody via their stateless function calls. Iterative solutions often depend on mutable states (e.g., loop variables), which can introduce side effects contrary to functional programming paradigms.
- **Parallelism and Concurrency**: Recursive approaches can be more easily adapted for parallel processing frameworks, such as MapReduce or Fork/Join frameworks, since many recursive algorithms naturally decompose into parallelizable sub-tasks. Iterative solutions, relying on a single thread's loop, tend to be less amenable to automatic parallelization.

Consider the following recursive and iterative implementations for computing the Fibonacci sequence. The recursive method illustrates the straightforward but potentially inefficient nature of simple recursion, while the iterative approach emphasizes performance optimization through state management:

```
public class Fibonacci {

    // Recursive implementation
    public static int fibRecursive(int n) {
        if (n <= 1) {
            return n;
        } else {
            return fibRecursive(n - 1) + fibRecursive(n - 2);
        }
    }

    // Iterative implementation
    public static int fibIterative(int n) {
        if (n <= 1) {
            return n;
        }
        int fib = 1;
        int prevFib = 1;
        for (int i = 2; i < n; i++) {
            int temp = fib;
            fib += prevFib;
            prevFib = temp;
        }
        return fib;
    }
}
```

Though the recursive implementation of Fibonacci directly reflects its mathematical definition, it suffers from exponential time complexity due to repeated calculations of the same subproblems. In contrast, the iterative implementation achieves linear time complexity by storing and updating previous results in a constant space loop.

Efficient recursion can be achieved through techniques such as memoization, which stores previously computed values to avoid redundant calculations, thus optimizing performance while preserving the declarative nature of recursion.

When choosing between recursion and iteration, consider the problem constraints, readability, maintainability, and performance requirements. Recursive solutions may offer elegance and alignment with functional programming principles, while iterative solutions often provide optimized and stack-saving alternatives suitable for performance-critical applications.

2.8 Lazy Evaluation

Lazy evaluation, also termed as call-by-need, is a critical concept in functional programming with profound implications on the efficiency and behavior of programs. It refers to the postponement of the evaluation of an expression until its value is required, and avoiding repeated evaluations by storing the results of expressions, also known as memoization.

In functional programming, the lazy evaluation paradigm enables the creation of potentially infinite data structures and the improvement of program efficiency by eliminating unnecessary calculations.

Example Illustration

To illustrate lazy evaluation, consider a scenario where we define an infinite list of Fibonacci numbers in Java using a lazy function. This task can be accomplished using streams in Java 8 or later.

```
import java.util.stream.Stream;

public class LazyFibonacci {
    public static void main(String[] args) {
        Stream<long[]> fib = Stream.iterate(new long[]{0, 1}, f -> new long[]{f[1], f[0]
            + f[1]});

        // Printing the first 10 Fibonacci numbers
        fib.limit(10)
            .map(f -> f[0])
            .forEach(System.out::println);
    }
}
```

```
0
1
1
2
3
5
8
13
21
34
```

In this example, the Stream.iterate method is used to generate an infinite stream of Fibonacci numbers. The evaluation of the Fibonacci sequence elements happens only when the limit operation is called, demonstrating lazy evaluation.

Advantages of Lazy Evaluation

- **Efficiency**: Lazy evaluation can make programs more efficient by avoiding unnecessary computations. Expressions are only evaluated when needed, reducing the computation overhead.

- **Memory Utilization**: By evaluating expressions on demand, lazy evaluation can lead to more optimal memory usage, especially when dealing with large data structures or streams.
- **Infinite Data Structures**: Lazy evaluation facilitates the usage of infinite data structures. Infinite lists or streams can be defined without causing the program to run out of memory, as elements are generated on-demand.

Potential Hazards and Mitigation

While lazy evaluation offers significant benefits, it introduces certain complexities and potential pitfalls:

- **Thunks**: A thunk is essentially a suspended expression waiting to be evaluated. Overreliance on lazy evaluation can cause an excessive accumulation of thunks, leading to memory overhead and potential performance degradation.
- **Debugging**: Lazy evaluation complicates debugging efforts as the actual computation occurs at runtime, possibly making it difficult to trace the flow of execution and identify bugs.
- **Strictness**: Developers often need to discern between strict and lazy evaluation contexts. Misunderstanding strictness properties can lead to unexpected behavior and inefficiencies.

Mitigation Strategies

To optimize lazy evaluation while mitigating potential hazards, consider the following strategies:

- **Strictness Analysis**: Analyze your program to determine which parts can benefit from lazy evaluation and which would be more efficient if evaluated strictly. Use tools and libraries that provide support for strictness analysis and visualization.
- **Memoization**: Use memoization judiciously to prevent recomputation of the same expressions. Memoization stores the results of expensive function calls and returns the cached result when the same inputs occur again.

- **Profiling and Optimization**: Employ profiling tools to monitor the performance and runtime behavior of your program. Identify bottlenecks where lazy evaluation might introduce inefficiency and optimize accordingly.

Lazy evaluation is a powerful technique that, when used correctly, can substantially enhance the performance and capabilities of functional programs. Understanding its principles, benefits, and potential pitfalls enables developers to leverage lazy evaluation effectively.

2.9 Referential Transparency

Referential transparency is a fundamental concept in functional programming. It simplifies reasoning about code by ensuring that expressions can be substituted with their corresponding values without altering the program's behavior. An expression is referentially transparent if it consistently produces the same result given the same inputs, meaning it behaves like a pure mathematical function.

Consider a function square, defined as follows:

```
int square(int x) {
    return x * x;
}
```

Here, the expression $\mathrm{square}(4)$ will always evaluate to 16, regardless of where or how many times it is invoked. This implies that $\mathrm{square}(4)$ is referentially transparent because it can be substituted with 16 throughout the program without changing the behavior.

Referential transparency contrasts with functions that produce side effects, such as modifying global variables, I/O operations, or mutating their arguments. These functions are not referentially transparent because their output or behavior can depend on the program's state or produce changes observable outside the function's scope.

To illustrate this, consider the following function $\mathrm{incrementCounter}$, which modifies a global variable:

```
int counter = 0;

int incrementCounter() {
    counter += 1;
    return counter;
}
```

Calling incrementCounter() will yield different results each time it's invoked, depending on the value of counter prior to the call. Therefore, incrementCounter() is not referentially transparent.

Maintaining referential transparency offers several advantages:

- **Simplified Reasoning**: Developers can reason about code more easily, making it easier to understand, debug, and verify.
- **Enhanced Predictability**: Functions' behavior will be consistent, promoting predictability and reliability.
- **Enabling Optimization**: Compilers can perform optimizations like common subexpression elimination and function memoization more effectively.
- **Facilitating Parallelization**: Without side effects, functions can be executed in parallel safely as they do not depend on shared mutable state.

Consider another example where referential transparency is preserved using immutable data structures. Assume we have a function addElement that adds an element to a list:

```
import java.util.List;
import java.util.ArrayList;
import java.util.Collections;

List<Integer> addElement(List<Integer> list, int element) {
    List<Integer> newList = new ArrayList<>(list);
    newList.add(element);
    return Collections.unmodifiableList(newList);
}
```

In this scenario, addElement does not modify the original list but returns a new list with the added element. Given the same list and element, it will always return an identical new list, thereby maintaining referential transparency.

Let's now consider a code example demonstrating the concept within the broader context of function composition:

```
int multiplyByTwo(int x) {
    return x * 2;
}

int addThree(int x) {
    return x + 3;
}

int composedFunction(int x) {
```

```
    return addThree(multiplyByTwo(x));
}
```

The function composedFunction can be reasoned about systematically. For composedFunction(5), we first evaluate multiplyByTwo(5) which gives 10, followed by addThree(10) which yields 13. This chains of calls, facilitated by referential transparency, ensure predictability and ease of understanding.

The adherence to referential transparency and pure functions empowers functional programming paradigms and facilitates techniques like lazy evaluation. Since expressions are guaranteed to yield the same values irrespective of evaluation time, computations can be deferred until their results are needed, optimizing performance.

Even in the context of state, functional programming approaches state management through concepts like monads (as seen in languages like Haskell). In essence, monads encapsulate state changes and side effects, ensuring code remains pure and referentially transparent from the functional programming perspective. The Java equivalent is managing side effects through constructs like the Optional class and streams.

Ultimately, referential transparency is a cornerstone for achieving robust and maintainable software, enabling developers to build systems where component behaviors are consistent, predictable, and easy to compose.

2.10 Declarative Programming

Declarative programming is a paradigm that expresses the logic of a computation without describing its control flow. Unlike imperative programming, which explicitly outlines every step in an algorithm, declarative programming focuses on the desired outcome and lets the underlying language mechanisms determine how to achieve this outcome. This approach aligns well with functional programming principles and reinforces immutability, pure functions, and higher-order functions.

Characteristics of Declarative Programming:

- **Expression of Logic:** In declarative programming, you articulate what you want to accomplish rather than how to accomplish it. This intrinsic separation allows developers to focus on problem-solving rather than procedure formulation.

- **Abstraction:** Declarative programming emphasizes a higher level of abstraction. This abstraction can encapsulate complex behavior behind simple expressions, making code more readable and maintainable.
- **Side Effect Minimization:** By favoring pure functions, declarative programming significantly reduces side effects, which are alterations in state that do not depend solely on the function inputs.

Differences from Imperative Programming: Imperative programming emphasizes explicit commands for the computer to follow with a clear sequence of steps. Examples of imperative languages include C, Java, and Python when used in a conventional procedural manner. In contrast, declarative programming is exemplified by languages like SQL, which describes *what* data to retrieve rather than *how* to retrieve it.

Declarative Constructs in Java: Java is traditionally an imperative language, but with the introduction of features such as the Stream API in Java 8, it supports more declarative constructs. Consider the following imperative approach to filter and collect names:

```
// Imperative approach
List<String> names = Arrays.asList("Alice", "Bob", "Charlie", "Dave");
List<String> result = new ArrayList<>();
for (String name : names) {
    if (name.startsWith("A")) {
        result.add(name);
    }
}
```

The equivalent declarative version utilizes Java Streams:

```
// Declarative approach with Streams
List<String> names = Arrays.asList("Alice", "Bob", "Charlie", "Dave");
List<String> result = names.stream()
                           .filter(name -> name.startsWith("A"))
                           .collect(Collectors.toList());
```

The declarative version expresses *what* to filter in a more concise manner, improving readability and reducing potential errors associated with mutating state.

Functional Style in Java: With Java Streams, one can leverage functional programming techniques to implement various operations declaratively. Common operations include map, filter, and reduce:

- map: Applies a given function to each element of the stream.

- filter: Produces a stream containing elements that match a given predicate.
- reduce: Aggregates stream elements into a single result by iteratively applying a combining function.

Consider a functional style example that combines these operations:

```
// Functional style example
List<String> names = Arrays.asList("Alice", "Bob", "Charlie", "Dave");
String concatenatedNames = names.stream()
                    .filter(name -> name.length() > 3)
                    .map(String::toUpperCase)
                    .reduce("", (s1, s2) -> s1 + s2);
```

This code filters names longer than three characters, converts them to uppercase, and concatenates them into a single string, demonstrating a composition of declarative operations.

Recursive Structures: Recursion inherently suits declarative paradigms, as it emphasizes expressing solutions in terms of simpler sub-problems. Consider the factorial function:

Imperative version:

```
// Imperative factorial
int factorial(int n) {
    int result = 1;
    for (int i = 1; i <= n; i++) {
        result *= i;
    }
    return result;
}
```

Declarative (recursive) version:

```
// Declarative factorial
int factorial(int n) {
    if (n == 0) return 1;
    return n * factorial(n - 1);
}
```

The recursive version succinctly expresses the definition of factorial, aligning with the declarative paradigm.

Declarative Data Querying with SQL: SQL (Structured Query Language) is a prime example of declarative programming. When querying a database, you specify the *what* rather than the *how*. Consider the SQL statement:

```
// SQL query
SELECT name FROM employees WHERE department = 'Engineering';
```

This query indicates what information to retrieve from the database without specifying the underlying mechanics of data access and retrieval.

Declarative programming favours abstraction, reduces side effects, and provides a concise way to write code, making it an advantageous paradigm in functional programming contexts. As Java continues to evolve, it increasingly incorporates declarative constructs like Streams and lambdas, enabling developers to leverage the benefits of functional programming while maintaining Java's robustness.

2.11 Side Effects and How to Avoid Them

Side effects occur in a program when functions interact with factors outside their local environment or when their execution depends on external states. Common examples of side effects include modifying a global variable, I/O operations such as reading from or writing to a file, and changing the state of mutable objects. In functional programming, side effects are avoided to maintain referential transparency, making reasoning about the program easier and enhancing modularity and testability.

The primary method of avoiding side effects in functional programming is to write pure functions—functions where the return value is determined solely by its input values, without observable side effects. To illustrate this, consider a simple example of a pure function and an impure function:

```
public int add(int x, int y) {
    return x + y;
}

public int impureAdd(int x, int y) {
    globalSum += x + y; // globalSum is a global variable
    return globalSum;
}
```

In the code above, the add function is pure because its output depends only on its input arguments. In contrast, the impureAdd function is impure as it alters the state of the global variable globalSum.

There are several strategies to avoid side effects in functional programming:

- **Immutability:** Ensure that data structures are immutable. Any operation on an immutable structure results in a new structure rather than modifying the existing one.

- **Pure Functions:** Design functions to depend solely on their input arguments and avoid modifying anything outside their scope.
- **Avoid Shared States:** Do not use shared states between functions; instead, pass the necessary data explicitly through function arguments.
- **Functional Interfaces:** Use functional interfaces that promote stateless operations, such as Java's Function, Supplier, Consumer, etc.
- **Local State Encapsulation:** Encapsulate state within functions or objects to prevent unwanted modifications.

Immutability in Practice Immutability can be implemented using immutable data structures. For instance, Java offers the Collections.unmodifiableList for lists that cannot be modified:

```
List<Integer> mutableList = Arrays.asList(1, 2, 3);
List<Integer> immutableList = Collections.unmodifiableList(mutableList);

// Throws UnsupportedOperationException
immutableList.add(4);
```

Example of a Pure Function To emphasize the importance of pure functions, consider the following implementation of a function that calculates the sum of elements in a list:

```
public int sumOfList(List<Integer> numbers) {
    return numbers.stream().reduce(0, Integer::sum);
}
```

This function leverages Java Streams to compute the sum without side effects, as it does not modify the input list.

Avoiding Shared States Shared states can lead to unpredictable behavior in the presence of concurrent executions. Here is how to avoid shared states by using function arguments:

```
public int computeSum(int[] numbers) {
    return IntStream.of(numbers).sum();
}
```

In this example, the function computeSum works directly with the numbers passed as an argument, avoiding any global variables or shared states.

Using Functional Interfaces Utilize Java's functional interfaces to ensure stateless operations:

```
Function<Integer, Integer> square = x -> x * x;
List<Integer> numbers = Arrays.asList(1, 2, 3, 4);
List<Integer> squares = numbers.stream()
                               .map(square)
                               .collect(Collectors.toList());
```

Local State Encapsulation Encapsulate state within functions or objects to prevent external modifications:

```
public class Counter {
    private int count = 0;

    public int increment() {
        return ++count;
    }

    public int getCount() {
        return count;
    }
}
```

Even though the Counter class maintains a state, it is encapsulated within the class, and external code cannot directly modify it.

To further illustrate the avoidance of side effects, consider an algorithm designed to filter even numbers from a list and collect them into a new list without modifying the input list:

Algorithm 2: Filter Even Numbers

Input: List of integers $numbers$
Output: List of integers $evenNumbers$

$evenNumbers \leftarrow$ new empty list;
for num *in* $numbers$ **do**
  if $num \mod 2 == 0$ **then**
    $evenNumbers.add(num)$;
  end
end
return $evenNumbers$;

This algorithm encapsulates its operations without side effects, returning a new list of even numbers instead of modifying the input list.

Adherence to these principles not only helps in avoiding side effects but also aligns with the broader goals of functional programming by emphasizing pure functions, immutability, and greater modularity.

Chapter 3

Functional Interfaces and Lambda Expressions

This chapter explores functional interfaces and lambda expressions, pivotal elements in Java's functional programming landscape. It covers the definition and use of built-in and custom functional interfaces, the syntax and utilization of lambda expressions, and how they interact with functional interfaces. Additionally, method and constructor references, the java.util.function package, scopes, closures, higher-order functions, and best practices for using lambda expressions are discussed to provide a thorough understanding of these fundamental concepts.

3.1 Introduction to Functional Interfaces

A functional interface in Java is an interface that contains a single abstract method, also known as a SAM (Single Abstract Method). These interfaces can be used with lambda expressions, method references, and constructor references, enabling a functional programming style in Java. The conceptual foundation lies in representing a single functionality with the abstract method and allowing it to be implemented with concise, event-driven, and often anonymous code.

Java 8 introduced the '@FunctionalInterface' annotation to indicate that an interface type declaration is intended to be a functional interface.

This annotation is not mandatory but highly recommended as it allows the compiler to enforce this intent, throwing a compilation error if the interface does not adhere to the constraints of a functional interface. For clarity and maintainability, leveraging this annotation is a best practice.

Functional interfaces have played a crucial role in streamlining the API of Java. Consider the following example of a functional interface:

```
@FunctionalInterface
public interface MyFunctionalInterface {
    void execute();
}
```

Here, MyFunctionalInterface contains a single abstract method execute(). This interface enables the use of lambda expressions to provide a concrete implementation of execute(), thus facilitating cleaner and more readable code.

```
MyFunctionalInterface myFunc = () -> System.out.println("Execution in progress");
myFunc.execute(); // Outputs: Execution in progress
```

In this context, the lambda expression () -> System.out.println("Execution in progress") provides an implementation of the execute() method. This implementation approach is succinct and avoids the boilerplate code associated with anonymous inner classes.

Functional interfaces also serve as the foundational elements for many operations in the java.util.function package. For example, the java.util.function.Predicate interface is defined as follows:

```
@FunctionalInterface
public interface Predicate<T> {
    boolean test(T t);
}
```

The test method is the single abstract method within this interface, making it functional. This interface can be used with lambda expressions to perform operations such as filtering collections:

```
List<String> names = Arrays.asList("Alice", "Bob", "Charlie");
Predicate<String> startsWithA = (name) -> name.startsWith("A");
names.stream().filter(startsWithA).forEach(System.out::println);
// Outputs: Alice
```

In this example, the lambda expression (name) -> name.startsWith("A") provides a concrete implementation of the test method in the Predicate interface, enabling the filter operation to be elegantly passed in a functional manner.

The power of functional interfaces extends beyond simple scenarios. They facilitate higher-order functions, which are functions that can take other functions as parameters or return them as results. This brings us into paradigms previously less accessible in Java before functional programming was introduced more robustly in Java 8.

A deeper understanding of functional interfaces can best be appreciated by exploring the differences between standard interfaces and functional interfaces. Here are the key points:

- A functional interface contains exactly one abstract method.
- Functional interfaces may contain multiple default or static methods.
- The @FunctionalInterface annotation is optional but enforces the intended design.
- Functional interfaces can leverage lambda expressions, method references, and constructor references.

Consider the following example with default methods:

```
@FunctionalInterface
public interface Calculator {
    int calculate(int a, int b);

    default int add(int a, int b) {
        return a + b;
    }

    default int subtract(int a, int b) {
        return a - b;
    }
}
```

In this example, Calculator is still a functional interface since it has a single abstract method calculate. The additional default methods add and subtract do not affect its functional interface status. This example also showcases the flexibility added in Java 8 to allow interfaces to have concrete methods, striking a balance between functionality and simplicity.

Using a functional interface with a lambda expression:

```
Calculator multiply = (a, b) -> a * b;
int result = multiply.calculate(5, 3); // Outputs: 15
```

The lambda expression (a, b) -> a * b effectively implements the calculate method in the Calculator interface, illustrating the conciseness and clarity functional programming introduces to the Java language.

The move towards functional programming in Java through constructs like functional interfaces represents a significant shift towards more flexible, expressive, and cleaner code patterns, allowing for the leveraging of lambda expressions to model behaviors with precision and readability.

3.2 Built-in Functional Interfaces in Java

Java provides several built-in functional interfaces that facilitate the use of functional programming constructs. These interfaces are collectively located in the java.util.function package, and they encompass a variety of common use-cases and operational paradigms. Understanding these built-in functional interfaces is crucial for effective functional programming in Java as they offer a standardized way to manipulate and process data using lambda expressions.

The java.util.function package includes several core functional interfaces, many of which are generic and parameterized for specific data types. Here are the most commonly used built-in functional interfaces:

- Function<T, R>
- Consumer<T>
- Supplier<T>
- Predicate<T>
- BiFunction<T, U, R>

Each of these interfaces targets different functional programming scenarios:

Function<T, R> represents a function that takes an input of type T and returns a result of type R. It includes one abstract method apply:

```
@FunctionalInterface
public interface Function<T, R> {
    R apply(T t);
}
```

This interface is useful for transforming an input type T to an output type R, which is commonly required in operations such as map-reduce or stream transformations.

Consumer<T> represents an operation that takes an input of type T and returns no result (i.e., it operates via side-effects). The main method provided in this interface is accept:

```
@FunctionalInterface
public interface Consumer<T> {
    void accept(T t);
}
```

Consumer<T> is particularly useful for operations where we need to perform an action on an element but don't need to return any value, such as logging or printing values from a list.

Supplier<T> represents a supplier of results, essentially providing a mechanism to generate or supply values without taking any input. It differs significantly from Function<T, R> in that it does not consume any arguments. The functional method defined in the Supplier interface is get:

```
@FunctionalInterface
public interface Supplier<T> {
    T get();
}
```

Supplier<T> is often used for lazy evaluation or deferred execution scenarios. For example, generating a random value or fetching data from an external service.

Predicate<T> represents a single argument function that returns a boolean value. It is used for evaluating a condition or making a decision based on an input argument. The core method in this interface is test:

```
@FunctionalInterface
public interface Predicate<T> {
    boolean test(T t);
}
```

Predicate<T> is instrumental in filtering streams or collections and implementing conditional checks.

BiFunction<T, U, R> represents a function that accepts two arguments T and U and produces a result of type R. The main method provided by this interface is apply:

```
@FunctionalInterface
public interface BiFunction<T, U, R> {
    R apply(T t, U u);
```

```
}
```

BiFunction<T, U, R> is particularly useful when an operation depends on two inputs and results in an output. For instance, adding two numbers or concatenating two strings.

To illustrate, let's consider practical examples for each of these interfaces.

Example Usage of Function<T, R>:

```
Function<Integer, String> intToString = integer -> "Number: " + integer;
String result = intToString.apply(5); // result is "Number: 5"
```

Example Usage of Consumer<T>:

```
Consumer<String> printConsumer = str -> System.out.println(str);
printConsumer.accept("Hello, World!"); // prints "Hello, World!"
```

Example Usage of Supplier<T>:

```
Supplier<Double> randomSupplier = () -> Math.random();
Double randomValue = randomSupplier.get(); // gets a random number
```

Example Usage of Predicate<T>:

```
Predicate<Integer> isEven = number -> number % 2 == 0;
boolean check = isEven.test(4); // check is true
```

Example Usage of BiFunction<T, U, R>:

```
BiFunction<String, String, String> concatStrings = (str1, str2) -> str1 + str2;
String concatenated = concatStrings.apply("Hello, ", "World!"); // concatenated is "
    Hello, World!"
```

These examples highlight the simplicity and power of using built-in functional interfaces in Java. Each interface caters to specific functional requirements, enabling developers to write concise, readable, and maintainable code. By leveraging these built-in interfaces, programmers can harness the full potential of lambda expressions and functional programming paradigms in Java.

3.3 Defining Custom Functional Interfaces

In Java, a functional interface is an interface that contains only one abstract method, known as the functional method. This single abstract method defines the function's signature that a lambda expression can provide. Although the interface might include other methods, such as default or static methods, only one abstract method is permitted. To comprehensively define custom functional interfaces, we start by understanding the @FunctionalInterface annotation and proceed to create custom functional interfaces as illustrated through examples.

A functional interface must adhere to specific conventions in Java. The @FunctionalInterface annotation is typically used to signal that the interface is intended to be functional. This annotation is not obligatory but recommended as it guarantees compile-time checking, ensuring that the interface maintains the single abstract method constraint. Consider the following example:

```
@FunctionalInterface
public interface MyFunctionalInterface {
    void execute();
}
```

Here, MyFunctionalInterface is declared using the @FunctionalInterface annotation, and it contains exactly one abstract method called execute. A lambda expression targeting this interface must have a compatible signature.

Custom functional interfaces can be defined for various functional programming concepts, such as operations, predicates, suppliers, or consumers. For instance, if we want to define an operation that accepts two integer values and returns their sum, we might define a functional interface as follows:

```
@FunctionalInterface
public interface BinaryOperation {
    int operate(int a, int b);
}
```

This interface defines a binary operation using the operate method. To implement this using a lambda expression:

```
BinaryOperation sum = (a, b) -> a + b;
int result = sum.operate(5, 3);
System.out.println(result);
```

8

By employing a lambda expression (a, b) -> a + b, we succinctly define the logic of the operation. The type of the parameters and the return type are inferred from the method signature in the functional interface.

Additionally, custom functional interfaces can include default and static methods. These methods provide reusable implementations that concrete classes can inherit or use directly. Default methods enable backward compatibility for interfaces, allowing the addition of new methods to existing interfaces without breaking existing implementations.

```
@FunctionalInterface
public interface EnhancedBinaryOperation {
    int operate(int a, int b);

    default int identity() {
        return 0;
    }

    static int add(int a, int b) {
        return a + b;
    }
}
```

In the example above, EnhancedBinaryOperation includes a default method identity, which returns the identity element of addition (zero). Also, it has a static method add that provides a concrete implementation of the addition operation. The functional method operate remains the sole abstract method, keeping the interface functional.

Next, consider defining a custom functional interface to represent a predicate, which is a boolean-valued function of one argument. Here is a way to define such an interface:

```
@FunctionalInterface
public interface MyPredicate<T> {
    boolean test(T t);
}
```

In this interface, MyPredicate takes a generic type T and the method test evaluates the argument, returning a boolean. This interface can be implemented using lambda expressions to encapsulate various logical conditions.

```
MyPredicate<String> isEmpty = s -> s.isEmpty();
boolean result = isEmpty.test("");
System.out.println(result);
```

```
true
```

The lambda expression s -> s.isEmpty() checks if the string is empty, aligning with the functional interface MyPredicate<String>. Functional interfaces thus provide a powerful abstraction by capturing the essence of a function signature and its behavior.

The principles of defining custom functional interfaces open the door to creating sophisticated functional programming paradigms in Java. Custom functional interfaces enrich the language's expressiveness, enhance code reusability, and support the declarative programming style facilitated by lambda expressions. Such interfaces are fundamental to adopting functional programming techniques in Java, leveraging type inference, and ensuring clearer, more concise code constructs.

3.4 Introduction to Lambda Expressions

Lambda expressions are a core feature introduced in Java 8, designed to enhance the language's expressiveness and facilitate functional programming. They enable you to treat code as data, allowing methods to be passed as arguments, stored in variables, and returned from other methods. This section introduces lambda expressions, emphasizing their syntax, utility, and integration with functional interfaces.

A lambda expression in Java provides a clear and concise way to represent an anonymous function—that is, a function without a declared name. The primary goal of lambda expressions is to enable functional programming patterns by providing syntactic sugar that simplifies writing instances of functional interfaces.

Consider the example of sorting a list using a comparator. Before the advent of lambda expressions in Java, implementing a Comparator interface required either creating a new class or using an anonymous class:

```
List<String> names = Arrays.asList("John", "Alice", "Bob");

Collections.sort(names, new Comparator<String>() {
    @Override
    public int compare(String s1, String s2) {
        return s1.compareTo(s2);
    }
});
```

This approach, while functional, is verbose and clutters the code with boilerplate. Lambda expressions, on the other hand, provide a more succinct notation:

```
List<String> names = Arrays.asList("John", "Alice", "Bob");

Collections.sort(names, (s1, s2) -> s1.compareTo(s2));
```

The lambda expression `(s1, s2) -> s1.compareTo(s2)` succinctly captures the behavior of the comparator. Here, `s1` and `s2` are the parameters of the lambda expression, and `s1.compareTo(s2)` is the body that defines the operation.

Syntax of Lambda Expressions The syntax of lambda expressions consists of three main parts: 1. Comma-separated list of formal parameters enclosed in parentheses. 2. The "arrow token" (->) separating the parameters and the body. 3. The body, which can either be a single expression or a block of code.

A lambda expression expressing a single statement does not require curly braces:

```
(param1, param2) -> expression
```

For example:

```
(int a, int b) -> a + b
```

When the body of the lambda expression contains multiple statements, curly braces are necessary:

```
(param1, param2) -> {
    statement1;
    statement2;
    return result;
}
```

For example:

```
(int a, int b) -> {
    System.out.println("Adding values");
    return a + b;
}
```

Type Inference in Lambda Expressions Java compiler uses type inference to deduce the types of lambda parameters. This means explicit type declarations can often be omitted if they can be inferred from the context. Compare the following declarations:

```
Comparator<String> comp = (String s1, String s2) -> s1.compareTo(s2);
Comparator<String> comp = (s1, s2) -> s1.compareTo(s2);
```

Both declarations are valid, but the latter leverages type inference for more concise code. Note, however, that if the context doesn't provide enough information for type inference, explicit types may still be required.

Lambda Expressions and Functional Interfaces Lambda expressions are closely tied to functional interfaces, interfaces with a single abstract method, also known as SAM interfaces (Single Abstract Method interfaces). The functional interface serves as the target type for a lambda expression, providing the context in which the lambda can

be used. For instance, `java.util.Comparator<String>` interfaces with a single method `compare()` can be assigned a lambda expression like:

```
Comparator<String> comparator = (s1, s2) -> s1.compareTo(s2);
```

The Comparator interface here is a functional interface, and the lambda expression provides the implementation of the abstract method compare().

Using Lambda Expressions in Collections API The power of lambda expressions becomes evident when used with the Java Collections framework, which includes several methods designed to accept functional interfaces. For example, the List interface provides the forEach method to perform an action for each element of the list:

```
List<String> names = Arrays.asList("John", "Alice", "Bob");

names.forEach(name -> System.out.println(name));
```

Similarly, stream operations like filter, map, and reduce can process collections in a functional manner:

```
List<String> filteredNames = names.stream()
                                  .filter(name -> name.startsWith("A"))
                                  .collect(Collectors.toList());
```

The lambda expression `name -> name.startsWith("A")` serves as the predicate for the filter method, demonstrating its seamless integration into the Collections API for functional-style data processing.

Understanding how to effectively use lambda expressions in conjunction with functional interfaces is a foundational aspect of mastering functional programming in Java. This capability facilitates the development of clean, readable, and maintainable code, leveraging the functional programming paradigm within the object-oriented landscape of Java.

3.5 Syntax of Lambda Expressions

Lambda expressions in Java provide a clear and concise way to represent one-method interfaces (commonly referred to as functional interfaces). The syntax and utilization of lambda expressions enable developers to express instances of single-method interfaces more succinctly. The general structure of a lambda expression can be broken down as follows:

```
(parameters) -> expression
```

where:

- parameters refer to the input parameters, identical to those in a method declaration.
- arrow operator (->) separates the parameters from the body of the lambda expression.
- expression is the body of the lambda, which can be either a single expression or a block of statements.

We can classify the syntax of a lambda expression into several forms, depending on specific cases:

No Parameters:

When the lambda expression does not take any parameters, we utilize empty parentheses. For example, a simple lambda that returns a fixed string can be written as:

```
() -> "Fixed Output"
```

Single Parameter without Type Declaration:

For lambdas with a single parameter, we may omit its type, relying on the compiler's type inference:

```
x -> x * x
```

Here, the parameter x is squared.

Single Parameter with Type Declaration:

Specifying the type of the single parameter could enhance readability or be necessary in certain contexts. For example:

```
(int x) -> x * x
```

Multiple Parameters:

When dealing with multiple parameters, both the types and parentheses are required:

```
(int a, int b) -> a + b
```

Alternatively, we can omit the parameter types for simplicity, allowing type inference to manage them:

```
(a, b) -> a + b
```

Multiple Statements:

In more complex scenarios where the lambda body comprises multiple statements, braces {} must enclose the body, and a return statement is used if necessary:

```
(int x, int y) -> {
    int sum = x + y;
    int product = x * y;
    return sum + product;
}
```

The Syntax of Lambda Block:

When a lambda body is a block, any statements within the block must be enclosed by braces and, if the block does not explicitly return a value, the lambda's return type is void. For instance:

```
(int a, int b) -> {
    System.out.println("Sum: " + (a + b));
}
```

In this example, no return value is expected from the lambda expression, hence it serves as a void lambda block.

Type Inference:

One of the benefits of lambda expressions is type inference, which allows the omission of parameter types where the compiler can deduce them. Using the following example:

```
Comparator<String> comparator = (s1, s2) -> s1.compareTo(s2);
```

Instead of explicitly declaring the parameter types for s1 and s2, the compiler infers them based on the context provided by the Comparator<String> interface.

Utilizing Var in Lambda Parameters:

Java 11 introduced the option of using var in lambda parameters, enabling more uniform parameter declaration syntax. Consider the example:

```
(var x, var y) -> x + y
```

Note that var cannot be mixed with explicit type declarations; it must be consistently used for all parameters in the lambda expression if opted.

Advanced Use Cases:

Lambda expressions maintain a robust interaction with other features in Java, including exception handling and generics.

For instance, a lambda expression can handle exceptions within its body:

```
(fileName) -> {
    try {
        return new String(Files.readAllBytes(Paths.get(fileName)));
    } catch (IOException e) {
        throw new UncheckedIOException(e);
    }
}
```

It can also be generic, where the lambda's types are inferred from a generic functional interface:

```
Function<Integer, Integer> square = x -> x * x;
Function<Double, Double> half = x -> x / 2;
```

Both examples illustrate lambdas with specific contexts, demonstrating their flexibility across various real-world scenarios.

Overall, understanding the syntax of lambda expressions lays a foundational role in effectively leveraging Java's functional programming features. The concise syntax and type inference capabilities align with write-less, do-more principles, paralleling Java's goal of enhancing developer productivity and code readability.

3.6 Using Lambda Expressions with Functional Interfaces

Lambda expressions serve as a powerful mechanism to define the behavior of functional interfaces in a concise and readable manner. This section details the process of utilizing lambda expressions with various functional interfaces in Java. It begins by examining the syntax and fundamental components before delving into practical examples leveraging the java.util.function package.

A lambda expression essentially provides an implementation of the abstract method defined in a functional interface. This makes the functional interface a target type for lambda expressions. Syntax of a lambda expression typically follows this structure:

```
// (parameters) -> expression or block of statements
(parameters) -> { statements }
```

Consider the java.util.function.Predicate interface, which is a one-parameter function returning a boolean value. The test method is its solitary abstract method:

```
@FunctionalInterface
public interface Predicate<T> {
    boolean test(T t);
}
```

To use a lambda expression with Predicate<T>, you can implement the test method as follows:

```
Predicate<String> isEmpty = (String s) -> s.isEmpty();
System.out.println(isEmpty.test("")); // prints: true
System.out.println(isEmpty.test("Hello, World!")); // prints: false
```

The lambda expression (String s) -> s.isEmpty() is equivalent to implementing the test method of Predicate<String> using an anonymous class. This shows the succinctness and readability benefit of lambdas in contrast to traditional anonymous classes.

Using Predicates with Collections

One common use case for lambda expressions with functional interfaces is filtering collections. For example, the Collection interface in Java provides an removeIf method, which accepts a Predicate to decide which elements should be removed:

```
List<String> names = new ArrayList<>(Arrays.asList("Alice", "", "Bob", "Charlie"));
names.removeIf((String s) -> s.isEmpty());
System.out.println(names); // prints: [Alice, Bob, Charlie]
```

You can achieve the same functionality with method references, which further enhances readability:

```
names.removeIf(String::isEmpty);
System.out.println(names); // prints: [Alice, Bob, Charlie]
```

Using Consumers

The java.util.function.Consumer<T> interface represents an operation that accepts a single input argument and returns no result. Its functional method accept is implemented using a lambda expression as illustrated:

```
Consumer<String> printUpperCase = (String s) -> System.out.println(s.toUpperCase
    ());
printUpperCase.accept("lambda"); // prints: LAMBDA
```

The forEach method in the Iterable interface can also use lambda expressions:

```
List<String> letters = Arrays.asList("a", "b", "c");
letters.forEach(letter -> System.out.print(letter.toUpperCase() + " ")); // prints: A B
    C
```

Using Functions

The java.util.function.Function<T, R> interface represents a function that accepts one argument and produces a result. The apply method is implemented using a lambda expression:

```
Function<String, Integer> lengthFunction = (String s) -> s.length();
System.out.println(lengthFunction.apply("lambda")); // prints: 6
```

Using Suppliers

The java.util.function.Supplier<T> interface represents a supplier of results. Implementing the get method with a lambda expression is straightforward:

```
Supplier<String> helloSupplier = () -> "Hello, functional interfaces!";
System.out.println(helloSupplier.get()); // prints: Hello, functional interfaces!
```

Using BinaryOperators

The java.util.function.BinaryOperator<T> interface represents an operation upon two operands of the same type, producing a result of the same type as the operands. Example usage with a lambda expression:

```
BinaryOperator<Integer> sum = (Integer x, Integer y) -> x + y;
System.out.println(sum.apply(2, 3)); // prints: 5
```

These examples illustrate how lambda expressions seamlessly integrate with functional interfaces, leveraging built-in interfaces from the java.util.function package for various tasks. Embracing lambda expressions in conjunction with functional interfaces significantly enhances code readability and maintainability.

3.7 Method References and Constructor References

Method references and constructor references are shorthand notations that enhance readability and conciseness when working with lambda expressions. They allow us to refer to methods and constructors directly by their names using a double colon '::'. This syntactic sugar was introduced in Java 8, significantly simplifying code that merely invokes existing methods or constructors.

Method references can be categorized into four types:

- Static Method References
- Instance Method References of a Particular Object
- Instance Method References of an Arbitrary Object of a Particular Type
- Constructor References

Static Method References refer to static methods of a class. The syntax includes the class name followed by '::' and the method name.

```
interface Converter<F, T> {
    T convert(F from);
}

public class StaticMethodReference {
    public static Integer parse(String str) {
        return Integer.parseInt(str);
    }

    public static void main(String[] args) {
        Converter<String, Integer> converter = StaticMethodReference::parse;
        Integer converted = converter.convert("123");
        System.out.println(converted); // Output: 123
    }
}
```

In this example, the static method parse is referenced using StaticMethodReference::parse.

Instance Method References of a Particular Object refer to non-static methods of an existing object.

```
public class InstanceMethodReference {
    public void print(String str) {
        System.out.println(str);
    }

    public static void main(String[] args) {
        InstanceMethodReference instance = new InstanceMethodReference();
        Printable printable = instance::print;
        printable.print("Hello, World!"); // Output: Hello, World!
    }
}

interface Printable {
    void print(String str);
}
```

Here, instance::print references the print method of an InstanceMethodReference object named instance.

Instance Method References of an Arbitrary Object of a Particular Type refer to instance methods of a given type without specifying the specific object.

```
import java.util.Arrays;

public class ArbitraryObjectMethodReference {
    public static void main(String[] args) {
        String[] strings = { "C", "A", "B" };
        Arrays.sort(strings, String::compareToIgnoreCase);
        System.out.println(Arrays.toString(strings)); // Output: [A, B, C]
    }
}
```

In this scenario, String::compareToIgnoreCase references the compareToIgnoreCase method applicable to any String object instance.

Constructor References are used to refer to constructors. They enable us to instantiate an object using a lambda expression.

```
class Person {
    String name;

    Person(String name) {
        this.name = name;
    }
}

interface PersonFactory {
    Person create(String name);
}

public class ConstructorReference {
    public static void main(String[] args) {
        PersonFactory factory = Person::new;
        Person person = factory.create("John");
        System.out.println(person.name); // Output: John
    }
}
```

Here, Person::new references the Person class constructor, providing a succinct way to create new Person instances.

Method and constructor references improve code readability and streamline expressions where methods or constructors are passed around. An understanding of these references fosters the development of concise and expressive code in functional programming using Java.

3.8 Functional Interfaces in the java.util.function Package

The java.util.function package is a comprehensive suite of functional interfaces designed to facilitate functional programming in Java. These interfaces encompass a wide array of functional paradigms, enabling developers to leverage pre-defined behavior patterns without the necessity to craft bespoke functional interfaces. This section elucidates the various functional interfaces contained within the java.util.function package, illustrating their definitions, typical use cases, and practical applications in Java programming.

1. Predicate

The Predicate interface encapsulates a boolean-valued function that accepts a single argument. It is typically used for evaluating a condition or a filter criterion.

```
@FunctionalInterface
public interface Predicate<T> {
    boolean test(T t);
}
```

A common application of Predicate is in stream filtering operations. For example, to filter a list of integers to retain only even numbers:

```
List<Integer> numbers = Arrays.asList(1, 2, 3, 4, 5, 6);
List<Integer> evenNumbers = numbers.stream()
                                   .filter(n -> n % 2 == 0)
                                   .collect(Collectors.toList());
System.out.println(evenNumbers);
```

```
[2, 4, 6]
```

2. Consumer

The Consumer interface represents an operation that accepts a single input argument and returns no result.

```
@FunctionalInterface
public interface Consumer<T> {
    void accept(T t);
}
```

Consumer is often used for operations involving a single input. For instance, printing each element in a list:

```
List<String> names = Arrays.asList("Alice", "Bob", "Charlie");
names.forEach(name -> System.out.println(name));
```

```
Alice
Bob
Charlie
```

3. Function

The Function interface applies a function to an input and produces an output. It is parametrized with the input type and the result type.

```
@FunctionalInterface
public interface Function<T, R> {
    R apply(T t);
}
```

An instance where Function is beneficial includes mapping elements from one type to another. A common use case is extracting the length of strings:

```
List<String> names = Arrays.asList("Alice", "Bob", "Charlie");
List<Integer> nameLengths = names.stream()
                                 .map(name -> name.length())
                                 .collect(Collectors.toList());
System.out.println(nameLengths);
```

```
[5, 3, 7]
```

4. Supplier

The Supplier interface represents a supplier of results, typically used for generating or providing a value without any input argument.

```
@FunctionalInterface
public interface Supplier<T> {
    T get();
}
```

In many scenarios, Supplier is utilized to produce or supply values when needed. For example, creating a random number generator:

```
Supplier<Double> randomValueSupplier = () -> Math.random();
System.out.println(randomValueSupplier.get());
```

```
0.7367249861648982
```

5. BiFunction

The BiFunction interface is akin to the Function interface but extends the concept to accepting two input arguments and providing a result.

```
@FunctionalInterface
public interface BiFunction<T, U, R> {
    R apply(T t, U u);
}
```

A use case for BiFunction involves operations on two parameters, such as concatenating two strings:

```
BiFunction<String, String, String> concatFunction = (a, b) -> a + b;
System.out.println(concatFunction.apply("Hello, ", "World!"));
```

Hello, World!

6. UnaryOperator and BinaryOperator

UnaryOperator and BinaryOperator are specializations of Function and BiFunction, respectively. UnaryOperator operates on a single operand and returns a result of the same type, while BinaryOperator operates on two operands of the same type and produces a result of the same type.

```
@FunctionalInterface
public interface UnaryOperator<T> extends Function<T, T> { }

@FunctionalInterface
public interface BinaryOperator<T> extends BiFunction<T, T, T> { }
```

For instance, implementing an increment operation using UnaryOperator:

```
UnaryOperator<Integer> increment = x -> x + 1;
System.out.println(increment.apply(5));
```

6

And utilizing BinaryOperator to find the maximum of two integers:

```
BinaryOperator<Integer> maxOperator = (a, b) -> a > b ? a : b;
System.out.println(maxOperator.apply(3, 7));
```

7

7. Additional Functional Interfaces

The java.util.function package provides several other functional interfaces tailored for various specific tasks, such as:

- BiConsumer<T, U>: Accepts two input arguments and performs an operation without returning a result.
- DoubleFunction<R> and other primitive-specific variants: Like Function but optimized for primitive types.
- IntPredicate, LongPredicate, and other predicate variants: Offer specialized predicates for primitive types.

Each of these interfaces serves to streamline functional programming in Java, providing a robust foundation for writing concise, expressive code. Integrating these functional interfaces in practical scenarios empowers developers to utilize the full potential of Java's functional programming capabilities, enabling elegant and efficient solutions to complex programming tasks through lambda expressions and method references.

3.9 Scopes and Closures in Lambda Expressions

In Java, understanding variable scope and closures is paramount when working with lambda expressions. These concepts dictate how variables are accessed and how lambda expressions operate within their enclosing context. To establish a clear comprehension, let's delve into scopes first, followed by closures.

Variable Scope describes the region within a program where a variable is accessible. The scope of variables can be broadly categorized into three types in the context of lambda expressions:

- **Local Variables** - Variables that are declared within a method.
- **Instance Variables** - Variables that are declared within a class but outside any method.
- **Static Variables** - Variables that belong to the class rather than any particular instance.

Consider the following example to illustrate variable scope within lambda expressions:

```
public class ScopeExample {
    private static int staticNum = 5; // Static variable
    private int instanceNum = 10; // Instance variable

    public void demoScope() {
        int localNum = 20; // Local variable

        // Lambda expression accessing different variable scopes
        Runnable r = () -> {
            System.out.println("Static Num: " + staticNum);
            System.out.println("Instance Num: " + instanceNum);
            System.out.println("Local Num: " + localNum);
        };

        r.run();
    }
```

```
}
```

Output:
Static Num: 5
Instance Num: 10
Local Num: 20

In the demoScope method, the lambda expression accesses a static variable (staticNum), an instance variable (instanceNum), and a local variable (localNum). This capability to access variables from different scopes is facilitated by closures.

Closures are constructs that allow a lambda expression to capture variables from its enclosing scope. In Java, this is achieved through the mechanism known as "effective finality". For a local variable to be accessed within a lambda expression, it must be effectively final. This means that the variable should not be modified after being assigned.

Consider the following example to delve further into closures:

```
public class ClosureExample {

    public static void main(String[] args) {
        int num = 30; // This must be effectively final

        // Local variable capture using lambda expression
        Runnable r = () -> System.out.println("Captured Num: " + num);

        r.run();
    }
}
```

Output:
Captured Num: 30

In this example, the variable num is captured by the lambda expression. If we attempt to modify num after its declaration, we would encounter a compile-time error:

```
public class ClosureExample {

    public static void main(String[] args) {
        int num = 30;

        // Local variable capture using lambda expression
        Runnable r = () -> System.out.println("Captured Num: " + num);

        num = 40; // This will cause a compile-time error

        r.run();
    }
}
```

The Java compiler will produce an error indicating that num should be effectively final. This restriction ensures that the lambda expression captures a snapshot of the variable's value at the moment the lambda is created, safeguarding against inconsistent or unexpected behavior.

It's essential to comprehend how lambda expressions maintain references to the captured variables. For instance, if a lambda captures an instance variable or a static variable, it holds a reference to the instance or class containing those variables. This referencing can, in certain scenarios, prevent objects from being garbage-collected, leading to potential memory management issues.

Understanding the interplay between scopes and closures is crucial, especially within the context of concurrency. When employing lambda expressions in multi-threaded applications, one must ensure thread safety of the captured variables. Mutating captured variables from multiple threads, either directly or by invoking non-thread-safe methods, can lead to concurrency issues.

To illustrate the importance of thread safety, consider the following example:

```
public class ConcurrentExample {
    private int count = 0; // Shared instance variable

    public void incrementConcurrently() {
        Runnable r = () -> {
            for (int i = 0; i < 1000; i++) {
                count++; // Not thread-safe
            }
        };

        Thread t1 = new Thread(r);
        Thread t2 = new Thread(r);
        t1.start();
        t2.start();
    }
}
```

In this scenario, the count variable is incremented by multiple threads. Given that count++ is not an atomic operation, it may lead to inconsistent results. To ensure thread safety, one would need to synchronize access to the shared variable or use atomic variables provided by the java.util.concurrent.atomic package.

In the implementation below, the shared variable is an AtomicInteger to ensure atomic operations:

```
import java.util.concurrent.atomic.AtomicInteger;

public class ConcurrentExample {
    private AtomicInteger count = new AtomicInteger(0); // Shared Atomic variable

    public void incrementConcurrently() {
        Runnable r = () -> {
```

```
            for (int i = 0; i < 1000; i++) {
                count.incrementAndGet(); // Thread-safe increment
            }
        };

        Thread t1 = new Thread(r);
        Thread t2 = new Thread(r);
        t1.start();
        t2.start();
    }
}
```

Output:
Final count: 2000 (due to atomic and thread-safe operations)

These principles of scope and closures, integrated into the functional paradigm with lambda expressions, provide powerful capabilities that, when properly understood, can lead to expressive and efficient code.

3.10 Higher-Order Functions with Lambdas

In functional programming, higher-order functions are functions that can take other functions as arguments or return them as results. This allows for a more flexible and expressive approach to function composition, abstraction, and reuse. In Java, lambda expressions provide a concise way to define and pass behavior, making higher-order functions both powerful and easy to use.

Definition and Examples

A higher-order function (HOF) is defined as follows:

- A function that takes one or more functions as parameters.
- A function that returns a function as its result.

To illustrate, consider the following example of a higher-order function in Java:

```
import java.util.function.Function;

public class HigherOrderFunctions {

    // Higher-order function that takes a function and an integer, applies the function,
        and returns the result
    public static Integer apply(Function<Integer, Integer> func, Integer value) {
        return func.apply(value);
    }

    public static void main(String[] args) {
```

```
        // Lambda expression that doubles a number
        Function<Integer, Integer> doubler = x -> x * 2;

        // Passing the lambda expression to the higher-order function
        Integer result = apply(doubler, 5);

        // Output the result
        System.out.println(result);
    }
}
```

10

In this example, the apply method is a higher-order function that takes a Function<Integer, Integer> and an Integer, applies the function to the integer, and returns the result. The lambda expression x -> x * 2 is passed to apply along with the integer value 5. The function doubles the integer, resulting in an output of 10.

Returning Functions from Functions

A higher-order function can also return another function. Consider the following example:

```
import java.util.function.Function;

public class FunctionReturningFunction {

    // Higher-order function that returns a function to add a constant value
    public static Function<Integer, Integer> adder(Integer addTo) {
        return x -> x + addTo;
    }

    public static void main(String[] args) {
        // Create an adder function that adds 10 to its input
        Function<Integer, Integer> addTen = adder(10);

        // Apply the function to a value
        Integer result = addTen.apply(5);

        // Output the result
        System.out.println(result);
    }
}
```

15

Here, the adder function is a higher-order function that takes an integer addTo and returns a lambda expression, which adds addTo to its input. The function adder(10) returns a lambda that adds 10, and when it is applied to the value 5, the output is 15.

Function Composition

Higher-order functions enable function composition, allowing developers to create new functions by combining existing ones. The following example demonstrates function composition using Java's Function interface:

```
import java.util.function.Function;

public class FunctionComposition {

    public static void main(String[] args) {
        // Define two simple functions
        Function<Integer, Integer> square = x -> x * x;
        Function<Integer, Integer> increment = x -> x + 1;

        // Compose a new function by combining square and increment
        Function<Integer, Integer> squareAndIncrement = square.andThen(increment);

        // Apply the composed function to a value
        Integer result = squareAndIncrement.apply(4);

        // Output the result
        System.out.println(result);
    }
}
```

17

In this example, we define two functions: square and increment. Using the andThen method provided by the Function interface, we compose a new function squareAndIncrement. When this composed function is applied to the value 4, it first squares it (resulting in 16) and then increments it by 1, producing an output of 17.

Practical Applications

Higher-order functions with lambdas play a crucial role in many real-world scenarios. Consider a problem where we need to filter and transform a list of integers:

```
import java.util.Arrays;
import java.util.List;
import java.util.function.Predicate;
import java.util.function.Function;
import java.util.stream.Collectors;

public class FilterAndTransform {

    // Higher-order function that takes a predicate and a function
    public static List<Integer> filterAndTransform(List<Integer> list, Predicate<
            Integer> filter, Function<Integer, Integer> transformer) {
        return list.stream()
                   .filter(filter)
                   .map(transformer)
                   .collect(Collectors.toList());
    }

    public static void main(String[] args) {
        List<Integer> numbers = Arrays.asList(1, 2, 3, 4, 5, 6);
```

```
        // Define a predicate to filter even numbers
        Predicate<Integer> isEven = x -> x % 2 == 0;

        // Define a function to double the number
        Function<Integer, Integer> doubler = x -> x * 2;

        // Use the higher-order function to filter and transform the list
        List<Integer> result = filterAndTransform(numbers, isEven, doubler);

        // Output the result
        System.out.println(result);
    }
}
```

```
[4, 8, 12]
```

In this example, the filterAndTransform function is a higher-order function that takes a Predicate<Integer>, a Function<Integer, Integer>, and a list of integers. It filters the list using the predicate, transforms the filtered elements using the function, and collects the results into a new list. The predicate isEven filters for even numbers, and the function doubler doubles the numbers. The resulting list contains 4, 8, and 12.

Higher-order functions with lambdas provide a powerful abstraction for function composition, transformation, and combination. They facilitate code reusability, modularity, and clarity when dealing with complex functional programming tasks in Java.

3.11 Best Practices for Using Lambda Expressions

Using lambda expressions effectively in Java requires adherence to best practices that can enhance code readability, maintainability, and performance. Presented here are several guidelines to consider when incorporating lambda expressions into your functional programming workflow.

Lambda expressions should be concise and focused. The primary motive of lambda expressions is to provide a compact and straightforward way to represent instances of functional interfaces. To achieve this, lambda expressions should be succinct and perform a single task ideally. Overly complex lambda expressions can obscure the code's intent and make maintenance difficult.

```
// Optimal: Single, clear task
Function<Integer, Integer> square = x -> x * x;
```

```
// Suboptimal: Multiple tasks leading to complexity
Function<Integer, String> describeAndSquare = x -> {
    System.out.println("Received: " + x);
    return "Square: " + (x * x).toString();
};
```

Maintain type inference by letting the compiler deduce types. The type of the parameters can typically be derived from the context, making explicit parameter type declarations redundant and verbose.

```
// Optimal: Using type inference
BiFunction<Integer, Integer, Integer> sum = (a, b) -> a + b;
// Suboptimal: Explicit type declaration
BiFunction<Integer, Integer, Integer> sumExplicit = (Integer a, Integer b) -> a + b;
```

Avoid using lambda expressions where method references provide a clearer alternative. Method references can improve code readability and reduce verbosity, especially when the lambda expression simply calls another method.

```
// Using a lambda expression
Consumer<String> print = x -> System.out.println(x);
// Using a method reference
Consumer<String> printMethodReference = System.out::println;
```

When lambdas get too complex, refactor them to named methods. If a lambda expression grows beyond a few lines, consider extracting it to a named method to enhance code readability and maintainability.

```
// Complex lambda
Predicate<String> complexLambda = s -> {
    if (s == null) return false;
    return s.startsWith("A");
};
// Refactored to a method
Predicate<String> refactoredLambda = this::isStartingWithA;

private boolean isStartingWithA(String s) {
    if (s == null) return false;
    return s.startsWith("A");
}
```

Use lambda expressions judiciously in APIs. Designing APIs that leverage lambda expressions can make the code more powerful and expressive. However, the usage should be intuitive and not force the user to create lambda expressions unless necessary. Ensure that the functional interfaces used in the API are clear in their intentions and naming.

Emphasize immutability and side-effect-free operations within lambda expressions. Lambda expressions used as functional arguments should ideally avoid altering state, maintaining the principles of functional programming. Ensure lambda expressions do not rely on or modify variables outside their scope. Such practices help in avoiding unintended side effects and concurrency issues.

```
// Suboptimal: Modifying external state
List<String> results = new ArrayList<>();
Function<String, Integer> lengthUpdater = s -> {
    results.add(s);
    return s.length();
};
// Optimal: No side effects
Function<String, Integer> lengthCalculator = String::length;
```

Optimize lambda expressions for performance when necessary. While lambdas introduce minimal overhead and provide performance comparable to anonymous classes, be aware of the underlying considerations like capturing external variables which may necessitate additional object creation. Utilize lambda expressions where they provide clear advantages but remain cautious about potential pitfalls regarding performance in high-frequency or critical operations.

Apply appropriate commenting and documentation for lambda expressions that perform non-trivial operations. Although part of lambda's appeal is reduced verbosity, uncommented complex lambdas can become a maintenance headache. Documenting their purpose can aid future developers in understanding the logic encapsulated within.

```
// Lambda requiring explanation
Function<Map<String, Integer>, Map<String, Integer>> incrementValues = map ->
        map.entrySet().stream()
    .collect(Collectors.toMap(Map.Entry::getKey, entry -> entry.getValue() + 1));
// Comment to make intent clear
// This lambda increments each value in the map by 1
```

In summary, the above guidelines can enhance the effectiveness of lambda expressions, making them a powerful, readable, and maintainable part of Java's functional programming capabilities. Following these best practices ensures that lambda expressions are used to their full potential without sacrificing code clarity or efficiency.

Chapter 4

Streams and Data Processing

This chapter introduces streams and their role in data processing within Java. It covers stream creation, distinguishing between intermediate and terminal operations, and demonstrates techniques for filtering and mapping data. The chapter also explores working with primitive streams, collecting results using collectors, grouping and partitioning data, and reduction operations. Additionally, the concepts of parallel streams, performance considerations, and common use cases and patterns are discussed to provide a comprehensive understanding of streams and their application in data processing.

4.1 Introduction to Streams in Java

Streams in Java are a powerful tool for processing sequences of elements with a focus on functional programming patterns. Introduced in Java 8 under the java.util.stream package, streams facilitate bulk operations on collections of data with a syntax and set of operations inspired by functional programming paradigms.

A stream is a sequence of elements supporting sequential and parallel aggregate operations. Unlike collections, streams do not store elements; they use a pipeline of computations to process data. A stream pipeline consists of a source, zero or more intermediate operations, and a terminal operation. Most intermediate operations return a new stream, allowing operations to be chained in a fluent interface style.

Code snippet for creating a simple stream from a list:

```
List<String> myList = Arrays.asList("a", "b", "c", "d");
Stream<String> myStream = myList.stream();
```

Streams can be created from various data sources, including collections, arrays, or even I/O channels. For example, using the Stream.of method:

```
Stream<String> streamOfStrings = Stream.of("a", "b", "c", "d");
```

Intermediate operations are those that transform a stream into another stream. These operators are lazy; they are not executed until a terminal operation is invoked. Common intermediate operations include filter, map, and distinct:

```
Stream<String> filteredStream = myStream.filter(s -> s.startsWith("a"));
Stream<Integer> lengthStream = myList.stream().map(String::length);
```

Terminal operations produce a result from the stream. They trigger the processing of all intermediate operations. Examples include collect, count, findFirst, and forEach:

```
long count = myList.stream().filter(s -> s.startsWith("a")).count();
List<String> collected = myList.stream().filter(s -> s.startsWith("a")).collect(
    Collectors.toList());
```

Another critical aspect of streams is that they can be either sequential or parallel. Sequential streams process elements one at a time, whereas parallel streams divide the processing among multiple threads:

```
Stream<String> parallelStream = myList.parallelStream();
```

Streams are particularly useful for their capacity to process large data sets efficiently, allowing for operations like filtering, mapping, and reducing without requiring explicit iteration. This enables a more readable and concise code structure, which is a significant advantage over traditional loop constructs.

A diagram depicting the structure of a typical stream pipeline may help in understanding the execution flow:

```
Source -> Intermediate Operations -> Terminal Operation
```

For instance, consider the following stream pipeline:

```
List<Integer> numbers = Arrays.asList(1, 2, 3, 4, 5);
int sum = numbers.stream()
                 .filter(n -> n % 2 == 1)
                 .mapToInt(n -> n * n)
                 .sum();
```

In this pipeline, the source is a list of integers. The intermediate operations involve filtering out even numbers and mapping each remaining number to its square. The terminal operation sums the squared values.

Understanding streams is crucial for leveraging the full potential of Java's functional programming capabilities. By using streams, developers can create more efficient, readable, and maintainable code, facilitating easier data manipulation and processing.

4.2 Creating Streams

In this section, we delve into the various methods of creating streams in Java, providing a comprehensive understanding of the different techniques available and their appropriate use cases. Streams are essential for functional-style operations on sequences of elements, providing a powerful abstraction over data processing.

1. Stream Sources

Streams can be created from a variety of sources, including collections, arrays, and generated data. The most common way to create streams is from collections, using the stream() or parallelStream() methods provided by the Collection interface.

```
List<String> list = Arrays.asList("a", "b", "c");
Stream<String> stream = list.stream(); // Sequential stream
Stream<String> parallelStream = list.parallelStream(); // Parallel stream
```

Collections such as List, Set, and Map support these methods, facilitating the creation of streams from widely used data structures.

2. Arrays

Streams can also be created from arrays using the Arrays.stream() method or the Stream.of() method. These methods are particularly useful for processing primitive arrays with IntStream, LongStream, and DoubleStream.

```
String[] array = {"a", "b", "c"};
Stream<String> stream = Arrays.stream(array);
// or alternatively
```

```
Stream<String> streamOfArray = Stream.of(array);

int[] intArray = {1, 2, 3};
IntStream intStream = Arrays.stream(intArray);
```

These approaches provide flexibility in creating streams directly from arrays without needing to convert them to collections first.

3. Stream.of() Method

The Stream.of() method can create streams from a sequence of elements directly. It is useful for small numbers of elements or when the data is already known and fixed at runtime.

```
Stream<String> stream = Stream.of("a", "b", "c");
Stream<Integer> intStream = Stream.of(1, 2, 3, 4, 5);
```

This method helps quickly instantiate streams with a specific set of values, simplifying code and enhancing readability.

4. Stream.builder() Method

For more controlled stream creation, especially when elements need to be added conditionally or in a sequence, the Stream.builder() method is appropriate.

```
Stream<String> streamBuilder = Stream.<String>builder()
    .add("a")
    .add("b")
    .add("c")
    .build();
```

The builder() method provides an intermediate step where elements are incrementally added before the stream is constructed, ensuring that a stream is built programmatically.

5. Generating Streams

Streams can also be generated using the Stream.generate() and Stream.iterate() methods. These methods are powerful for creating infinite streams or streams based on a function.

Stream.generate() creates a stream based on a supplier.

```
Stream<String> generatedStream = Stream.generate(() -> "element").limit(10);
```

In the above code, the stream will contain ten identical elements, which is useful for testing or generating repetitive data patterns.

Stream.iterate() creates a stream using an initial seed and an iterative function.

```
Stream<Integer> iteratedStream = Stream.iterate(1, n -> n + 2).limit(10);
```

Here, the stream starts from 1 and iterates by adding 2 to the previous element, generating a sequence of ten odd numbers.

6. Other Sources

Streams can also be created from files, ranges, and patterns. For example, the Files.lines() method from the java.nio.file package reads all lines from a file as a Stream<String>.

```
Stream<String> lines = Files.lines(Paths.get("file.txt"));
```

Using IntStream.range() or IntStream.rangeClosed() generates streams for numeric ranges.

```
IntStream rangeStream = IntStream.range(1, 10); // 1 to 9
IntStream rangeClosedStream = IntStream.rangeClosed(1, 10); // 1 to 10
```

Streams from patterns can be created using the Pattern.splitAsStream() method, which splits the input sequence around matches of a pattern.

```
Stream<String> patternStream = Pattern.compile(",").splitAsStream("a,b,c");
```

In practice, choosing the right stream source depends on the data type and the context in which the stream is required. Understanding these diverse methods of stream creation lays the foundation for effective data processing using the Stream API in Java.

4.3 Stream Operations: Intermediate and Terminal

In Java Streams, operations are classified into two main categories: intermediate and terminal. Understanding the distinction between these operations is crucial as it forms the foundation for effective stream manipulation and data processing.

Intermediate operations transform a stream into another stream. They are lazy in nature; meaning, they do not perform any processing until a terminal operation is invoked. Intermediate operations enable method chaining and can be composed together to form complex data processing pipelines.

Common intermediate operations include filter, map, flatMap, distinct, sorted, peek, limit, and skip. Here, we will explore each in detail and provide relevant examples.

```
List<String> names = Arrays.asList("Alice", "Bob", "Charlie", "David", "Edward");
// Example of intermediate operation
List<String> modifiedNames = names.stream()
  .filter(name -> name.startsWith("A"))
  .map(String::toUpperCase)
  .collect(Collectors.toList());
System.out.println(modifiedNames);
```

```
[Alice, Amanda, Albert]
```

1. filter(Predicate<? super T> predicate): This operation produces a stream containing elements that match a given predicate.

```
Stream<String> filteredStream = names.stream()
  .filter(name -> name.length() > 3);
```

2. map(Function<? super T,? extends R> mapper): This operation transforms each element of the stream into another form using a function.

```
Stream<String> upperCaseStream = names.stream()
  .map(String::toUpperCase);
```

3. flatMap(Function<? super T,? extends Stream<? extends R» mapper): This operation is used to flatten a stream of collections into a single stream containing all the elements of the nested collections.

```
List<List<String>> listOfLists = Arrays.asList(
  Arrays.asList("a", "b"),
  Arrays.asList("c", "d", "e"),
  Arrays.asList("f", "g"));
Stream<String> flatMapStream = listOfLists.stream()
  .flatMap(Collection::stream);
```

4. distinct(): This operation returns a stream with duplicate elements removed.

```
Stream<String> distinctStream = names.stream()
  .distinct();
```

5. sorted(): This operation returns a stream with elements sorted by their natural order or by a provided comparator.

```
Stream<String> sortedStream = names.stream()
  .sorted();
Stream<String> reverseSortedStream = names.stream()
  .sorted(Collections.reverseOrder());
```

6. peek(Consumer<? super T> action): This operation is mainly used for debugging purposes. It allows performing an action on each element as it is encountered.

```
Stream<String> peekStream = names.stream()
  .peek(System.out::println);
```

7. limit(long maxSize): This operation returns a stream containing a maximum of a given number of elements.

```
Stream<String> limitedStream = names.stream()
  .limit(3);
```

8. skip(long n): This operation returns a stream with the first n elements discarded.

```
Stream<String> skippedStream = names.stream()
  .skip(2);
```

Terminal operations, on the other hand, are responsible for stream traversal and produce a result or a side-effect. They trigger the processing of the lazy intermediate operations.

Common terminal operations include collect, count, forEach, forEachOrdered, toArray, reduce, findAny, findFirst, and allMatch, noneMatch, anyMatch. Here, we will explore each in detail with examples.

```
List<String> result = names.stream()
  .filter(name -> name.startsWith("C"))
  .collect(Collectors.toList());
System.out.println(result);
```

[Charlie]

1. collect(Collector<? super T,A,R> collector): This terminal operation is used to collect the elements of the stream into a destination, such as a List, Set, or Map.

```
List<String> collectedList = names.stream()
  .collect(Collectors.toList());
```

2. count(): This operation returns the count of elements in the stream.

```
long count = names.stream()
  .count();
```

3. forEach(Consumer<? super T> action): This operation performs an action for each element in the stream.

```
names.stream()
  .forEach(System.out::println);
```

4. forEachOrdered(Consumer<? super T> action): This operation performs an action for each element in the encounter order of the stream if the stream has a defined encounter order.

```
names.stream()
  .forEachOrdered(System.out::println);
```

5. toArray(): This operation returns an array containing the elements of the stream.

```
Object[] namesArray = names.stream()
  .toArray();
```

6. reduce(BinaryOperator<T> accumulator): This operation performs a reduction on the elements of the stream using an associative accumulation function.

```
Optional<String> reduced = names.stream()
  .reduce((name1, name2) -> name1 + ", " + name2);
reduced.ifPresent(System.out::println);
```

```
Alice, Bob, Charlie, David, Edward
```

7. findAny(): This operation returns an Optional describing some element of the stream, or an empty Optional if the stream is empty.

```
Optional<String> anyElement = names.stream()
  .findAny();
anyElement.ifPresent(System.out::println);
```

8. findFirst(): This operation returns an Optional describing the first element of the stream, or an empty Optional if the stream is empty.

```
Optional<String> firstElement = names.stream()
  .findFirst();
firstElement.ifPresent(System.out::println);
```

9. allMatch(Predicate<? super T> predicate): This operation returns true if all elements of the stream match the provided predicate; otherwise, false.

```
boolean allMatch = names.stream()
  .allMatch(name -> name.length() > 2);
System.out.println(allMatch);
```

10. noneMatch(Predicate<? super T> predicate): This operation returns true if no elements of the stream match the provided predicate; otherwise, false.

```
boolean noneMatch = names.stream()
  .noneMatch(name -> name.length() > 10);
```

```
System.out.println(noneMatch);
```

11. anyMatch(Predicate<? super T> predicate): This operation returns true if any element of the stream matches the provided predicate; otherwise, false.

```
boolean anyMatch = names.stream()
  .anyMatch(name -> name.equals("Alice"));
System.out.println(anyMatch);
```

Understanding the distinction and use-cases of intermediate versus terminal operations is essential for proficient stream-based data processing and manipulation. Recognizing that intermediate operations are lazy and terminal operations are eager allows for crafting efficient and effective data transformation pipelines.

4.4 Filtering and Mapping Data

Filtering and mapping are fundamental operations when working with streams in Java. These operations enable selective processing and transformation of data, respectively, and are core to harnessing the power and flexibility of streams. This section delves into the functionalities provided for filtering and mapping data within streams, offering detailed examples to elucidate each concept.

To begin with, consider the basic syntax for filtering and mapping operations in a Java stream. Filtering is performed using the filter method, which takes a Predicate as a parameter. A predicate is a functional interface representing a condition that each element of the stream must satisfy. If an element satisfies the condition, it remains in the stream; otherwise, it is excluded.

Example:

```
// List of integers
List<Integer> numbers = Arrays.asList(1, 2, 3, 4, 5, 6, 7, 8, 9, 10);

// Filtering out only even numbers
List<Integer> evenNumbers = numbers.stream()
                                   .filter(n -> n % 2 == 0)
                                   .collect(Collectors.toList());

System.out.println(evenNumbers);
```

```
[2, 4, 6, 8, 10]
```

In this example, the filter method is used to retain only even numbers from the original list. The predicate n -> n % 2 == 0 is a lambda expression that evaluates each number to determine if it is even.

Mapping, on the other hand, is designed for transforming stream elements. The map method applies a function to each element of the stream, which transforms the element and returns a new stream of transformed elements. The function passed to map is a Function, another functional interface that takes an input and produces an output.

Example:

```
// List of strings
List<String> words = Arrays.asList("lambda", "stream", "filter", "map", "collect");

// Mapping each word to its uppercase equivalent
List<String> upperCaseWords = words.stream()
                                   .map(String::toUpperCase)
                                   .collect(Collectors.toList());

System.out.println(upperCaseWords);
```

```
[LAMBDA, STREAM, FILTER, MAP, COLLECT]
```

Here, each string in the list is converted to its uppercase form using the map method, with String::toUpperCase serving as the mapping function.

Combining filtering and mapping operations can yield powerful data transformations. For instance, consider a list of integers where we want to first filter out even numbers and then square each remaining number:

Example:

```
// List of integers
List<Integer> numbers = Arrays.asList(1, 2, 3, 4, 5, 6, 7, 8, 9, 10);

// Filtering odd numbers and squaring them
List<Integer> squaredOddNumbers = numbers.stream()
                                         .filter(n -> n % 2 != 0)
                                         .map(n -> n * n)
                                         .collect(Collectors.toList());

System.out.println(squaredOddNumbers);
```

```
[1, 9, 25, 49, 81]
```

In this example, the stream is first filtered to retain only odd numbers, and then each odd number is squared using the mapping function n -> n * n.

It is also worth noting the distinction between map and flatMap. While map transforms each element into another form, flatMap is used when each element itself is a stream, and we want to flatten all resulting streams into a single continuous stream.

Consider the case where we have a list of lists, and we want to create a single list containing all elements:

Example:

```
// List of lists of integers
List<List<Integer>> listOfLists = Arrays.asList(
    Arrays.asList(1, 2, 3),
    Arrays.asList(4, 5, 6),
    Arrays.asList(7, 8, 9)
);

// Flattening the list of lists into a single list
List<Integer> flattenedList = listOfLists.stream()
                                          .flatMap(List::stream)
                                          .collect(Collectors.toList());

System.out.println(flattenedList);
```

```
[1, 2, 3, 4, 5, 6, 7, 8, 9]
```

In this example, flatMap is used to convert each list within the main list into a stream, and then all these streams are flattened into a single continuous stream.

Understanding filtering and mapping is critical to effective data processing using streams in Java. These operations are declarative, meaning they emphasize what should be done rather than how it should be done, leading to code that is cleaner, more readable, and easier to maintain.

4.5 Working with Primitives: IntStream, LongStream, and DoubleStream

Java provides specific stream classes—IntStream, LongStream, and DoubleStream—to handle primitive data types efficiently. These specialized streams help in avoiding the overhead associated with boxing and unboxing operations when working with primitive data types such as int, long, and double. This section delves into the creation and manipulation of these streams and illustrates their usage through practical examples.

Creating Primitive Streams

Primitive streams can be created in several ways, similar to object streams. The following examples demonstrate various methods for creating IntStream, LongStream, and DoubleStream:

```
IntStream intStream = IntStream.of(1, 2, 3, 4, 5);
LongStream longStream = LongStream.of(1L, 2L, 3L, 4L, 5L);
DoubleStream doubleStream = DoubleStream.of(1.0, 2.0, 3.0, 4.0, 5.0);
```

These streams can also be created using arrays:

```
int[] intArray = {1, 2, 3, 4, 5};
IntStream intStreamFromArray = Arrays.stream(intArray);

long[] longArray = {1L, 2L, 3L, 4L, 5L};
LongStream longStreamFromArray = Arrays.stream(longArray);

double[] doubleArray = {1.0, 2.0, 3.0, 4.0, 5.0};
DoubleStream doubleStreamFromArray = Arrays.stream(doubleArray);
```

Additionally, the static range and rangeClosed methods allow creating streams of sequentially ordered numbers:

```
IntStream intRangeStream = IntStream.range(1, 6); // 1, 2, 3, 4, 5
LongStream longRangeStream = LongStream.rangeClosed(1, 5); // 1, 2, 3, 4, 5
DoubleStream doubleRangeStream = IntStream.range(1, 6).asDoubleStream(); // 1.0,
    2.0, 3.0, 4.0, 5.0
```

Intermediate Operations on Primitive Streams

Primitive streams support several intermediate operations similar to those available for object streams. The following examples highlight some of the commonly used operations:

```
// Filter example
IntStream filteredIntStream = intStream.filter(value -> value % 2 == 0);

// Map example
IntStream mappedIntStream = intStream.map(value -> value * value);

// FlatMap example
IntStream flatMappedIntStream = intStream.flatMap(value -> IntStream.range(0,
    value));
```

Terminal Operations on Primitive Streams

Like object streams, primitive streams also provide terminal operations to produce a result or a side-effect:

```
// Sum example
int sum = intStream.sum();

// Max example
OptionalInt max = intStream.max();

// Average example
OptionalDouble average = intStream.average();

// Reduce example
int product = intStream.reduce(1, (a, b) -> a * b);
```

Specialized Operations

Primitive streams also come with specialized operations that are not present on object streams. These operations are tailored to the nature of primitive types and can lead to more concise and efficient code. For instance:

```
// Collect statistics
IntSummaryStatistics statistics = intStream.summaryStatistics();
System.out.println(statistics);

// Generate random numbers
IntStream randomIntStream = new Random().ints(5); // 5 random int values
LongStream randomLongStream = new Random().longs(5); // 5 random long values
DoubleStream randomDoubleStream = new Random().doubles(5); // 5 random double
    values
```

```
IntSummaryStatistics stats = intStream.summaryStatistics();
System.out.println(stats);
```

The example above displays statistics such as count, sum, min, average, and max of the values in the stream. These statistics can be useful for various analytical tasks.

Conversions Between Streams

Primitive streams can be converted to object streams and vice versa. This flexibility allows for hybrid processing, combining the performance benefits of primitive streams with the generality of object streams:

```
IntStream intStream = IntStream.range(1, 6);
Stream<Integer> boxedStream = intStream.boxed();

Stream<String> stringStream = Stream.of("1", "2", "3");
IntStream unboxedStream = stringStream.mapToInt(Integer::parseInt);
```

asDoubleStream converts a primitive stream into a DoubleStream:

```
IntStream intStream = IntStream.range(1, 6);
DoubleStream doubleStream = intStream.asDoubleStream();

LongStream longStream = LongStream.range(1, 6);
DoubleStream doubleStreamFromLong = longStream.asDoubleStream();
```

These conversions enable combining multiple processing steps that may require various types of streams.

Performance Considerations

Using primitive streams can significantly enhance performance by reducing the overhead associated with boxing and unboxing operations. For instance, consider the following performance-focused experiment:

```
// Using boxed stream
```

```
Stream<Integer> boxedIntStream = IntStream.range(1, 1000000).boxed();
int boxedSum = boxedIntStream.reduce(0, Integer::sum);

// Using primitive stream
IntStream primitiveIntStream = IntStream.range(1, 1000000);
int primitiveSum = primitiveIntStream.sum();
```

```
Time taken for boxed sum: xxx ms
Time taken for primitive sum: xxx ms
```

The time taken for the boxed sum is generally higher due to the overhead of boxing and unboxing each integer.

The section provides a comprehensive overview of working with primitive streams, emphasizing the creation, manipulation, and performance benefits of using IntStream, LongStream, and DoubleStream. The examples and descriptions given aim to equip the reader with practical knowledge for effectively leveraging these specialized streams in data processing tasks.

4.6 Collecting Results with Collectors

In Java's Stream API, collecting results is a fundamental operation that enables the transformation of streams into various forms such as lists, sets, maps, or summary statistics. The java.util.stream.Collectors utility class provides a vast set of methods designed specifically for this purpose. This section delves into the usage and nuances of collectors, shedding light on their importance in functional-style programming with Java.

The most common collector is Collectors.toList. This collector accumulates the elements of the stream into a List. Consider the following example:

```
List<String> collectedNames = Stream.of("Alice", "Bob", "Charlie")
                                    .collect(Collectors.toList());
```

In this snippet, a stream of strings is created using Stream.of. The collect method then gathers these elements into a List.

Another frequently used collector is Collectors.toSet, which collects the stream elements into a Set, removing any duplicates:

```
Set<String> collectedNamesSet = Stream.of("Alice", "Bob", "Charlie", "Alice")
                                      .collect(Collectors.toSet());
```

The resultant Set will contain "Alice", "Bob", and "Charlie", since sets do not allow duplicates.

Collectors also support more advanced transformations such as joining, which concatenates the stream's elements into a single String. This can be particularly useful when dealing with streams of strings as shown:

```
String concatenatedNames = Stream.of("Alice", "Bob", "Charlie")
        .collect(Collectors.joining(", "));
```

The output will be:

```
Alice, Bob, Charlie
```

For grouping elements of a stream by a certain criterion, the Collectors.groupingBy method proves indispensable. Here's an example that groups strings by their length:

```
Map<Integer, List<String>> groupedByLength = Stream.of("Alice", "Bob", "Charlie"
    )
        .collect(Collectors.groupingBy(String::
            length));
```

This will produce a Map where the keys represent string lengths and the values are lists of strings with the corresponding length:

```
{
  3=[Bob],
  5=[Alice],
  7=[Charlie]
}
```

Similarly, partitioning is a specialized form of grouping. The partitioningBy collector method divides elements into two groups based on a predicate. For example:

```
Map<Boolean, List<String>> partitionedByLength = Stream.of("Alice", "Bob", "
    Charlie")
        .collect(Collectors.partitioningBy(s ->
            s.length() > 3));
```

The resulting map will partition the elements based on whether their length is greater than 3:

```
{
  false=[Bob],
  true=[Alice, Charlie]
}
```

In scenarios requiring more intricate collection, the Collectors.collectingAndThen method allows for post-processing of the result. For instance, to collect the elements into a List and then make it unmodifiable:

```
List<String> unmodifiableList = Stream.of("Alice", "Bob", "Charlie")
                                .collect(Collectors.collectingAndThen(Collectors.
                                    toList(),
                                                Collections::
                                                    unmodifiableList
                                                ));
```

It is also feasible to use downstream collectors for more elaborate transformations. For example, when grouping elements and mapping the results into sets:

```
Map<Integer, Set<String>> groupedByLengthToSet = Stream.of("Alice", "Bob", "
    Charlie")
                                        .collect(Collectors.groupingBy(String::
                                            length,
                                                        Collectors.
                                                            toSet
                                                            ()));
```

The key abstraction here is that collectors can significantly affect the final shape and representation of the data, attesting to their versatility in stream processing. Examples include sum, count, and average calculations, which can be performed using summary statistics collectors like Collectors.summarizingInt, Collectors.summarizingDouble, and Collectors.summarizingLong. For example:

```
IntSummaryStatistics summary = Stream.of(1, 2, 3, 4, 5)
                            .collect(Collectors.summarizingInt(Integer::intValue));
```

Inspecting the summary object will reveal statistical values such as sum, count, min, average, and max:

```
IntSummaryStatistics{count=5, sum=15, min=1, average=3.000000, max=5}
```

Collectors also offer flexibility in combination, creating powerful data aggregation pipelines. As shown by the examples, understanding collectors enables effective transformation and manipulation of stream data in functional programming with Java.

4.7 Grouping and Partitioning Data

Java streams provide sophisticated mechanisms for grouping and partitioning data, which are essential when working with large datasets that need organized categorization. The Collectors utility class in the java.util.stream package offers the necessary tools to perform these operations efficiently.

Grouping data in Java streams can be achieved using the Collectors.groupingBy method. This method takes a classifier function and returns a Collector that collects elements to a Map whose keys are the result of applying the classification function on the input elements, and the values are Lists containing the respective grouped items.

For instance, consider a list of Person objects, where each Person has a getAge() method. To group persons by their age, you can perform the following operation:

```
List<Person> people = ...;
Map<Integer, List<Person>> peopleByAge = people.stream()
    .collect(Collectors.groupingBy(Person::getAge));
```

The above code leverages the Person::getAge method reference as the classifier function, grouping all Person objects with the same age into lists. The resulting Map will have the ages as keys and their corresponding lists of Person objects as values.

To handle more complex grouping, you can utilize a downstream collector that performs additional operations on the grouped results. For example, grouping by age and then collecting the names of people in those groups into sets can be achieved as follows:

```
Map<Integer, Set<String>> namesByAge = people.stream()
    .collect(Collectors.groupingBy(
        Person::getAge,
        Collectors.mapping(Person::getName, Collectors.toSet())
    ));
```

The Collectors.mapping method is used to transform the grouped elements, extracting the names of Person objects and collecting them into Sets.

Partitioning is a special case of grouping that splits the dataset into two distinct groups based on a predicate. This is performed using the Collectors.partitioningBy method. For instance, partitioning people into adults and minors based on whether their age is at least 18 can be written as:

```
Map<Boolean, List<Person>> partitionedByAge = people.stream()
    .collect(Collectors.partitioningBy(person -> person.getAge() >= 18));
```

The predicate person -> person.getAge() >= 18 determines the partitioning, resulting in a Map with Boolean keys. The true key maps to the list of adults, and the false key maps to the list of minors.

Like grouping, partitioning can also utilize downstream collectors for more advanced partitioned data processing. For example, to partition people into adults and minors and then count the number of people in each partition, you can use:

```
Map<Boolean, Long> countByPartition = people.stream()
   .collect(Collectors.partitioningBy(
        person -> person.getAge() >= 18,
        Collectors.counting()
   ));
```

This code partitions the list of Person objects by the predicate and applies the Collectors.counting() collector downstream to count the number of elements in each partition.

Furthermore, the ability to combine grouping and partitioning can be powerful for multi-level categorization. Suppose we want to group people by gender and, within each gender, partition by adult status. Assuming Person has a getGender() method, the following setup will achieve this:

```
Map<String, Map<Boolean, List<Person>>> groupAndPartition = people.stream()
   .collect(Collectors.groupingBy(
        Person::getGender,
        Collectors.partitioningBy(person -> person.getAge() >= 18)
   ));
```

This code groups people by gender first, then partitions each gender group into adults and minors using nested collectors.

Handling custom containers or specialized collection results can be achieved by specifying additional parameters to the collector methods. For instance, to group people by age but store the results in a custom TreeMap for sorted keys, you can do:

```
Map<Integer, List<Person>> sortedPeopleByAge = people.stream()
   .collect(Collectors.groupingBy(
        Person::getAge,
        TreeMap::new,
        Collectors.toList()
   ));
```

In this example, a TreeMap is used to maintain a sorted order of ages, ensuring the result map is sorted by age.

Understanding these techniques for grouping and partitioning is crucial for effective data processing using Java streams. These operations provide flexibility in organizing and summarizing data, making them indispensable for real-world data processing tasks.

4.8 Reduction Operations

Reduction operations in Java Streams are terminal operations that transform the elements of a stream into a single summary result, typically producing a scalar value such as a sum, average, or maximum. The concept of reduction stems from functional programming and parallel processing where it aggregates the stream items into fewer values based on a predefined operation.

Reduction is performed using the reduce method, among others, provided by the Stream API. The reduce method comes in three forms:

- Optional<T> reduce(BinaryOperator<T> accumulator)
- T reduce(T identity, BinaryOperator<T> accumulator)
- <U> U reduce(U identity, BiFunction<U, ? super T, U> accumulator, BinaryOperator<U> combiner)

Each form serves a different purpose and provides versatility in usage.

```
List<Integer> numbers = Arrays.asList(1, 2, 3, 4, 5);
Optional<Integer> sum = numbers.stream()
                               .reduce((a, b) -> a + b);
sum.ifPresent(System.out::println); // Output: 15
```

In this example, the reduce(BinaryOperator<T> accumulator) method applies the provided BinaryOperator to the sequence of elements in the stream. The BinaryOperator defines how two elements are combined, in this case using the addition operator.

Identity and Associativity

The accumulator function used in reduce needs to be both associative and stateless. Associativity means that the function produces the same result regardless of the grouping of operands, for example, addition and multiplication are associative, whereas subtraction and division are not.

The identity value is a default or initial value which serves as a neutral starting point for the reduction operation. It has the following properties:

- It embodies an identity element for the accumulator function.
- It is the initial value within the reduction operation.
- Combining any value with the identity should return the same value.

The composition of identity with the accumulator should not alter outcomes:

```
int sum = numbers.stream()
                .reduce(0, (a, b) -> a + b);
System.out.println(sum); // Output: 15
```

Here, the reduce method is initiated with an identity value of 0.

Collect with Parallel Streams

The third form of reduce is particularly useful for parallel streams and consists of three arguments: identity, accumulator, and combiner. The combiner is used when the stream is processed in parallel, to combine partial results generated in parallel tasks.

```
List<Integer> numbers = Arrays.asList(1, 2, 3, 4, 5);
Integer sum = numbers.parallelStream()
                    .reduce(0, (a, b) -> a + b, (a, b) -> a + b);
System.out.println(sum); // Output: 15
```

Reduction with Collectors

Reduction isn't limited to reduce. The Collectors utility provides prebuilt collectors for common reduction operations. For instance, Collectors.summingInt, Collectors.averagingDouble, and Collectors.maxBy are predefined collectors that succinctly express reductions.

```
import static java.util.stream.Collectors.*;

List<Integer> numbers = Arrays.asList(1, 2, 3, 4, 5);
int sum = numbers.stream()
                .collect(summingInt(Integer::intValue));

double average = numbers.stream()
                .collect(averagingDouble(Integer::doubleValue));

Optional<Integer> max = numbers.stream()
                .collect(maxBy(Comparator.naturalOrder()));

System.out.println("Sum: " + sum); // Output: Sum: 15
System.out.println("Average: " + average); // Output: Average: 3.0
max.ifPresent(value -> System.out.println("Max: " + value));
```

Reduction Operations on Primitive Streams

Primitive stream interfaces such as IntStream, LongStream, and DoubleStream offer specialized reduction operations to avoid boxing overhead. For these primitive streams, reduction examples include sum, average, max, and min:

```
IntStream intStream = IntStream.range(1, 6);
int intSum = intStream.sum();
System.out.println(intSum); // Output: 15
```

```
LongStream longStream = LongStream.of(1L, 2L, 3L, 4L, 5L);
OptionalLong maxLong = longStream.max();
maxLong.ifPresent(System.out::println); // Output: 5

DoubleStream doubleStream = DoubleStream.of(1.0, 2.0, 3.0, 4.0, 5.0);
double average = doubleStream.average().orElse(Double.NaN);
System.out.println(average); // Output: 3.0
```

Understanding and appropriately using reduction operations allows developers to efficiently summarize stream data, enhancing functional programming approaches in Java. Proficiency with these operations paves the way for effectively managing and processing complex datasets.

4.9 Parallel Streams

Parallel streams in Java leverage the fork/join framework to execute stream operations in parallel, utilizing multiple cores to potentially enhance performance for large datasets. Understanding how to implement and effectively use parallel streams can significantly affect the performance of data processing tasks.

Parallel streams are created using the parallelStream() method instead of the standard stream() method. The following example demonstrates how to create a parallel stream from a list:

```
List<String> myList = Arrays.asList("apple", "banana", "cherry", "date", "elderberry"
    );

// Creating a parallel stream
Stream<String> parallelStream = myList.parallelStream();
```

Parallel streams can also be created by invoking the parallel() method on an existing stream:

```
// Converting a sequential stream to a parallel stream
Stream<String> sequentialStream = myList.stream();
Stream<String> parallelStream = sequentialStream.parallel();
```

A critical aspect of parallel streams is their potential to improve performance. However, it is essential to balance the performance benefits against the overhead introduced by creating and managing multiple threads. The following example shows a non-trivial computation performed on a large dataset using both sequential and parallel streams:

```
import java.util.List;
import java.util.stream.Collectors;
```

```
import java.util.stream.IntStream;

public class ParallelStreamExample {
    public static void main(String[] args) {
        List<Integer> intList = IntStream.range(0, 1000000)
                                         .boxed()
                                         .collect(Collectors.toList());

        // Sequential stream
        long startTime = System.currentTimeMillis();
        intList.stream().mapToInt(ParallelStreamExample::compute).sum();
        long endTime = System.currentTimeMillis();
        System.out.println("Time taken with sequential stream: " + (endTime -
            startTime) + "ms");

        // Parallel stream
        startTime = System.currentTimeMillis();
        intList.parallelStream().mapToInt(ParallelStreamExample::compute).sum();
        endTime = System.currentTimeMillis();
        System.out.println("Time taken with parallel stream: " + (endTime - startTime)
            + "ms");
    }

    private static int compute(int value) {
        // Some time-consuming computation
        return value * 2;
    }
}
```

```
Output could be:
Time taken with sequential stream: 35ms
Time taken with parallel stream: 15ms
```

The success of parallel streams depends on several factors, including the nature of the task (CPU-bound vs. I/O-bound), size of the dataset, and the extent of data processing. Developers must also consider the following principles to exploit parallel streams effectively:

- Statelessness: Operations on parallel streams should be stateless to avoid issues with concurrent modifications.
- Associativity: Reduction operations performed on parallel streams should be associative to ensure consistency and correctness of results.
- Thread-Safety: Ensure that mutable data structures, if used, are thread-safe or appropriately synchronized to prevent data corruption.

A potential pitfall is treating all tasks as ideal candidates for parallel processing. For instance, tasks involving a significant amount of I/O operations might not benefit from parallel streams due to the overhead of context switching and thread management. Another consideration is the order of operations; certain ordered operations may not parallelize efficiently because maintaining order constrains the flexibility of task distribution.

One way to fine-tune parallel stream performance is by controlling the pool of threads employed during computation. By default, the parallel stream utilizes the common fork/join pool, which is shared among all parallel streams in the application. The size of this pool can be customized for optimal performance by setting the java.util.concurrent.ForkJoinPool.common.parallelism system property:

```
// Setting the parallelism level
System.setProperty("java.util.concurrent.ForkJoinPool.common.parallelism", "12");
```

Alternatively, for more granular control, a custom ForkJoinPool can be used:

```
import java.util.concurrent.ForkJoinPool;

public class CustomParallelStreamExample {
    public static void main(String[] args) {
        ForkJoinPool customThreadPool = new ForkJoinPool(12);

        customThreadPool.submit(() -> {
            // Parallel computation using a custom thread pool
            List<Integer> intList = IntStream.range(0, 1000000)
                                           .boxed()
                                           .collect(Collectors.toList());
            long startTime = System.currentTimeMillis();
            intList.parallelStream()
                   .mapToInt(CustomParallelStreamExample::compute)
                   .sum();
            long endTime = System.currentTimeMillis();
            System.out.println("Time taken with custom parallel stream: " + (endTime -
                   startTime) + "ms");
        }).join();
    }

    private static int compute(int value) {
        // Some time-consuming computation
        return value * 2;
    }
}
```

This code demonstrates the use of a custom ForkJoinPool with a parallel stream to optimize performance for specific requirements. Implementing and tuning parallel streams involves careful consideration of task dependencies, order, and resource management to fully leverage the parallel processing advantages.

4.10 Performance Considerations with Streams

Understanding performance considerations is crucial when working with streams in Java, especially when dealing with large datasets or computationally intensive operations. This section delves into various factors that impact the performance of stream operations and provides best practices to ensure efficient stream processing.

Lazy Evaluation: Streams in Java employ lazy evaluation, meaning that intermediate operations such as filter, map, and sorted are not executed until a terminal operation (like collect, forEach, or reduce) is invoked. This allows for potential optimization by combining or reordering operations for better performance.

```
Stream<Integer> stream = IntStream.range(1, 10)
    .filter(n -> {
        System.out.println("Filter: " + n);
        return n % 2 == 0;
    })
    .map(n -> {
        System.out.println("Map: " + n);
        return n * 2;
    })
    .boxed();

System.out.println("Starting terminal operation:");
stream.forEach(System.out::println);
```

An important aspect to take into consideration is that no filtering or mapping operations will be executed until the terminal operation forEach is called. This feature can optimize processing by minimizing unnecessary operations.

Short-Circuiting Operations: Some operations in streams can short-circuit and terminate the processing early. Common examples include anyMatch, allMatch, noneMatch, findFirst, and findAny.

```
boolean anyEven = IntStream.range(1, 10)
    .peek(n -> System.out.println("Processing: " + n))
    .anyMatch(n -> n % 2 == 0);
System.out.println("Any Even: " + anyEven);
```

Here, the stream will stop processing as soon as it encounters the first even number, saving computational resources.

Ordering and Parallel Processing: Maintaining order in streams can have a significant impact on performance, particularly in parallel streams. Operates like unordered can hint the JDK to potentially optimize parallel processing by disregarding element order.

```
List<Integer> list = IntStream.range(1, 1000).boxed().collect(Collectors.toList());
List<Integer> unorderedList = list.stream()
    .unordered()
    .parallel()
    .collect(Collectors.toList());
```

By using unordered, the stream can process elements without considering their original order, which can provide performance improvements especially in parallel streams.

Parallel Streams: Utilizing parallel streams can lead to significant performance improvement by leveraging multi-core processors. However, one must carefully consider the type of operations being performed. Overhead costs associated with parallel processing can sometimes outweigh benefits for simpler tasks or small data sizes.

```
List<Integer> numbers = IntStream.range(1, 1000000).boxed().collect(Collectors.toList
    ());
List<Integer> squaredNumbers = numbers.parallelStream()
    .map(n -> n * n)
    .collect(Collectors.toList());
```

parallelStream method divides the task across multiple threads, which can make a noticeable difference for computationally intensive operations on large datasets.

Splitting Strategy: Consider the cost of splitting for parallel streams; different data structures have different splitting characteristics. For instance, arrays and ArrayList have efficient splitting, whereas LinkedList and Stream.iterate might not.

```
List<Integer> arrayList = Arrays.asList(1, 2, 3, 4, 5);
List<Integer> linkedList = new LinkedList<>(arrayList);

arrayList.parallelStream().forEach(System.out::println); // Efficient splitting
linkedList.parallelStream().forEach(System.out::println); // Less efficient splitting
```

The performance difference stems from the data structure's ability to evenly partition itself for parallel processing.

Stateful vs Stateless Operations: Stateful operations (e.g., sorted, distinct) hold internal state which can affect performance, especially in parallel streams. Stateless operations are preferable for parallel processing.

```
List<Integer> numbers = IntStream.range(1, 100).boxed().collect(Collectors.toList());

List<Integer> sortedNumbers = numbers.stream()
    .parallel()
    .sorted() // Stateful operation
```

```
    .collect(Collectors.toList());

List<Integer> doubledNumbers = numbers.stream()
    .parallel()
    .map(n -> n * 2) // Stateless operation
    .collect(Collectors.toList());
```

sorted requires holding and organizing elements, which introduces overhead compared to a stateless operation like map.

For optimal stream performance, one should aim to minimize statefulness, prefer stateless operations, utilize parallel streams judiciously, and understand the subtleties of lazy evaluation and short-circuiting. This approach ensures efficient and effective use of streams for data processing tasks.

4.11 Common Stream Use Cases and Patterns

One of the most compelling aspects of streams in Java is their versatility and convenience in addressing common data processing tasks. The declarative style of streams promotes readable and maintainable code, adhering to the principles of functional programming. This section elucidates several prevalent use cases and patterns for employing streams effectively.

1. Filtering Collections

A frequent requirement is filtering elements from a collection based on certain predicates. By leveraging the filter intermediate operation, streams provide an elegant and concise solution for this task. Consider the following example where we filter a list of integers to retain only even numbers:

```
List<Integer> numbers = Arrays.asList(1, 2, 3, 4, 5, 6);
List<Integer> evenNumbers =
    numbers.stream()
        .filter(n -> n % 2 == 0)
        .collect(Collectors.toList());
```

The above code demonstrates the use of a lambda expression within the filter method to retain elements that satisfy the predicate (i.e., numbers divisible by 2).

2. Mapping Elements

Transforming elements of a collection from one form to another is another common task, efficiently handled using the map intermediate operation. For example, converting a list of strings to their uppercase equivalents can be accomplished as follows:

```
List<String> words = Arrays.asList("hello", "world");
List<String> upperCaseWords =
    words.stream()
        .map(String::toUpperCase)
        .collect(Collectors.toList());
```

Here, the map method applies the toUpperCase function to each element of the stream, and the transformed elements are collected into a new list.

3. Reducing Collections

Reduction operations aggregate the elements of a stream into a single result. The reduce terminal operation provides this functionality. For instance, summing a list of integers can be achieved as follows:

```
List<Integer> numbers = Arrays.asList(1, 2, 3, 4, 5);
int sum = numbers.stream()
                 .reduce(0, Integer::sum);
```

The reduce method here uses an initial value of 0 and the Integer::sum method reference to accumulate the elements of the stream.

4. Collecting Results into a Map

Streams also excel in tasks that involve collecting data into various forms, such as maps. Use cases include grouping elements or mapping keys to values. Suppose we have a list of Person objects and we want to create a map of persons by their IDs:

```
class Person {
    int id;
    String name;
    // constructor, getters, etc.
}

List<Person> people = Arrays.asList(
    new Person(1, "John"),
    new Person(2, "Jane"),
    new Person(3, "Jack")
);

Map<Integer, String> peopleMap =
    people.stream()
        .collect(Collectors.toMap(Person::getId, Person::getName));
```

In this example, Collectors.toMap is used to collect the stream elements into a map, with person IDs as keys and names as values.

5. Grouping Data

Grouping data based on a classifier function is seamlessly handled by the groupingBy collector. This pattern is particularly valuable for organizing data hierarchically. For instance, grouping a list of strings by their length:

```
List<String> words = Arrays.asList("apple", "banana", "cherry");
Map<Integer, List<String>> groupedByLength =
    words.stream()
        .collect(Collectors.groupingBy(String::length));
```

Here, Collectors.groupingBy is employed to create a map where the keys are string lengths and the values are lists of strings with the corresponding length.

6. Partitioning Data

Partitioning, a specialized form of grouping, involves dividing elements into two groups based on a predicate. The partitioningBy collector enables this functionality. For example, partitioning a list of integers into even and odd numbers:

```
List<Integer> numbers = Arrays.asList(1, 2, 3, 4, 5, 6);
Map<Boolean, List<Integer>> partitioned =
    numbers.stream()
        .collect(Collectors.partitioningBy(n -> n % 2 == 0));
```

In this scenario, Collectors.partitioningBy generates a map with Boolean keys, where true maps to even numbers and false maps to odd numbers.

7. Finding Maximum and Minimum

Finding the maximum or minimum element in a collection based on a comparator is straightforward using the max and min terminal operations. For instance, identifying the longest string in a list:

```
List<String> words = Arrays.asList("apple", "banana", "cherry");
Optional<String> longest =
    words.stream()
        .max(Comparator.comparingInt(String::length));
```

The max method in this code uses a comparator to determine the string with the greatest length, returning an Optional<String>.

These use cases illustrate the adaptability and conciseness of Java streams in various data processing scenarios. The patterns discussed not only simplify coding but also foster better readability, maintainability, and reduced error proneness in handling complex data manipulations.

Chapter 5

Java Functional Libraries

This chapter provides an overview of Java functional libraries, highlighting their significance in simplifying complex programming tasks. It explores the core functional utilities provided by libraries such as Guava, Apache Commons, and Vavr. Detailed discussions include common operations with Guava, using Apache Commons for functional programming, and advanced techniques with Vavr. The chapter also compares different functional libraries and offers guidance on integrating these libraries into real-world projects to enhance functional programming capabilities in Java.

5.1 Introduction to Java Functional Libraries

Java functional libraries serve as indispensable tools for developers aiming to implement functional programming paradigms within the Java ecosystem. These libraries extend the core capabilities of Java by introducing additional functional constructs that simplify complex programming tasks, enhance code readability, and promote more concise and expressive code. They provide facilities for immutability, higher-order functions, and powerful data structures that align with functional programming principles.

At the core, functional libraries for Java emphasize functions as first-class citizens. This means that functions can be passed as arguments to other functions, returned as values, and assigned to variables. Key features and constructs introduced by these libraries include immutable collections, lazy evaluation, pattern matching, and functional composition. These capabilities allow for a more declarative approach to solving programming problems, contrasting the traditional imperative style prevalent in Java.

Immutability is a cornerstone of functional programming. It ensures that data structures, once created, cannot be modified. This eliminates side effects, making programs easier to reason about and verifiable. Functional libraries in Java introduce immutable collections such as immutable lists, sets, and maps that can be manipulated via pure functions, preserving their immutable nature.

Higher-order functions are functions that take other functions as parameters or return them as results. These enable the creation of more abstract and reusable software components. Java's standard library supports higher-order functions through interfaces like Function<T, R>, Consumer<T>, Supplier<T>, and Predicate<T>. Functional libraries build upon these and provide richer abstractions and utilities for dealing with higher-order functions more effectively.

Consider the following example using Java's standard functional interfaces:

```
import java.util.function.Function;

public class HigherOrderFunctionExample {
    public static void main(String[] args) {
        Function<Integer, Integer> square = (x) -> x * x;
        System.out.println(applyFunction(square, 5)); // Should print 25
    }

    public static <T, R> R applyFunction(Function<T, R> func, T value) {
        return func.apply(value);
    }
}
```

The above code demonstrates a higher-order function applyFunction that takes a Function<T, R> and a value of type T, applying the function to the value and returning the result of type R.

Lazy evaluation is another significant feature. By deferring the evaluation of expressions until their values are needed, lazy evaluation can improve performance and allow for the definition of potentially infinite data structures. Libraries such as Vavr employ lazy evaluation to create streams and other data structures that do not compute their elements until required.

Pattern matching is often used to simplify complex decision-making processes. It provides a more readable and expressive means of comparing values and executing corresponding code. This is similar to switch-case statements but with more flexibility and power, especially with complex data types and conditions. Vavr's Match API is a prime example that facilitates pattern matching in Java:

```
import io.vavr.API.*;
import io.vavr.Predicates.*;

public class PatternMatchingExample {
    public static void main(String[] args) {
        int number = 8;
        String result = Match(number).of(
            Case($(1), "one"),
            Case($(2), "two"),
            Case($(), "other")
        );
        System.out.println(result); // Should print "other"
    }
}
```

This snippet defines a pattern matching mechanism where the variable number is compared against multiple cases, leading to more succinct and readable code.

Functional composition allows combining simple functions to create more complex operations. Libraries like Guava and Apache Commons provide utilities to compose functions, ensuring smoother transformation of data through multiple functional steps. For instance, Vavr's Function1 interface supports method chaining and advanced composition techniques:

```
import io.vavr.Function1;

public class FunctionCompositionExample {
    public static void main(String[] args) {
        Function1<Integer, Integer> addOne = (a) -> a + 1;
        Function1<Integer, Integer> square = (a) -> a * a;
        Function1<Integer, Integer> composed = addOne.andThen(square);
        System.out.println(composed.apply(4)); // Should print 25
    }
}
```

In this example, the function addOne is composed with square, first adding one to the input and then squaring the result.

Java functional libraries also enhance the manipulation of collections. While the standard Java library offers Stream API, which supports powerful operations like map, filter, and reduce, other libraries extend these capabilities with more advanced features, such as those found in Guava's FluentIterable, Apache Commons' CollectionUtils, and Vavr's List and Vector classes. These libraries facilitate operations like transforming, filtering, and reducing collections in a functional manner.

In practice, adopting functional libraries in Java enables developers to write more modular, expressive, and safer code. By leveraging immutability, higher-order functions, lazy evaluation, pattern matching, and functional composition, Java programmers can solve complex problems more efficiently and with less code. This chapter continues to explore these libraries in depth, highlighting their application and comparing their features to guide optimal usage in real-world projects.

5.2 Overview of Java Standard Library Functions

Java's standard library, often termed the Java Development Kit (JDK), includes extensive utility functions designed to facilitate many common programming tasks, establishing the foundation of Java's functional programming capabilities. This section delves into the core functional programming constructs and utilities provided by the JDK, focusing on java.util.function package and its pivotal role in enabling a functional style within Java.

The java.util.function package introduces several functional interfaces, categorized primarily based on their arities and expected operations. Functional interfaces are central to functional programming in Java as they enable the use of lambda expressions and method references. A functional interface is an interface with exactly one abstract method, and it may contain multiple default or static methods.

Key Functional Interfaces

- Function<T,R>: Represents a function that accepts one argument of type T and produces a result of type R. The abstract method apply is the key operation.
- BiFunction<T,U,R>: Extends Function to accept two arguments of types T and U, returning a result of type R.
- Consumer<T>: Denotes an operation that takes a single argument of type T and returns no result. It primarily implements the accept method.
- BiConsumer<T,U>: A variant of Consumer that takes two arguments of types T and U.

- Supplier<T>: Represents a supplier of results, returning a result of type T without accepting any arguments, implemented by the get method.
- Predicate<T>: Defines a boolean-valued function that accepts an argument of type T and returns a boolean. The primary method is test.
- BiPredicate<T,U>: Extends Predicate to operate on two arguments of types T and U.
- UnaryOperator<T>: A specialization of Function where the input and output are of the same type T.
- BinaryOperator<T>: A specialization of BiFunction for the case where all operands and the result are of the same type T.

Example Usage

The following example demonstrates the use of several functional interfaces from the java.util.function package:

```
import java.util.function.*;

public class FunctionalInterfaceExamples {
    public static void main(String[] args) {
        // Example of Function interface
        Function<Integer, String> intToString = Object::toString;
        System.out.println("Function Example: " + intToString.apply(5));

        // Example of BiFunction interface
        BiFunction<String, String, String> concat = (a, b) -> a + b;
        System.out.println("BiFunction Example: " + concat.apply("Hello, ", "World"));

        // Example of Consumer interface
        Consumer<String> print = System.out::println;
        print.accept("Consumer Example");

        // Example of Supplier interface
        Supplier<String> supplier = () -> "Supplier Example";
        System.out.println(supplier.get());

        // Example of Predicate interface
        Predicate<Integer> isEven = x -> x % 2 == 0;
        System.out.println("Predicate Example (is 4 even?): " + isEven.test(4));

        // Example of UnaryOperator interface
        UnaryOperator<Integer> square = x -> x * x;
        System.out.println("UnaryOperator Example: " + square.apply(4));

        // Example of BinaryOperator interface
        BinaryOperator<Integer> sum = (a, b) -> a + b;
        System.out.println("BinaryOperator Example: " + sum.apply(4, 5));
    }
}
```

```
Function Example: 5
BiFunction Example: Hello, World
Consumer Example
Supplier Example
Predicate Example (is 4 even?): true
UnaryOperator Example: 16
BinaryOperator Example: 9
```

Stream API

The Stream API, introduced in Java 8, significantly leverages these functional interfaces to enable functional-style operations on sequences of elements. Streams support operations such as map, filter, reduce, collect, and more, which can be performed sequentially or in parallel.

Key methods include:

- Stream.map(Function mapper): Applies a function to each element and returns a new stream of the results.
- Stream.filter(Predicate predicate): Returns a stream consisting of the elements that match the given predicate.
- Stream.reduce(BinaryOperator accumulator): Combines the stream's elements using an associative combining function, producing a single result.
- Stream.collect(Collector collector): Performs a mutable reduction operation on the elements of the stream using a Collector.

The following example demonstrates the use of the Stream API:

```java
import java.util.List;
import java.util.stream.Collectors;
import java.util.stream.IntStream;

public class StreamAPIExamples {
    public static void main(String[] args) {
        List<Integer> numbers = IntStream.rangeClosed(1, 10).boxed().collect(
                Collectors.toList());

        // Example of map operation
        List<Integer> squared = numbers.stream()
                .map(x -> x * x)
                .collect(Collectors.toList());
        System.out.println("Map Example: " + squared);

        // Example of filter operation
        List<Integer> evens = numbers.stream()
                .filter(x -> x % 2 == 0)
                .collect(Collectors.toList());
        System.out.println("Filter Example: " + evens);

        // Example of reduce operation
```

```
        int sum = numbers.stream()
                .reduce(0, Integer::sum);
        System.out.println("Reduce Example: " + sum);

        // Example of collect operation
        List<Integer> collected = numbers.stream()
                .collect(Collectors.toList());
        System.out.println("Collect Example: " + collected);
    }
}
```

```
Map Example: [1, 4, 9, 16, 25, 36, 49, 64, 81, 100]
Filter Example: [2, 4, 6, 8, 10]
Reduce Example: 55
Collect Example: [1,2,3,4,5,6,7,8,9,10]
```

This section has covered the essential functional interfaces and the Stream API in Java's standard library, providing the foundational tools required for effective functional programming within Java applications.

5.3 Guava: Google's Core Libraries for Java

Guava is an open-source set of common libraries for Java, developed by Google. These libraries provide a variety of utilities for collections, caching, primitives support, concurrency, common annotations, string processing, I/O, and, most importantly for this context, functional programming. Guava enhances Java's built-in library with more versatile and powerful tools tailored for functional programming paradigms.

Functional Utilities in Guava

One of the primary modules in Guava that is relevant for functional programming is the com.google.common.base package. This package offers several classes and interfaces that support functional operations, such as Function, Predicate, and Supplier. Let's explore these key elements and how they contribute to functional programming.

Function is a straightforward interface representing a function that takes an input of type T and returns an output of type R.

```
public interface Function<T, R> {
    R apply(T input);
}
```

This interface can be instantiated using lambda expressions or anonymous classes, enabling functional-style transformations.

The Predicate interface represents a predicate (boolean-valued function) of one argument.

```
public interface Predicate<T> {
    boolean apply(T input);
}
```

Predicates are useful for filtering collections or streams of data.

Supplier is an interface that supplies values of a given type without taking any input.

```
public interface Supplier<T> {
    T get();
}
```

Suppliers can be used to generate or supply values on-demand, useful in lazy initialization and caching patterns.

Example: Transforming and Filtering with Guava

To illustrate how Guava can be employed for functional programming, consider a scenario where we have a list of students and we wish to filter out those who have passed based on their grades and then transform the remaining list to obtain their names.

First, define a Student class:

```
public class Student {
    private String name;
    private int grade;

    // Constructor, getters, and setters
    public Student(String name, int grade) {
        this.name = name;
        this.grade = grade;
    }

    public String getName() {
        return name;
    }

    public int getGrade() {
        return grade;
    }
}
```

Next, use the Guava Predicate to filter out students who have passed:

```
List<Student> students = Arrays.asList(
    new Student("Alice", 85),
    new Student("Bob", 67),
    new Student("Charlie", 55)
);

Predicate<Student> passedPredicate = new Predicate<Student>() {
    @Override
    public boolean apply(Student student) {
        return student.getGrade() >= 60;
```

```
    }
};

List<Student> passedStudents = Lists.newArrayList(
    Iterables.filter(students, passedPredicate)
);
```

This code filters the list, retaining only students with grades greater than or equal to 60. Using the Function interface, we can then transform this list to extract the names:

```
Function<Student, String> getNameFunction = new Function<Student, String>() {
    @Override
    public String apply(Student student) {
        return student.getName();
    }
};

List<String> passedStudentNames = Lists.newArrayList(
    Iterables.transform(passedStudents, getNameFunction)
);
```

Combining these two operations establishes a functional approach to manipulating and processing the list of students.

Immutable Collections

Immutability is a core concept in functional programming. Guava provides a suite of immutable collections. These collections help to ensure that once they are initialized, they cannot be modified. This immutability leads to safer code by preventing unintended changes to data.

Example of creating an immutable list:

```
List<String> immutableList = ImmutableList.of("Alice", "Bob", "Charlie");
try {
    immutableList.add("David");
} catch (UnsupportedOperationException e) {
    System.out.println("Cannot modify immutable list.");
}
```

The attempt to modify the immutable list will result in an UnsupportedOperationException, thereby preserving data integrity.

Optional Type

Guava's Optional class is a robust replacement for null references, inspired by the functional programming languages. The Optional type acts as a container for an optional (i.e., possibly null) value. This feature allows for a more expressive and safer handling of potentially absent values.

Creating and using an Optional:

```
Optional<String> optionalValue = Optional.of("Hello, World!");
if (optionalValue.isPresent()) {
    System.out.println(optionalValue.get());
}

Optional<String> absentValue = Optional.absent();
System.out.println(absentValue.or("Default Value"));
```

Here, Optional provides a means to avoid null checks and can specify default values if the contained value is absent.

Guava's rich set of utilities not only expands the standard Java library but also embraces functional programming paradigms, offering enhanced tools for transformations, filtering, and immutability. This enables Java developers to write clearer, more expressive, and safer code.

5.4 Apache Commons: Functional Utilities

Apache Commons is a comprehensive collection of reusable Java components designed to facilitate a variety of programming tasks. Among these, Apache Commons Collections and Apache Commons Lang are particularly relevant for functional programming. This section expounds on the functional utilities offered by these libraries, elucidating their use with concrete examples.

Apache Commons Collections provides sophisticated enhancements to the Java Collections Framework. One of the most salient functional components is the CollectionUtils class, which furnishes utility methods for functional-style operations on collections.

```
import org.apache.commons.collections4.CollectionUtils;
import java.util.Arrays;
import java.util.List;

public class CollectionUtilsExample {
    public static void main(String[] args) {
        List<String> list = Arrays.asList("one", "two", "three", "four");
        CollectionUtils.filter(list, item -> item.startsWith("t"));
        list.forEach(System.out::println); // Output: two, three
    }
}
```

In this example, the filter method of CollectionUtils is employed to retain only the elements that start with the letter 't'. The lambda expression item -> item.startsWith("t") serves as the filtering criterion. This paradigm aligns with functional programming by treating functions as first-class citizens.

Another pivotal utility in Apache Commons Collections is the Transformer interface. This interface enables the transformation of objects in a collection, which can be highly useful in functional programming.

```
import org.apache.commons.collections4.CollectionUtils;
import org.apache.commons.collections4.Transformer;
import java.util.Arrays;
import java.util.List;

public class TransformerExample {
    public static void main(String[] args) {
        List<String> list = Arrays.asList("one", "two", "three", "four");
        Transformer<String, String> toUpperCase = String::toUpperCase;
        CollectionUtils.transform(list, toUpperCase);
        list.forEach(System.out::println); // Output: ONE, TWO, THREE, FOUR
    }
}
```

Here, the transform method applies a transformation to each element in the list, converting all strings to uppercase. The use of method references String::toUpperCase exemplifies the concise expression of functional transformations.

Apache Commons Lang supplements the core functionality of the Java standard library. The ArrayUtils class, for instance, extends array handling capabilities, making functional operations more approachable.

```
import org.apache.commons.lang3.ArrayUtils;
import java.util.Arrays;

public class ArrayUtilsExample {
    public static void main(String[] args) {
        String[] array = {"one", "two", "three", "four"};
        String[] reversedArray = ArrayUtils.reverse(array);
        System.out.println(Arrays.toString(reversedArray)); // Output: [four, three, two,
              one]
    }
}
```

The reverse method from ArrayUtils demonstrates an elegant way to reverse an array, a task that would otherwise require considerable boilerplate code.

Apache Commons Lang also includes the StringUtils class, which offers a plethora of string manipulation utilities. In functional programming, such utilities can dramatically reduce the verbosity of code.

```
import org.apache.commons.lang3.StringUtils;

public class StringUtilsExample {
    public static void main(String[] args) {
```

```
        String str = " apache commons ";
        String trimmedStr = StringUtils.trim(str);
        System.out.println(trimmedStr); // Output: apache commons
    }
}
```

In this snippet, the trim method from StringUtils is utilized to remove leading and trailing whitespace from a string, an operation frequently required in data processing tasks.

In addition to collections and strings, Apache Commons Lang provides utilities for handling objects via the ObjectUtils class. The defaultIfNull method is particularly useful in functional programming to provide default values.

```
import org.apache.commons.lang3.ObjectUtils;

public class ObjectUtilsExample {
    public static void main(String[] args) {
        String nullStr = null;
        String nonNullStr = ObjectUtils.defaultIfNull(nullStr, "default");
        System.out.println(nonNullStr); // Output: default
    }
}
```

The defaultIfNull method from ObjectUtils allows for a concise and readable way to handle null values by specifying a default value when the primary value is null, thus preventing the often cumbersome null-checking code.

Lastly, **Apache Commons Functor** is a dedicated component for functional programming within the Apache Commons suite. It defines interfaces for functors, which are objects that represent functions. Key interfaces include Predicate, Function, and Procedure.

```
import org.apache.commons.functor.Predicate;
import org.apache.commons.functor.core.composite.FilteredIterable;
import java.util.Arrays;
import java.util.List;

public class FunctorExample {
    public static void main(String[] args) {
        List<Integer> list = Arrays.asList(1, 2, 3, 4, 5);
        Predicate<Integer> isEven = item -> item % 2 == 0;
        FilteredIterable<Integer> filtered = new FilteredIterable<>(list, isEven);
        filtered.forEach(System.out::println); // Output: 2, 4
    }
}
```

In this example, a Predicate is employed to filter a list of integers, keeping only the even numbers. The FilteredIterable class demonstrates the effective combination of functional interfaces to achieve concise and expressive code.

By utilizing Apache Commons Collections and Lang, developers can leverage functional programming paradigms within the Java ecosystem, significantly enhancing the readability, maintainability, and expressiveness of their code.

5.5 Javaslang (Vavr): Functional Programming in Java

Javaslang, which has been rebranded as Vavr, is a popular functional programming library for Java that aims to provide persistent data types and functional control structures. It is designed to bring some of the benefits of functional programming found in languages like Scala to the Java ecosystem. By using Vavr, developers can write more concise, expressive, and bug-resistant code.

The library introduces several key concepts and data structures that enable functional programming paradigms. These include, but are not limited to, immutable collections, tuples, and functional control structures like Try, Option, and Either.

Option is a container type that represents an optional value, i.e., a value that might be present or absent. It helps to avoid NullPointerException and make the code more expressive.

```
import io.vavr.control.Option;

public class VavrExample {
    public static void main(String[] args) {
        Option<String> maybeFoo = Option.of("foo");
        Option<String> maybeEmpty = Option.none();

        // Accessing the value
        String value = maybeFoo.getOrElse("default");
        System.out.println(value); // prints "foo"

        value = maybeEmpty.getOrElse("default");
        System.out.println(value); // prints "default"
    }
}
```

The Either type represents a value of one of two possible types, delineating success from failure without resorting to exceptions.

```
import io.vavr.control.Either;

public class VavrExample {
    public static void main(String[] args) {
```

```
        Either<String, Integer> right = Either.right(5);
        Either<String, Integer> left = Either.left("error");

        // Using Either
        String resultRight = right.map(i -> i * 2)
                                  .getOrElse("default");
        System.out.println(resultRight); // prints "10"

        String resultLeft = left.map(i -> i * 2)
                                .getOrElse("default");
        System.out.println(resultLeft); // prints "default"
    }
}
```

The Try type is inspired by Scala's Try and it represents a computation that may either result in an exception or return a successfully computed value.

```
import io.vavr.control.Try;

public class VavrExample {
    public static void main(String[] args) {
        Try<Integer> result = Try.of(() -> 1 / 0);
        Integer value = result.getOrElse(-1);
        System.out.println(value); // prints "-1"

        result = Try.of(() -> 1 / 1);
        value = result.getOrElse(-1);
        System.out.println(value); // prints "1"
    }
}
```

Vavr also offers immutable collections such as List, Map, and Set. These collections promote safe programming practices by ensuring that the data structures cannot be altered once they are created.

```
import io.vavr.collection.List;

public class VavrExample {
    public static void main(String[] args) {
        List<Integer> list = List.of(1, 2, 3);
        List<Integer> newList = list.append(4);

        System.out.println(list); // prints "(1, 2, 3)"
        System.out.println(newList); // prints "(1, 2, 3, 4)"
    }
}
```

Algorithms are an integral aspect of Vavr's usage to facilitate more streamlined and expressive code. Consider a functional approach to manipulating lists using Vavr.

Algorithm 3: Functional Mapping Using Vavr

Input: A list of integers list

Output: A new list where each integer is multiplied by 2

$newList = list.\mathrm{map}(x \Rightarrow x \times 2);$

return $newList;$

By leveraging the above functional approach, developers can achieve more transparent and expressive data transformations.

Vavr's integration with Java enhances its functional programming capabilities while maintaining compatibility with existing Java frameworks and tools. It facilitates the implementation of robust, maintainable, and concise functional programs.

5.6 Functional Java Project

In this section, we will explore how to create a functional Java project by employing the principles and utilities of various functional libraries discussed in the preceding chapters. The focus will be on using the libraries Guava, Apache Commons, and Vavr to implement a functional programming approach in a real-world scenario. We will walk through the entire process, from setting up the project to writing and executing the code.

To build this project, we will implement a functional pipeline for processing and transforming a collection of data. This project will demonstrate practical applications of functional programming concepts such as immutability, higher-order functions, and declarative programming.

Project Setup

First, create a new Java project using your preferred IDE. Ensure that Maven or Gradle is configured to manage dependencies. The following Maven configuration can be added to the pom.xml file to include the necessary libraries:

```
<dependencies>
    <!-- Guava: Google's Core Libraries for Java -->
    <dependency>
        <groupId>com.google.guava</groupId>
        <artifactId>guava</artifactId>
        <version>31.0.1-jre</version>
    </dependency>
    <!-- Apache Commons Lang -->
```

```
    <dependency>
        <groupId>org.apache.commons</groupId>
        <artifactId>commons-lang3</artifactId>
        <version>3.12.0</version>
    </dependency>
    <!-- Vavr: Functional Library for Java -->
    <dependency>
        <groupId>io.vavr</groupId>
        <artifactId>vavr</artifactId>
        <version>0.10.3</version>
    </dependency>
</dependencies>
```

Data Model

We will start by defining our data model. Assume we are processing a collection of Person objects. Each Person object has attributes name, age, and email. The class definition is as follows:

```
public class Person {
    private final String name;
    private final int age;
    private final String email;

    public Person(String name, int age, String email) {
        this.name = name;
        this.age = age;
        this.email = email;
    }

    public String getName() {
        return name;
    }

    public int getAge() {
        return age;
    }

    public String getEmail() {
        return email;
    }

    @Override
    public String toString() {
        return "Person{name='" + name + "', age=" + age + ", email='" + email + "
            '}";
    }
}
```

Data Transformation Pipeline

We will construct a functional pipeline to filter, transform, and collect a list of Person objects. The following steps will illustrate the use of each functional library.

Step 1: Filtering with Vavr

We will first filter the list to include only persons older than 18 years old using Vavr's List and filter methods:

```
import io.vavr.collection.List;

public class FunctionalPipeline {

    public static List<Person> filterAdults(List<Person> persons) {
        return persons.filter(person -> person.getAge() > 18);
    }

    public static void main(String[] args) {
        List<Person> persons = List.of(
            new Person("Alice", 20, "alice@example.com"),
            new Person("Bob", 17, "bob@example.com"),
            new Person("Charlie", 23, "charlie@example.com")
        );

        List<Person> adults = filterAdults(persons);
        System.out.println(adults);
    }
}
```

The output will be:

```
List(Person{name='Alice', age=20, email='alice@example.com'}, Person{name='Charlie', age=23, email='charlie@example.com'})
```

Step 2: Transforming with Guava

Next, we will use Guava's Function and Futures to transform the list of Person objects into a list of their names:

```
import com.google.common.base.Function;
import com.google.common.collect.FluentIterable;
import java.util.List;
import java.util.stream.Collectors;

public class GuavaTransformation {

    public static List<String> transformToNames(List<Person> persons) {
        return FluentIterable.from(persons)
                .transform(new Function<Person, String>() {
                    @Override
                    public String apply(Person person) {
                        return person.getName();
                    }
                })
                .toList();
    }

    public static void main(String[] args) {
```

```
        List<Person> persons = List.of(
            new Person("Alice", 20, "alice@example.com"),
            new Person("Bob", 17, "bob@example.com"),
            new Person("Charlie", 23, "charlie@example.com")
        );

        List<String> names = transformToNames(persons);
        System.out.println(names);
    }
}
```

The output will be:

```
[Alice, Bob, Charlie]
```

Step 3: Collecting with Apache Commons

Finally, we will collect the transformed names into a single string separated by commas using Apache Commons' StringUtils:

```
import org.apache.commons.lang3.StringUtils;
import java.util.List;

public class CommonsCollection {

    public static String collectNames(List<String> names) {
        return StringUtils.join(names, ", ");
    }

    public static void main(String[] args) {
        List<String> names = List.of("Alice", "Bob", "Charlie");
        String collectedNames = collectNames(names);
        System.out.println(collectedNames);
    }
}
```

The output will be:

```
Alice, Bob, Charlie
```

Putting It All Together

Integrating all the steps into a single functional pipeline provides a comprehensive view of how each library facilitates different functional operations:

```
import io.vavr.collection.List;
import com.google.common.base.Function;
import com.google.common.collect.FluentIterable;
import org.apache.commons.lang3.StringUtils;

public class FunctionalPipeline {
```

```
    public static List<Person> filterAdults(List<Person> persons) {
        return persons.filter(person -> person.getAge() > 18);
    }

    public static java.util.List<String> transformToNames(List<Person> persons) {
        return FluentIterable.from(persons.toJavaList())
                .transform(new Function<Person, String>() {
                    @Override
                    public String apply(Person person) {
                        return person.getName();
                    }
                })
                .toList();
    }

    public static String collectNames(java.util.List<String> names) {
        return StringUtils.join(names, ", ");
    }

    public static void main(String[] args) {
        List<Person> persons = List.of(
            new Person("Alice", 20, "alice@example.com"),
            new Person("Bob", 17, "bob@example.com"),
            new Person("Charlie", 23, "charlie@example.com")
        );

        List<Person> adults = filterAdults(persons);
        java.util.List<String> names = transformToNames(adults);
        String collectedNames = collectNames(names);

        System.out.println(collectedNames);
    }
}
```

The final output will be:

```
Alice, Charlie
```

This project demonstrates the application of Vavr for filtering, Guava for transforming, and Apache Commons for collecting data. It exemplifies how different functional programming libraries can be integrated to create a seamless and efficient functional pipeline in Java.

5.7 Common Operations with Guava

Guava, a set of core libraries developed by Google, vastly simplifies Java programming by providing a myriad of utilities for common tasks. In functional programming, Guava's utilities become indispensable, offering methods that compose, transform, and handle collections in ways that align with functional paradigms.

Predicates form the cornerstone of functional programming in Guava, enabling the creation of composable, reusable conditions. Below is an example demonstrating how to filter a list of integers using predicates.

```
import com.google.common.base.Predicate;
import com.google.common.collect.Collections2;

import java.util.Arrays;
import java.util.Collection;

public class GuavaExample {
    public static void main(String[] args) {
        Collection<Integer> numbers = Arrays.asList(1, 2, 3, 4, 5, 6, 7, 8, 9, 10);

        Predicate<Integer> evenPredicate = new Predicate<Integer>() {
            public boolean apply(Integer number) {
                return number % 2 == 0;
            }
        };

        Collection<Integer> evenNumbers = Collections2.filter(numbers, evenPredicate)
            ;
        System.out.println(evenNumbers);
    }
}
```

```
Output:
[2, 4, 6, 8, 10]
```

In this example, Predicate<Integer> evenPredicate defines the condition for filtering. Collections2.filter() applies this predicate to the collection, yielding a new collection of even numbers.

Continuing with collection manipulations, the Function interface allows transformation of elements. Here is an example of transforming a list of integers by squaring each element.

```
import com.google.common.base.Function;
import com.google.common.collect.Lists;

import java.util.List;

public class GuavaExample {
    public static void main(String[] args) {
        List<Integer> numbers = Arrays.asList(1, 2, 3, 4, 5);

        Function<Integer, Integer> squareFunction = new Function<Integer, Integer>()
            {
            public Integer apply(Integer number) {
                return number * number;
            }
        };

        List<Integer> squaredNumbers = Lists.transform(numbers, squareFunction);
        System.out.println(squaredNumbers);
    }
}
```

```
Output:
[1, 4, 9, 16, 25]
```

Lists.transform() applies the squareFunction to each element, transforming the list to squaredNumbers, where each integer is squared. Such transformations demonstrate the power and conciseness of functional programming with Guava.

Multimaps in Guava facilitate the mapping of keys to multiple values, simplifying the construction of complex data structures. The following example illustrates the usage of Multimap.

```
import com.google.common.collect.ArrayListMultimap;
import com.google.common.collect.Multimap;

public class GuavaExample {
    public static void main(String[] args) {
        Multimap<String, String> multimap = ArrayListMultimap.create();

        multimap.put("fruit", "apple");
        multimap.put("fruit", "banana");
        multimap.put("vegetable", "carrot");

        System.out.println(multimap.get("fruit"));
    }
}
```

```
Output:
[apple, banana]
```

The ArrayListMultimap conveniently maps the category "fruit" to multiple values, "apple" and "banana." Accessing multimap.get("fruit") returns a collection of all associated values.

Next, consider the Immutable Collections, which represent a structural consistency crucial in functional programming. Below is an example to create an immutable list and map.

```
import com.google.common.collect.ImmutableList;
import com.google.common.collect.ImmutableMap;

public class GuavaExample {
    public static void main(String[] args) {
        ImmutableList<String> immutableList = ImmutableList.of("a", "b", "c");
        System.out.println(immutableList);

        ImmutableMap<Integer, String> immutableMap = ImmutableMap.of(1, "one",
              2, "two", 3, "three");
        System.out.println(immutableMap);
    }
}
```

```
Output:
[a, b, c]
{1=one, 2=two, 3=three}
```

ImmutableList.of() and ImmutableMap.of() create unmodifiable collections that guarantee data integrity. Since these collections cannot be altered, they prevent bugs related to concurrent access or accidental modifications.

Optional in Guava is yet another utility that encapsulates the presence or absence of a value. The following example demonstrates the usage of Optional.

```
import com.google.common.base.Optional;

public class GuavaExample {
    public static void main(String[] args) {
        Optional<Integer> optional = Optional.of(5);
        System.out.println(optional.isPresent()); // true
        System.out.println(optional.get()); // 5

        Optional<Integer> absentOptional = Optional.absent();
        System.out.println(absentOptional.isPresent()); // false
    }
}
```

```
Output:
true
5
false
```

Optional.of(5) creates an Optional object containing the value 5, while Optional.absent() represents an absent value. Optional.isPresent() checks if a value is contained, and Optional.get() retrieves the value, eliminating null checks and potential NullPointerException.

Finally, the Ordering class provides powerful, fluent mechanisms for sorting collections with various criteria. Here is a brief example of its capabilities.

```
import com.google.common.collect.Ordering;
import java.util.Arrays;
import java.util.List;

public class GuavaExample {
    public static void main(String[] args) {
        List<Integer> numbers = Arrays.asList(5, 3, 15, 8, 1);
        Ordering<Integer> naturalOrdering = Ordering.natural();

        List<Integer> sortedNumbers = naturalOrdering.immutableSortedCopy(
                numbers);
        System.out.println(sortedNumbers);
    }
}
```

```
Output:
[1, 3, 5, 8, 15]
```

Ordering.natural() creates an Ordering instance for natural order sorting. immutableSortedCopy() sorts the numbers list immutably, demonstrating an easy way to sort collections while adhering to functional programming principles.

These operations illustrate Guava's capacity to handle functional programming tasks efficiently and elegantly, becoming an essential tool in any Java programmer's toolkit.

5.8 Using Apache Commons for Functional Programming

The Apache Commons library provides several utilities that facilitate functional programming in Java. Notably, the library includes Commons Collections and Commons Lang, which offer a number of operations and transforms that align with functional programming paradigms. This section delves into these utilities, emphasizing how they can be used to enhance code readability, reduce boilerplate, and promote a functional style.

Predicate and Transformer Classes

Apache Commons provides the Predicate and Transformer interfaces, enabling you to write code that is more expressive and adaptable. A Predicate is an object that defines a boolean condition, often used to filter collections. A Transformer applies a transformation to an input object and returns a result. These are analogous to Java 8's Predicate and Function interfaces, respectively, but can be used in environments where Java 8 features are not available.

```
// Example of Predicate
Predicate<String> isEmpty = new Predicate<String>() {
    public boolean evaluate(String str) {
        return str == null || str.isEmpty();
    }
};

// Example of Transformer
Transformer<String, Integer> stringLength = new Transformer<String, Integer>() {
    public Integer transform(String input) {
        return input.length();
    }
};
```

Filtering Collections

Using Predicate, collections can be filtered in a functional style. The CollectionUtils.filter() method applies the predicate to each item in the collection, retaining items that match the condition.

```
List<String> names = Arrays.asList("Alice", "", "Bob", "Charlie", "");
```

```
Predicate<String> nonEmpty = new Predicate<String>() {
    public boolean evaluate(String str) {
        return str != null && !str.isEmpty();
    }
};

CollectionUtils.filter(names, nonEmpty);
System.out.println(names); // Output: [Alice, Bob, Charlie]
```

Transforming Collections

Applying transformations to elements in a collection is straightforward using the Transformer interface and the CollectionUtils.transform() method.

```
List<String> words = Arrays.asList("functional", "programming", "java");
Transformer<String, String> upperCase = new Transformer<String, String>() {
    public String transform(String input) {
        return input.toUpperCase();
    }
};

CollectionUtils.transform(words, upperCase);
System.out.println(words); // Output: [FUNCTIONAL, PROGRAMMING, JAVA]
```

Chained Functional Operations

Apache Commons also supports chaining functional operations, allowing multiple predicates and transformations to be applied sequentially. This can enhance the expressiveness of the code.

```
List<String> data = Arrays.asList("Functional", "", "Programming", "In", "Java", "");

Predicate<String> nonEmpty = new Predicate<String>() {
    public boolean evaluate(String str) {
        return str != null && !str.isEmpty();
    }
};

Transformer<String, String> toUpperCase = new Transformer<String, String>() {
    public String transform(String input) {
        return input.toUpperCase();
    }
};

CollectionUtils.filter(data, nonEmpty);
CollectionUtils.transform(data, toUpperCase);

System.out.println(data); // Output: [FUNCTIONAL, PROGRAMMING, IN, JAVA]
```

Using Functions Module

The org.apache.commons.functions package is specifically designed to provide functional utilities. It includes various predefined predicates, transformers, and factory methods.

```
List<Integer> numbers = Arrays.asList(1, -2, 3, -4, 5);
Predicate<Integer> isPositive = PredicateUtils.notNullPredicate()
    .and(PredicateUtils.truePredicate())
    .and(PredicateUtils.uniquePredicate());
Transformer<Integer, Integer> negate = TransformerUtils.invokerTransformer("negate"
    );

CollectionUtils.filter(numbers, isPositive);
CollectionUtils.transform(numbers, negate);

System.out.println(numbers); // Output: [-1, -3, -5]
```

Functional Interfaces

For users familiar with Java 8, org.apache.commons.functions also provides support for java.util.function. This integration allows users to leverage the efficiencies of Java 8 while maintaining compatibility with Apache Commons.

```
List<String> elements = Arrays.asList("one", "two", "three");
Function<String, Integer> stringLengthFunctional = String::length;

Transformer<String, Integer> commonTransformer = TransformerUtils.asTransformer(
    stringLengthFunctional);

CollectionUtils.transform(elements, commonTransformer);
System.out.println(elements); // Output: [3, 3, 5]
```

Advanced Usage

Combining the predicates and transformers with other Apache Commons functionalities, such as collections or map operations, can substantially reduce the complexity of code that engages with data transformations and filtering.

```
List<String> phrases = Arrays.asList(" Apache Commons", " is useful ", " for
    functional programming ");
Predicate<String> trimmedNotEmpty = new Predicate<String>() {
    public boolean evaluate(String input) {
        return input != null && !input.trim().isEmpty();
    }
};

Transformer<String, String> trimTransformer = new Transformer<String, String>() {
    public String transform(String input) {
        return input.trim();
    }
};

CollectionUtils.transform(phrases, trimTransformer);
CollectionUtils.filter(phrases, trimmedNotEmpty);

System.out.println(phrases); // Output: [Apache Commons, is useful, for functional
    programming]
```

This section integrates seamlessly into our exploration of advanced

Java functionalities, reflecting the power and flexibility of the Apache Commons library. Its predicates and transformers offer elegant solutions to common programming tasks, emphasizing maintainability and functional purity.

5.9 Advanced Techniques with Vavr

Vavr, formerly known as Javaslang, is an open-source functional library for Java that enhances the language's capabilities with a rich set of immutable data types and functional control structures. This section delves into advanced techniques that can be leveraged using Vavr to write more expressive and maintainable Java code. We will examine advanced usage patterns, custom data types, and efficient functional programming constructs provided by Vavr.

Using Vavr's Tuples

Tuples in Vavr are a data structure that can store a fixed number of elements of different types. They are particularly useful when dealing with functions that return multiple values without the overhead of creating a custom class. Vavr's Tuple class provides up to Tuple8, which allows storing eight elements.

```
import io.vavr.Tuple;
import io.vavr.Tuple2;

public class TupleExample {
    public static void main(String[] args) {
        Tuple2<String, Integer> person = Tuple.of("Jane", 28);

        // Accessing tuple elements
        String name = person._1();
        Integer age = person._2();

        System.out.println("Name: " + name);
        System.out.println("Age: " + age);
    }
}
```

```
Name: Jane
Age: 28
```

In this example, Tuple2 is used to store a person's name and age. The elements are accessed using the _1() and _2() methods.

Pattern Matching

Vavr's pattern matching provides a versatile approach for handling complex conditions without extensive if-else or switch-case statements. Pattern matching in Vavr is performed using the Match class.

```
import io.vavr.API;
import io.vavr.Predicates;
import static io.vavr.API.*;
import static io.vavr.Predicates.*;

public class PatternMatchingExample {
    public static void main(String[] args) {
        int input = 3;

        String result = Match(input).of(
            Case($(1), "one"),
            Case($(2), "two"),
            Case($(isIn(3, 4, 5)), "three to five"),
            Case($(), "other")
        );

        System.out.println("Result: " + result);
    }
}
```

```
Result: three to five
```

In this code, the Match class is used to map an integer input to a string output based on the value of the input. The Case statements provide patterns for matching specific conditions.

Efficient Handling of Collections with Vavr's Persistent Data Types

Vavr provides immutable collections that ensure that any modification operation returns a new collection rather than modifying the existing one. This characteristic is crucial for functional programming as it promotes immutability and thread safety.

```
import io.vavr.collection.List;

public class PersistentCollections {
    public static void main(String[] args) {
        List<Integer> numbers = List.of(1, 2, 3);

        List<Integer> newNumbers = numbers.append(4);

        System.out.println("Original List: " + numbers);
        System.out.println("New List: " + newNumbers);
    }
}
```

```
Original List: List(1, 2, 3)
New List: List(1, 2, 3, 4)
```

Here, the append operation returns a new list with the additional element without altering the original list. This immutability allows for safer concurrent programming.

Advanced Functional Constructs: Try, Option, Either

Vavr provides classes such as Try, Option, and Either to handle computations that may fail, optional values, and computations with two possible outcomes respectively.

Try is used to encapsulate operations that may throw exceptions.

```
import io.vavr.control.Try;

public class TryExample {
    public static void main(String[] args) {
        Try<Integer> result = Try.of(() -> 1 / 0);

        System.out.println("Success: " + result.isSuccess());
        System.out.println("Failure: " + result.isFailure());
        result.onFailure(ex -> System.out.println("Exception: " + ex.getMessage()));
    }
}
```

```
Success: false
Failure: true
Exception: / by zero
```

Option is used to represent optional values, avoiding null checks.

```
import io.vavr.control.Option;

public class OptionExample {
    public static void main(String[] args) {
        Option<String> maybeName = Option.of("John Doe");

        String name = maybeName.getOrElse("Unknown");

        System.out.println("Name: " + name);
    }
}
```

```
Name: John Doe
```

Either is used to represent a value of one of two possible types, typically used for operations that can return a result or an error.

```
import io.vavr.control.Either;

public class EitherExample {
    public static void main(String[] args) {
        Either<String, Integer> computeResult = divide(4, 2);

        computeResult
            .peek(result -> System.out.println("Result: " + result))
            .peekLeft(error -> System.out.println("Error: " + error));
    }

    private static Either<String, Integer> divide(int dividend, int divisor) {
        if (divisor == 0) {
            return Either.left("Division by zero");
        } else {
            return Either.right(dividend / divisor);
        }
    }
```

```
}
```

Result: 2

These constructs allow for more robust error handling and result management in a functional programming style, ensuring that your code can gracefully handle different scenarios without cumbersome error-prone checks.

Advanced techniques with Vavr empower developers to write concise, expressive, and maintainable code by leveraging immutable data types, pattern matching, and powerful functional constructs like Try, Option, and Either.

5.10 Comparing Different Functional Libraries

Comparing functional libraries in Java involves analyzing various aspects such as available features, ease of use, performance, and interoperability with existing codebases. We will examine three prominent libraries: Guava, Apache Commons, and Vavr (formerly known as Javaslang). Each of these libraries brings unique capabilities to Java functional programming, and understanding their differences can guide developers in choosing the most appropriate tools for their projects.

Feature Set

Each library offers a robust set of features tailored to functional programming.

- **Guava:** Google's Guava provides a comprehensive collection of utilities for functional programming, including immutable collections, functional idioms (such as Function and Predicate), and enhancements to existing Java utility classes.
- **Apache Commons:** Apache Commons focuses on adding functionality that complements Java's standard libraries, with functional utilities mostly found in the Commons Collections and Commons Lang components. It provides utilities such as Closure, Predicate, Transformer, and Functor.
- **Vavr:** Vavr stands out by offering a dedicated functional programming library for Java, including immutable data structures

(like List, Map, Set), functional interfaces (complementing Java's java.util.function), and control structures like Option, Try, Either.

Ease of Use

The ease of using these libraries depends largely on their API design and documentation quality.

- **Guava:** Guava's APIs are designed to be intuitive, and it integrates seamlessly with Java's standard libraries. Its comprehensive documentation and widespread community support make it relatively easy to adopt.
- **Apache Commons:** While powerful, the functional utilities in Apache Commons can be more complex to use due to their design focusing on a wide variety of use cases. The documentation is thorough, but the learning curve can be steep.
- **Vavr:** Vavr offers a cohesive functional programming experience. Its APIs are designed with immutability and side-effect-free operations in mind, which align well with functional programming principles. Vavr's documentation is detailed and includes many examples, which eases the learning process.

Performance

Performance is a critical factor when evaluating functional libraries.

- **Guava:** Guava is well-optimized for performance, especially its collection utilities. However, the overhead introduced by some functional idioms might be non-trivial in performance-critical applications.
- **Apache Commons:** The design of Apache Commons utilities sometimes favors flexibility over performance. Consequently, performance may vary depending on the specific usage and context.
- **Vavr:** Vavr prioritizes immutability, which can introduce overhead, particularly in data transformation operations. However, Vavr provides efficient implementations for common functional data structures and lazy evaluation techniques to mitigate performance issues.

Interoperability

Interoperability with existing codebases ensures that these libraries can be integrated without major refactoring.

- **Guava:** Guava is highly interoperable with Java's standard libraries and other third-party libraries. Its functional utilities can be seamlessly incorporated into existing Java projects.
- **Apache Commons:** Apache Commons integrates well with Java's core libraries. Its modular nature allows selective adoption of functional utilities, ensuring minimal disruption to existing code.
- **Vavr:** Vavr is designed to complement Java's native functional interfaces, making it relatively easy to integrate. However, due to its extensive use of functional paradigms, some refactoring might be necessary to fully leverage its capabilities.

The following example demonstrates how to perform a map operation using Guava, Apache Commons, and Vavr, illustrating the practical differences in their APIs.

```
// Guava Example: Mapping a List of Strings to their lengths
List<String> strings = Arrays.asList("one", "two", "three");
List<Integer> lengths = Lists.transform(strings, new Function<String, Integer>() {
    public Integer apply(String input) {
        return input.length();
    }
});
System.out.println(lengths);
```

```
[3, 3, 5]
```

```
// Apache Commons Example: Mapping a List of Strings to their lengths
List<String> strings = Arrays.asList("one", "two", "three");
Collection<Integer> lengths = CollectionUtils.collect(strings, new Transformer<String,
      Integer>() {
    public Integer transform(String input) {
        return input.length();
    }
});
System.out.println(lengths);
```

```
[3, 3, 5]
```

```
// Vavr Example: Mapping a List of Strings to their lengths
List<String> strings = List.of("one", "two", "three");
List<Integer> lengths = strings.map(String::length);
System.out.println(lengths);
```

List(3, 3, 5)

These examples illustrate the differing approaches each library takes. Guava requires a more verbose definition of transformation functions, Apache Commons leverages its Transformer interface, while Vavr offers the most concise syntax due to its seamless integration with Java's functional programming features.

Choosing the right functional library for a Java project depends on specific requirements such as the desired feature set, ease of use, performance considerations, and how well the library can be integrated into the existing codebase. Each of these libraries offers distinct advantages, and understanding their key differences helps developers make informed decisions tailored to their particular needs.

5.11 Integrating Functional Libraries in Real Projects

Effective integration of functional libraries in real-world projects requires an understanding of both the capabilities of these libraries and the context in which they will be applied. By leveraging functional programming paradigms with libraries such as Guava, Apache Commons, and Vavr, developers can write cleaner, more maintainable, and efficient code. This section will discuss the practical steps and considerations involved in integrating functional libraries into existing and new projects.

Guava, provided by Google, simplifies many common programming tasks. To integrate Guava into a Maven project, add the following dependency to your pom.xml:

```
<dependency>
    <groupId>com.google.guava</groupId>
    <artifactId>guava</artifactId>
    <version>30.1.1-jre</version>
</dependency>
```

For Gradle users, add the dependency as follows in your build.gradle:

```
implementation 'com.google.guava:guava:30.1.1-jre'
```

With Guava integrated, developers can utilize a plethora of utilities for collections, caching, primitives support, concurrency, common annotations, string processing, and more. For instance, Guava provides a functional approach to filtering a list:

```
import com.google.common.collect.Lists;
import com.google.common.collect.Iterables;
import com.google.common.base.Predicate;

import java.util.List;

public class GuavaExample {
    public static void main(String[] args) {
        List<String> names = Lists.newArrayList("John", "Doe", "Jane", "Joe");
        Iterable<String> filtered = Iterables.filter(names, new Predicate<String>() {
            @Override
            public boolean apply(String input) {
                return input.startsWith("J");
            }
        });

        for (String name : filtered) {
            System.out.println(name);
        }
    }
}
```

The output:

```
John
Jane
Joe
```

Apache Commons focuses on providing reusable components that complement the Java standard library. To incorporate Apache Commons into a Maven project, insert the following dependency:

```
<dependency>
    <groupId>org.apache.commons</groupId>
    <artifactId>commons-lang3</artifactId>
    <version>3.12.0</version>
</dependency>
```

For Gradle:

```
implementation 'org.apache.commons:commons-lang3:3.12.0'
```

With Apache Commons, functional programming can be enhanced by using its utilities. For example, you can use the Commons Lang library to work with StringUtils to simplify string operations:

```
import org.apache.commons.lang3.StringUtils;

public class ApacheCommonsExample {
    public static void main(String[] args) {
        String input = " Hello, Apache Commons!";
        String abbreviated = StringUtils.abbreviate(input, 10);
        System.out.println(abbreviated);
    }
}
```

The output:

...Common

Vavr, formerly known as Javaslang, introduces functional programming concepts directly into Java. Adding Vavr to a Maven project involves the following addition to the pom.xml:

```
<dependency>
    <groupId>io.vavr</groupId>
    <artifactId>vavr</artifactId>
    <version>0.10.3</version>
</dependency>
```

For Gradle:

```
implementation 'io.vavr:vavr:0.10.3'
```

With Vavr, you can use immutable collections and pattern matching, among other functional constructs. An example illustrating Vavr's Try monad for handling exceptions functionally:

```
import io.vavr.control.Try;

public class VavrExample {
    public static void main(String[] args) {
        Try<Integer> result = Try.of(() -> divide(10, 0))
                                 .recover(ArithmeticException.class, 0);

        System.out.println(result.get());
    }

    private static int divide(int dividend, int divisor) {
        return dividend / divisor;
    }
}
```

The output:

```
0
```

Real-world integration involves context-specific considerations:

- **Compatibility**: Ensure that the functional library is compatible with your existing project's libraries and frameworks. This can be checked by validating library versions and testing for any dependency conflicts.
- **Performance Impact**: Functional libraries often introduce abstractions that can have performance implications. Profiling and benchmarking your application after integration can help to identify and mitigate performance hotspots.
- **Learning Curve**: Introducing functional libraries can require a

shift in programming paradigms. Ensuring that the team is adequately trained and adopting a gradual integration approach can alleviate potential challenges.

- **Refactoring**: Existing code can usually benefit from functional paradigms such as immutability, higher-order functions, and monads. Evaluating the complexity and feasibility of refactoring can guide the extent of integration.
- **Testing and Validation**: Comprehensive unit and integration testing is crucial to ensure that the functional library integration does not introduce regressions or bugs.

Selecting the appropriate points for integration can depend on various factors such as project size, team expertise, and specific requirements. For example, smaller modules or new features can first adopt these libraries as a proof of concept before a broader application integration.

Chapter 6

Immutability and Persistent Data Structures

This chapter examines the concepts of immutability and persistent data structures in Java. It details the benefits of immutability and provides techniques for creating immutable objects, including the use of final variables and addressing deep versus shallow immutability. The chapter also explores persistent data structures such as lists, maps, and sets, including their implementation and performance considerations. Common patterns and best practices for working with immutability are discussed to ensure robust and efficient data management in functional programming.

6.1 Introduction to Immutability

Immutability, within the context of programming, refers to objects whose state cannot be altered after they have been instantiated. An immutable object, once created, will always hold the same data. This concept plays a crucial role in functional programming, wherein data consistency and reliability are paramount.

To understand immutability, first consider a standard object in Java. Typically, such an object has fields that can be changed throughout its lifecycle. For example, consider a simple class Person:

```
public class Person {
  private String name;
  private int age;

  public Person(String name, int age) {
    this.name = name;
    this.age = age;
  }

  public String getName() {
    return name;
  }

  public void setName(String name) {
    this.name = name;
  }

  public int getAge() {
    return age;
  }

  public void setAge(int age) {
    this.age = age;
  }
}
```

In the above example, it is possible to modify the fields name and age after a Person object is created using the setName and setAge methods. This mutable characteristic can lead to unpredictable behavior, particularly in concurrent or multi-threaded applications.

Immutability eliminates such issues by ensuring that once an object is initialized, it cannot be changed. Immutable objects provide several advantages:

- **Thread-Safety**: As immutable objects cannot be changed, they are inherently thread-safe. This means multiple threads can access immutable objects simultaneously without synchronization.
- **Ease of Understanding**: Immutable objects are simpler to comprehend because their state does not change over time.
- **Failure-Resistance**: Since immutable objects cannot be altered, they reduce the chances of undesired side-effects, leading to fewer bugs and more predictable code behavior.

To contrast with the mutable example, consider an immutable version of the Person class:

```
public final class Person {
  private final String name;
```

```
  private final int age;

  public Person(String name, int age) {
    this.name = name;
    this.age = age;
  }

  public String getName() {
    return name;
  }

  public int getAge() {
    return age;
  }
}
```

In this immutable version:

- The class is marked as final, preventing it from being subclassed.
- The fields name and age are also marked as final, ensuring their values are set once and never changed.
- There are no setter methods.

Through immutability, objects are restricted from any form of alteration post-instantiation. This method encourages a programming style that results in safer, more maintainable code.

It is necessary to emphasize that immutability does not inherently come without its own challenges. For instance, immutability often requires creating new instances of objects rather than modifying existing ones. This can initially seem inefficient, but optimizations and persistent data structures (discussed later in the chapter) alleviate potential performance concerns.

Java provides built-in support for creating immutable objects via the use of the String class, which is a prime example of efficient immutable design.

```
String s1 = "hello";
String s2 = s1.concat(" world");
System.out.println(s1); // Outputs: hello
System.out.println(s2); // Outputs: hello world
```

In this example, invoking the concat method results in a new String being created. The original String s1 remains unchanged, demonstrating immutability in action.

Understanding immutability lays the foundation for both functional programming and concurrent computing. As we advance through the chapter, we will explore how to build on these principles with effective techniques and structures, ensuring robust and efficient Java applications.

6.2 Benefits of Immutability

Immutability, a core principle within functional programming, offers numerous benefits that can significantly enhance the predictability, maintainability, and performance of code. Understanding these benefits lays a strong foundation for applying immutability effectively in Java.

Thread Safety: One of the most significant advantages of immutable objects is their inherent thread safety. Since the state of an immutable object cannot be altered once it is created, multiple threads can safely read the same immutable object simultaneously without synchronization. This eliminates complex locking mechanisms and reduces the possibility of concurrency-related bugs.

```
// Example of thread safety with immutable objects
public final class ImmutablePoint {
    private final int x;
    private final int y;

    public ImmutablePoint(int x, int y) {
        this.x = x;
        this.y = y;
    }

    public int getX() {
        return x;
    }

    public int getY() {
        return y;
    }
}

// Safe usage in multithreaded context
ImmutablePoint point = new ImmutablePoint(1, 2);
Thread t1 = new Thread(() -> System.out.println(point.getX()));
Thread t2 = new Thread(() -> System.out.println(point.getY()));
t1.start();
t2.start();
```

Ease of Reasoning: Immutability simplifies reasoning about program behavior. With immutable objects, you can be confident that an object's state remains consistent throughout its lifetime. This predictability reduces the cognitive load on developers, making it easier to understand and trace the flow of data within an application.

Elimination of Defensive Copying: In traditional mutable object design, it is often necessary to create defensive copies of objects to avoid unexpected modification. This practice can lead to performance overhead and increased memory usage. Immutable objects naturally eliminate the need for defensive copying because their state cannot change.

```
// Without immutability, defensive copying is required
public class MutablePoint {
    private int x;
    private int y;

    public MutablePoint(int x, int y) {
        this.x = x;
        this.y = y;
    }

    public synchronized int getX() {
        return x;
    }

    public synchronized int getY() {
        return y;
    }

    public synchronized void setX(int x) {
        this.x = x;
    }

    public synchronized void setY(int y) {
        this.y = y;
    }
}

// Potentially creating defensive copies
public class Shape {
    private MutablePoint center;

    public Shape(MutablePoint center) {
        this.center = new MutablePoint(center.getX(), center.getY());
    }

    public MutablePoint getCenter() {
        return new MutablePoint(center.getX(), center.getY());
    }
}

// Using immutability, no need for defensive copying
public final class ImmutablePoint {
    private final int x;
    private final int y;

    public ImmutablePoint(int x, int y) {
        this.x = x;
        this.y = y;
    }

    public int getX() {
        return x;
    }

    public int getY() {
        return y;
```

```
    }
}
public class Shape {
    private final ImmutablePoint center;

    public Shape(ImmutablePoint center) {
        this.center = center;
    }

    public ImmutablePoint getCenter() {
        return center;
    }
}
```

Prevention of Identity Mutability Bugs: In mutable object design, bugs can arise if the identity or equality of objects changes while they are used as keys in data structures like maps or sets. Immutable objects guarantee that their state—and thus their identity and hash code—remains constant, preventing such issues.

```
// Potential issue with mutable keys
import java.util.HashMap;
import java.util.Map;

public class MutableKey {
    private String key;

    public MutableKey(String key) {
        this.key = key;
    }

    public String getKey() {
        return key;
    }

    public void setKey(String key) {
        this.key = key;
    }

    @Override
    public int hashCode() {
        return key.hashCode();
    }

    @Override
    public boolean equals(Object obj) {
        if (this == obj) return true;
        if (obj == null || getClass() != obj.getClass()) return false;
        MutableKey that = (MutableKey) obj;
        return key.equals(that.key);
    }
}

// Using MutableKey as a Map key
public class Example {
    public static void main(String[] args) {
        Map<MutableKey, String> map = new HashMap<>();
        MutableKey key = new MutableKey("key1");
        map.put(key, "value1");
```

```
        // Modifying the key
        key.setKey("key2");

        // Inconsistent behavior: map lookup with modified key
        System.out.println(map.get(new MutableKey("key1"))); // prints null
        System.out.println(map.get(new MutableKey("key2"))); // prints null
    }
}

// With immutable keys, no such issue
public final class ImmutableKey {
    private final String key;

    public ImmutableKey(String key) {
        this.key = key;
    }

    public String getKey() {
        return key;
    }

    @Override
    public int hashCode() {
        return key.hashCode();
    }

    @Override
    public boolean equals(Object obj) {
        if (this == obj) return true;
        if (obj == null || getClass() != obj.getClass()) return false;
        ImmutableKey that = (ImmutableKey) obj;
        return key.equals(that.key);
    }
}

// Using ImmutableKey as a Map key
public class Example {
    public static void main(String[] args) {
        Map<ImmutableKey, String> map = new HashMap<>();
        ImmutableKey key = new ImmutableKey("key1");
        map.put(key, "value1");

        // No possibility to modify the key, consistent behavior
        System.out.println(map.get(new ImmutableKey("key1"))); // prints "value1"
    }
}
```

Improved Caching and Optimization: Immutable objects can be freely shared and reused, enabling more effective caching and optimization strategies. For example, if an immutable object represents a frequently occurring value, it can be cached and reused to avoid redundant object creation.

```
// Caching example with immutable objects
public final class Color {
    private static final Map<String, Color> CACHE = new HashMap<>();
    private final String colorCode;

    private Color(String colorCode) {
```

```
        this.colorCode = colorCode;
    }

    public static Color of(String colorCode) {
        return CACHE.computeIfAbsent(colorCode, Color::new);
    }

    public String getColorCode() {
        return colorCode;
    }
}

// Reusing the object instead of creating new instances
public class Example {
    public static void main(String[] args) {
        Color red1 = Color.of("#FF0000");
        Color red2 = Color.of("#FF0000");
        System.out.println(red1 == red2); // prints true, same instance reused
    }
}
```

Facilitation of Functional Programming Constructs: Immutability aligns naturally with the principles of functional programming, which emphasizes the use of pure functions and avoids side effects. Immutable objects ensure that functions remain pure by eliminating state changes.

```
// Pure function with immutable objects
public final class Coordinate {
    private final int x;
    private final int y;

    public Coordinate(int x, int y) {
        this.x = x;
        this.y = y;
    }

    public Coordinate translate(int dx, int dy) {
        return new Coordinate(this.x + dx, this.y + dy);
    }

    public int getX() {
        return x;
    }

    public int getY() {
        return y;
    }
}
public class Example {
    public static void main(String[] args) {
        Coordinate point = new Coordinate(1, 2);
        Coordinate newPoint = point.translate(3, 4);
        System.out.println("Original: (" + point.getX() + ", " + point.getY() + ")"); //
            (1, 2)
        System.out.println("Translated: (" + newPoint.getX() + ", " + newPoint.getY()
            + ")"); // (4, 6)
    }
}
```

Through these examples and considerations, it is evident that immutability provides a robust framework for developing safer, more efficient, and more understandable code. The consistent state, the elimination of concurrency issues, and the alignment with functional programming paradigms all underscore the importance of immutability in modern Java applications.

6.3 Creating Immutable Objects in Java

Immutability in Java is a powerful concept that ensures objects remain unchangeable once they have been instantiated. This characteristic is particularly beneficial in functional programming, allowing for more predictable and safer code. To create immutable objects in Java, several techniques and principles must be employed meticulously.

Characteristics of Immutable Objects:

- **Final Class:** An immutable object is typically part of a final class. Making the class final prevents inheritance, which could potentially introduce mutability.
- **Private Fields:** All fields of the class should be declared private. This restricts direct access to the fields of the object.
- **Final Fields:** Each field should be declared as final to ensure that the reference cannot be modified once it has been assigned.
- **No Mutative Methods:** The class must not provide any methods that modify the object's state. All state modifications should return new instances instead.
- **Deep Copying:** If the object contains mutable fields, it should perform deep copying to maintain immutability.

Implementing an Immutable Class:

Consider a simple example of an immutable class, ImmutablePoint, which represents a point in a 2D space with x and y coordinates.

```
public final class ImmutablePoint {
    private final int x;
    private final int y;

    public ImmutablePoint(int x, int y) {
        this.x = x;
```

```
        this.y = y;
    }
    public int getX() {
        return x;
    }
    public int getY() {
        return y;
    }
}
```

In this example, the ImmutablePoint class is immutable because:

- The class is declared as final, preventing it from being subclassed.
- Fields x and y are declared as private and final, ensuring they cannot be directly accessed or modified after construction.
- No mutative methods are provided. Only getters are available to access the field values.

Handling Mutable Objects:

When an immutable object needs to hold a reference to a mutable object, deeper considerations are required. The class should create defensive copies of the mutable fields to ensure that these fields cannot be modified externally.

Consider a complex immutable class, ImmutablePerson, containing a list of phone numbers:

```
import java.util.Collections;
import java.util.List;

public final class ImmutablePerson {
    private final String name;
    private final List<String> phoneNumbers;

    public ImmutablePerson(String name, List<String> phoneNumbers) {
        this.name = name;
        this.phoneNumbers = List.copyOf(phoneNumbers); // Creating a copy
    }

    public String getName() {
        return name;
    }

    public List<String> getPhoneNumbers() {
        return Collections.unmodifiableList(phoneNumbers); // Returning an
            unmodifiable view
    }
}
```

In this example:

- The constructor creates a defensive copy of the input list using List.copyOf, ensuring that any modifications made to the original list after the object's creation do not affect the internal state of the immutable object.
- The getPhoneNumbers method returns an unmodifiable view of the list by using Collections.unmodifiableList, preventing outside modifications to the internal list.

Using Builder Pattern for Immutable Objects:

When constructing complex immutable objects, the Builder Pattern can be very useful. It helps manage the creation process more cleanly, especially when dealing with numerous fields.

Examine the following implementation for an ImmutableCar class using the Builder Pattern:

```
public final class ImmutableCar {
    private final String make;
    private final String model;
    private final int year;

    private ImmutableCar(Builder builder) {
        this.make = builder.make;
        this.model = builder.model;
        this.year = builder.year;
    }

    public String getMake() {
        return make;
    }

    public String getModel() {
        return model;
    }

    public int getYear() {
        return year;
    }
    public static class Builder {
        private String make;
        private String model;
        private int year;

        public Builder setMake(String make) {
            this.make = make;
            return this;
        }

        public Builder setModel(String model) {
            this.model = model;
            return this;
```

```
        }

        public Builder setYear(int year) {
            this.year = year;
            return this;
        }

        public ImmutableCar build() {
            return new ImmutableCar(this);
        }
    }
}
```

The Builder Pattern exemplifies an elegant way to construct immutable objects:

- The ImmutableCar class has a private constructor that takes a Builder instance.
- The Builder class is a static nested class that allows the setting of fields through setter methods.
- The build method in the Builder class constructs and returns an instance of ImmutableCar.

Such patterns contribute to code clarity, especially as the complexity of the immutable object increases, allowing for a more maintainable and extendable approach to constructing instances.

Ensuring Immutability via Final Methods:

In addition to the previously discussed practices, enforcing immutability can also involve declaring methods as final. This ensures that subclasses cannot override methods, preserving the intended immutability constraints. These practices are pertinent not only to maintain immutability but also to provide a predictable structure for objects interacting within a functional programming paradigm.

Constructing immutable objects in Java demands a systematic approach focusing on immovable and inaccessible state, deep copying, and controlled instantiation pathways. Applying these principles rigorously secures the benefits of immutability, including thread-safety, simplicity in reasoning, and enhanced reliability.

6.4 Final and Effective Final Variables

In Java programming, the usage of final variables is crucial for maintaining immutability, ensuring the integrity and reliability of data throughout the lifecycle of an application. The keyword final can be applied to variables, methods, and classes. When applied to variables, it guarantees that the variable can be assigned only once. This restriction simplifies reasoning about the state of variables, making code easier to understand and debug.

Consider the following example demonstrating the use of a final variable in Java:

```
public class Example {
    public static void main(String[] args) {
        final int CONSTANT_VALUE = 42;
        // CONSTANT_VALUE = 50; // This line would produce a compilation error
        System.out.println(CONSTANT_VALUE);
    }
}
```

```
42
```

In the example above, the variable CONSTANT_VALUE is declared as final, meaning its value cannot be changed once assigned. Attempting to reassign it, as illustrated in the commented line, results in a compilation error. This immutability is fundamental in enforcing data consistency, especially in concurrent programming where multiple threads may interact with shared data.

It is also possible to use final with object references. However, this enforces immutability only on the reference itself, not on the object it points to. For instance:

```
public class Example {
    public static void main(String[] args) {
        final StringBuilder builder = new StringBuilder("Hello");
        // builder = new StringBuilder("World"); // This line would produce a
             compilation error
        builder.append(", World!");
        System.out.println(builder.toString());
    }
}
```

```
Hello, World!
```

In this scenario, the variable builder is final, and attempting to reassign it produces a compilation error. However, the object it references, a StringBuilder, can still be modified. Therefore, while the reference itself is immutable, the state of the object is not.

Beyond final variables, Java also supports what are known as **effectively final** variables. These are variables that are not explicitly declared as final, yet their values do not change after they are initialized. Effectively final variables are particularly relevant in the context of lambda expressions and inner classes. For instance:

```
public class Example {
    public static void main(String[] args) {
        int number = 100;
        Runnable printNumber = () -> System.out.println(number);
        // number = 200; // This line would produce a compilation error
        printNumber.run();
    }
}
```

```
100
```

In this example, number is not declared as final, but because its value does not change after initialization, it is considered effectively final. Attempting to reassign number after it has been captured by the lambda expression results in a compilation error. This effectively final nature ensures that the lambda expression sees a consistent value, avoiding potential concurrency issues.

Similarly, in the context of inner classes, effectively final variables allow for safe capture and usage when defining behavior that relies on the state established at the time of definition. Consider the following:

```
public class Example {
    public static void main(String[] args) {
        int initialValue = 10;
        class LocalClass {
            void printValue() {
                System.out.println(initialValue);
            }
        }
        LocalClass local = new LocalClass();
        local.printValue();
        // initialValue = 20; // This line would produce a compilation error
    }
}
```

```
10
```

In this scenario, initialValue is captured by the LocalClass inner class. As an effectively final variable, any attempt to reassign initialValue after its capture would result in a compilation error. This ensures that the inner class operates on a consistent value, fundamentally supporting the principles of immutability and thread-safety.

Thus, employing final and effectively final variables in Java is essential for preserving immutability, enabling safer concurrent programming, and minimizing the risk of state inconsistencies. Understanding and correctly applying these concepts contribute significantly to writing robust, maintainable, and side-effect-free code.

6.5 Deep vs Shallow Immutability

Understanding the distinction between deep and shallow immutability is essential for effective implementation of immutable objects.

Shallow immutability refers to the immutability of an object's immediate fields, meaning the top-level fields of the object cannot be altered once the object is constructed. However, if an object holds references to other mutable objects, shallow immutability does not prevent modifications to the state of those referenced objects.

On the other hand, deep immutability ensures that not only the immediate fields but also all nested objects and their fields are immutable. This involves creating immutable versions of all objects within the hierarchical structure of the initial object. Such rigor guarantees the entire object's immutability, irrespective of how deeply nested a mutable reference might be.

To illustrate these concepts, consider the following Java class definitions and instances.

```
public final class ShallowImmutable {
    private final int value;
    private final List<String> items;

    public ShallowImmutable(int value, List<String> items) {
        this.value = value;
        this.items = new ArrayList<>(items); // creating a defensive copy
    }

    public int getValue() {
        return value;
    }

    public List<String> getItems() {
        return new ArrayList<>(items); // returning a defensive copy
    }
}
```

In the ShallowImmutable class, the object references items are protected only at the initial level. Hence, items can still be modified after the object construction through its reference.

```
public class Main {
    public static void main(String[] args) {
        List<String> itemList = new ArrayList<>(Arrays.asList("item1", "item2"));
```

```
        ShallowImmutable shallowObj = new ShallowImmutable(42, itemList);

        // The object itself is immutable, but internal list is not
        List<String> items = shallowObj.getItems();
        items.add("item3");

        System.out.println(shallowObj.getItems()); // item3 appears in the list
    }
}
```

[Output]
[item1, item2, item3]

To achieve true immutability, also known as deep immutability, nested objects must be immutable. Implementing deep immutability requires defensive copies of mutable objects and potentially usage of immutable collections from libraries such as Guava or Java Collections Framework.

```
public final class DeepImmutable {
    private final int value;
    private final List<String> items;

    public DeepImmutable(int value, List<String> items) {
        this.value = value;
        // Using Java's built-in immutableList from Guava library
        this.items = Collections.unmodifiableList(new ArrayList<>(items));
    }

    public int getValue() {
        return value;
    }

    public List<String> getItems() {
        return items;
    }
}
```

In the DeepImmutable class, the items list is deeply immutable because it is wrapped in an unmodifiable list. Any attempt to modify the items list will result in an UnsupportedOperationException.

```
public class Main {
    public static void main(String[] args) {
        List<String> itemList = new ArrayList<>(Arrays.asList("item1", "item2"));
        DeepImmutable deepObj = new DeepImmutable(42, itemList);

        // The internal list cannot be modified
        List<String> items = deepObj.getItems();
        items.add("item3"); // this line will throw an exception

        System.out.println(deepObj.getItems());
    }
}
```

```
[Output]
Exception in thread "main" java.lang.UnsupportedOperationException
 at java.base/java.util.Collections$UnmodifiableList.add(Collections.java:1505)
 at Main.main(Main.java:10)
```

When designing deeply immutable objects, consider the following points:

- **Immutable Types:** Ensure that all fields are of immutable types or are deeply copied and wrapped in unmodifiable structures.
- **Constructor Copies:** Make defensive copies of mutable parameters in the constructor.
- **Unmodifiable Wrappers:** Use collections from the Java Collections Framework or other libraries (like Guava) that provide immutable wrappers.
- **Factory Methods:** Prefer factory methods to constructors, as they allow for complex logic to ensure immutability.

Deep immutability ensures thread-safety and makes an object truly immutable by preventing accidental modification at any nested level, thereby enhancing robustness and reliability in concurrent programming environments.

6.6 Persistent Data Structures Overview

Persistent data structures provide a mechanism for achieving immutability while maintaining efficient performance. A persistent data structure allows for the creation of a new version of a data structure when modifications are made, without altering the original structure. This is particularly useful in functional programming, where immutability is a core principle. In this section, we will delve into the properties, advantages, and typical uses of persistent data structures.

Persistent data structures, often referred to as immutable data structures, ensure that once a data structure is created, it cannot be changed. Any modification operations create a new data structure that incorporates the change alongside the existing data, often sharing much of the underlying structure to optimize for memory and processing time. This concept aligns well with the functional programming paradigm, wherein functions do not have side effects and data remains unchanged after being created.

To illustrate, let's consider the implementation of a basic persistent list. We'll provide an example in Java to elucidate the concept.

```
// Node class representing an element in the list
public final class Node {
    private final int value;
    private final Node next;

    // Constructor for Node
    public Node(int value, Node next) {
        this.value = value;
        this.next = next;
    }

    public int getValue() {
        return value;
    }

    public Node getNext() {
        return next;
    }

    // Method to add a new element to the list
    public Node add(int newValue) {
        return new Node(newValue, this);
    }
}
// Example usage in a main method
public class PersistentListExample {
    public static void main(String[] args) {
        Node head = new Node(1, null);
        head = head.add(2);
        head = head.add(3);

        // Iterating through the persistent list
        for (Node current = head; current != null; current = current.getNext()) {
            System.out.println(current.getValue());
        }
    }
}
```

In the example above, Node is a basic immutable element of a list containing an integer value and a reference to the next Node. The add method does not modify the existing list but rather returns a new list with the new element added to the front. This illustrates the concept of persistence as each call to add returns a new list with the additional element.

The creation of persistent maps and sets follows a similar pattern. These data structures leverage underlying mechanisms such as trees and hash arrays mapped tries (HAMT), which are specifically designed to optimize sharing and ensure immutability without significant performance compromises.

For instance, a persistent map can be implemented using a structure that allows for sub-linear time complexity operations, such as updates and lookups. This might involve techniques like path copying in trees, ensuring that only the necessary parts of the structure are duplicated and most of the data can be shared between versions.

```
// A simple implementation of a persistent map entry using a binary tree structure
public final class PersistentMap<K, V> {
    private final K key;
    private final V value;
    private final PersistentMap<K, V> left, right;

    public PersistentMap(K key, V value, PersistentMap<K, V> left, PersistentMap<K,
            V> right) {
        this.key = key;
        this.value = value;
        this.left = left;
        this.right = right;
    }

    public V get(K searchKey) {
        if (searchKey.equals(key)) {
            return value;
        } else if (searchKey.hashCode() < key.hashCode() && left != null) {
            return left.get(searchKey);
        } else if (searchKey.hashCode() > key.hashCode() && right != null) {
            return right.get(searchKey);
        } else {
            return null;
        }
    }

    public PersistentMap<K, V> put(K newKey, V newValue) {
        if (newKey.hashCode() < key.hashCode()) {
            return new PersistentMap<>(key, value, left == null ? new PersistentMap
                    <>(newKey, newValue, null, null) : left.put(newKey, newValue), right)
                    ;
        } else if (newKey.hashCode() > key.hashCode()) {
            return new PersistentMap<>(key, value, left, right == null ? new
                    PersistentMap<>(newKey, newValue, null, null) : right.put(newKey,
                    newValue));
        } else {
            return new PersistentMap<>(newKey, newValue, left, right);
        }
    }
}
```

This simple implementation uses a binary tree to manage the keys and values. The put method creates and returns a new map with the new key-value pair inserted, ensuring no modification of the original map takes place.

The use of persistent data structures is not without trade-offs. The additional overhead of creating new structures and the complexity of implementing structures that efficiently share data can result in increased memory and CPU utilization. However, these costs are often outweighed by the benefits of immutability, including easier reasoning about code, safe concurrent access without locks, and elimination of certain classes of bugs.

Studying persistent data structures equips developers with tools to write safer, more predictable code. Mastery of these concepts supports the creation of applications that gracefully handle and even benefit from immutability, ultimately leading to more robust and maintainable software systems.

6.7 Implementing Persistent Lists

In functional programming, persistent data structures are fundamental to ensure immutability and efficient data management. A persistent list is a type of data structure that preserves previous versions of itself when modified. This section focuses on the intricacies of implementing persistent lists in Java, leveraging the principles of immutability.

To begin with, we define a persistent list by creating a simple linked list structure. Below is the code to define an immutable node for our linked list:

```
public final class ListNode<T> {
    private final T value;
    private final ListNode<T> next;

    public ListNode(T value, ListNode<T> next) {
        this.value = value;
        this.next = next;
    }

    public T getValue() {
        return value;
    }

    public ListNode<T> getNext() {
        return next;
    }
}
```

In the ListNode class, both the value and next fields are final, ensuring that once a ListNode is created, its state cannot be altered. This immutability is crucial for achieving persistence.

Next, we define operations to manipulate the persistent list, such as adding elements. Consider the add method, which inserts a new element at the front of the list:

```
public final class PersistentList<T> {
    private final ListNode<T> head;
    private final int size;
```

```
    public PersistentList() {
        this.head = null;
        this.size = 0;
    }

    private PersistentList(ListNode<T> head, int size) {
        this.head = head;
        this.size = size;
    }

    public PersistentList<T> add(T value) {
        return new PersistentList<>(new ListNode<>(value, head), size + 1);
    }

    public T get(int index) {
        if (index < 0 || index >= size) {
            throw new IndexOutOfBoundsException();
        }
        ListNode<T> current = head;
        for (int i = 0; i < index; i++) {
            current = current.getNext();
        }
        return current.getValue();
    }

    public int size() {
        return size;
    }
}
```

The add method creates a new PersistentList by instantiating a new ListNode with the added value and linking it to the current head. This ensures that the original list remains unchanged.

A key aspect to note is the efficient sharing of structure between different versions of the list. For instance, appending an element does not require duplicating the entire list but rather, only creating new nodes that reflect the changes, leaving the old nodes intact. This provides significant memory efficiency.

Let us explore another fundamental operation: removing an element from the list. Below, we implement the remove function which removes the first occurrence of a specified value:

```
public PersistentList<T> remove(T value) {
    if (head == null) {
        return this;
    }

    if (head.getValue().equals(value)) {
        return new PersistentList<>(head.getNext(), size - 1);
    }

    ListNode<T> current = head;
    ListNode<T> previous = null;
    while (current != null && !current.getValue().equals(value)) {
        previous = current;
```

```
        current = current.getNext();
    }

    if (current == null) {
        return this; // Value not found
    }

    if (previous == null) {
        return new PersistentList<>(current.getNext(), size - 1);
    }

    previous.setNext(current.getNext());
    return new PersistentList<>(head, size - 1);
}
```

This remove method ensures immutability by constructing a new PersistentList each time an element is removed, without altering the original list. We use the previous node to traverse the list and update links efficiently.

Persistent data structures must provide mechanisms for iteration. An iterator can be implemented for PersistentList:

```
public Iterator<T> iterator() {
    return new Iterator<T>() {
        private ListNode<T> current = head;

        @Override
        public boolean hasNext() {
            return current != null;
        }

        @Override
        public T next() {
            if (!hasNext()) {
                throw new NoSuchElementException();
            }
            T value = current.getValue();
            current = current.getNext();
            return value;
        }
    };
}
```

The iterator implementation enables traversal through the list without modifying its structure, thus maintaining immutability.

For practical use, handling persistence in lists via these implementations balances efficiency and immutability. Using persistent lists, developers can ensure safer functional programming practices by preventing unintended side effects and preserving the history of data states for potential debugging and state recovery mechanisms.

6.8 Implementing Persistent Maps

In this section, we delve into the implementation of persistent maps in Java, which ensures that every modification returns a new map, leaving the original map unaltered. This concept leverages immutability to create efficient, thread-safe data structures suitable for functional programming. We will focus on the principles and techniques used, highlighting specific examples to foster comprehension.

Persistent maps, often referred to as functional maps, provide an immutable interface while allowing the underlying structure to share as much of its state as possible with previous versions. This sharing is crucial for efficiency, reducing the overhead associated with copying large data sets.

To implement a persistent map, one common approach is to use a trie (or prefix tree) structure, particularly a Hash Array Mapped Trie (HAMT). In contrast to traditional hash tables, where each entry is placed in a bucket indicated by hashing, a HAMT distributes the entries across an array of buckets and recursively applies the same mechanism to each bucket.

Let's explore a basic implementation of a persistent map using a HAMT. This involves understanding nodes in the trie and how insertions and lookups are managed.

```
public class PersistentMap<K, V> {

    private final TrieNode<K, V> root;

    public PersistentMap() {
        this.root = new EmptyNode<>();
    }

    private PersistentMap(TrieNode<K, V> root) {
        this.root = root;
    }

    public PersistentMap<K, V> put(K key, V value) {
        return new PersistentMap<>(root.put(key, value, key.hashCode(), 0));
    }

    public V get(K key) {
        return root.get(key, key.hashCode(), 0);
    }

    private interface TrieNode<K, V> {
        TrieNode<K, V> put(K key, V value, int hash, int depth);
        V get(K key, int hash, int depth);
    }

    private static class EmptyNode<K, V> implements TrieNode<K, V> {
```

```
        public TrieNode<K, V> put(K key, V value, int hash, int depth) {
            return new LeafNode<>(key, value);
        }
        public V get(K key, int hash, int depth) {
            return null;
        }
    }

    private static class LeafNode<K, V> implements TrieNode<K, V> {
        private final K key;
        private final V value;

        LeafNode(K key, V value) {
            this.key = key;
            this.value = value;
        }

        public TrieNode<K, V> put(K key, V value, int hash, int depth) {
            if (this.key.equals(key)) {
                return new LeafNode<>(key, value);
            } else {
                return new InnerNode<K, V>().put(this.key, this.value, this.key.
                    hashCode(), depth)
                                        .put(key, value, hash, depth);
            }
        }

        public V get(K key, int hash, int depth) {
            return this.key.equals(key) ? value : null;
        }
    }

    private static class InnerNode<K, V> implements TrieNode<K, V> {
        private static final int BUCKET_SIZE = 16;
        private final TrieNode<K, V>[] buckets;

        @SuppressWarnings("unchecked")
        InnerNode() {
            this.buckets = new TrieNode[BUCKET_SIZE];
        }

        public TrieNode<K, V> put(K key, V value, int hash, int depth) {
            int index = (hash >>> (depth * 4)) & (BUCKET_SIZE - 1);
            TrieNode<K, V> child = buckets[index];
            if (child == null) {
                child = new EmptyNode<>();
            }
            TrieNode<K, V> newChild = child.put(key, value, hash, depth + 1);
            if (newChild == child) return this;

            InnerNode<K, V> newNode = new InnerNode<>();
            System.arraycopy(this.buckets, 0, newNode.buckets, 0, BUCKET_SIZE);
            newNode.buckets[index] = newChild;
            return newNode;
        }

        public V get(K key, int hash, int depth) {
            int index = (hash >>> (depth * 4)) & (BUCKET_SIZE - 1);
            TrieNode<K, V> child = buckets[index];
            if (child == null) {
                return null;
            }
```

```
            return child.get(key, hash, depth + 1);
        }
    }
}
```

The PersistentMap class encapsulates the persistent map implementation, defining key operations such as put and get. The core of the trie structure is represented by the TrieNode interface and its various implementations: EmptyNode, LeafNode, and InnerNode.

To insert a key-value pair: 1. The put method computes the hash of the key and recursively navigates down the trie based on the hash's bits. 2. At each depth, it determines the appropriate bucket using bitwise operations. 3. When an empty node is encountered, it converts it into a leaf node. If a leaf node with a different key is found, it converts this into an inner node to handle hash collisions.

To retrieve a value: 1. The get method computes the hash and navigates through the trie similarly. 2. It inspects each node until it either finds the key or determines that the key is absent.

This implementation assures that each modification returns a new PersistentMap instance, leaving the original unchanged. Subparts of the path affected by the insertion are copied, ensuring minimal memory usage.

Given this, persistent maps can coexist without interference, making them inherently thread-safe. By leveraging this design, we retain both immutability and efficiency, fundamental principles in functional programming.

Next, we will address the performance considerations and optimizations for persistent data structures, ensuring their usability in real-world applications.

6.9 Implementing Persistent Sets

Implementing persistent sets in Java requires a keen understanding of how sets are traditionally structured in mutable environments and how these structures need to be transformed to uphold immutability.

A set is a collection of distinct elements, with no particular order. In mutable contexts, Java typically employs HashSet or TreeSet, the former providing average constant-time complexity for basic operations and the latter ensuring logarithmic time due to its sorted property. However, persistent sets necessitate a different approach.

To achieve immutability, one prominent method involves leveraging a persistent data structure known as a "Persistent Hash Array Mapped Trie" (HAMT). This ensures each 'modification' operation such as insertion or deletion does not alter the original set but rather returns a new set with the desired changes. This immutable behavior is realized through structural sharing, which allows the new set to reuse parts of the existing set's structure, thus optimizing memory usage and performance.

```
public class PSetNode<E> {
    final E value;
    final PSetNode<E> left;
    final PSetNode<E> right;

    public PSetNode(E value, PSetNode<E> left, PSetNode<E> right) {
        this.value = value;
        this.left = left;
        this.right = right;
    }

    public boolean contains(E element) {
        int cmp = element.compareTo(value);
        if (cmp < 0) return (left != null) && left.contains(element);
        else if (cmp > 0) return (right != null) && right.contains(element);
        else return true;
    }

    public PSetNode<E> add(E element) {
        int cmp = element.compareTo(value);
        if (cmp < 0) {
            return new PSetNode<>(value, left == null ? new PSetNode<>(element,
                    null, null) : left.add(element), right);
        } else if (cmp > 0) {
            return new PSetNode<>(value, left, right == null ? new PSetNode<>(
                    element, null, null) : right.add(element));
        } else {
            return this; // Element already in set
        }
    }
}
```

In this simplified example, PSetNode represents a node in a binary tree structure. Each PSetNode contains a value and references to left and right child nodes. The contains method checks if an element is present in the set by comparing the element recursively, while the add method creates a new node with structural sharing to maintain immutability.

For a complete persistent set implementation, a factory class handles operations and maintenance of the set structure:

```
import java.util.Iterator;
import java.util.NoSuchElementException;
```

```
public class PersistentSet<E extends Comparable<E>> implements Iterable<E> {
    private final PSetNode<E> root;

    public PersistentSet() {
        this.root = null;
    }

    private PersistentSet(PSetNode<E> root) {
        this.root = root;
    }

    public boolean contains(E element) {
        return root != null && root.contains(element);
    }

    public PersistentSet<E> add(E element) {
        if (root == null) {
            return new PersistentSet<>(new PSetNode<>(element, null, null));
        }
        return new PersistentSet<>(root.add(element));
    }

    @Override
    public Iterator<E> iterator() {
        return new Iterator<>() {
            // Stack based implementation for in-order traversal of binary tree
            private final Stack<PSetNode<E>> stack = new Stack<>();
            private PSetNode<E> current = root;

            @Override
            public boolean hasNext() {
                return current != null || !stack.isEmpty();
            }

            @Override
            public E next() {
                while (current != null) {
                    stack.push(current);
                    current = current.left;
                }
                if (stack.isEmpty()) throw new NoSuchElementException();
                PSetNode<E> node = stack.pop();
                E result = node.value;
                current = node.right;
                return result;
            }
        };
    }
}
```

PersistentSet class wraps around PSetNode to present a user-friendly interface while maintaining immutability. Each add operation generates a new instance of the set with the updated node structure, thus preserving the original set. Iteration is achieved through an in-order traversal using an internal stack-based iterator.

The implementation of persistent sets using HAMT or other structures like the Red-Black Trees, discussed in earlier sections, focuses on balancing immutability with performance. Structural sharing is the key to efficient memory usage, and operations are designed to maintain logarithmic time complexity.

A specific application of these principles ensures thread-safe operations inherent to functional programming paradigms without the need for explicit synchronization, enhancing performance in concurrent environments.

6.10 Performance Considerations with Immutability

Immutability offers significant advantages in terms of software reliability and simplicity. However, it is crucial to understand the performance implications when working with immutable objects and persistent data structures in Java. While immutability can reduce certain types of bugs, it may introduce performance bottlenecks if not managed correctly. This section delves into the performance considerations, including memory usage, computation overhead, garbage collection, and efficient implementation techniques.

Memory Usage. Immutability generally leads to increased memory usage because each modification to an immutable object typically results in the creation of a new object. For example, modifying a single element in an immutable list would require creating a whole new list. This can be particularly costly for large collections. To demonstrate this, consider the following code:

```
import java.util.ArrayList;
import java.util.Collections;
import java.util.List;

public class ImmutableListExample {
    public static void main(String[] args) {
        List<Integer> originalList = new ArrayList<>();
        Collections.addAll(originalList, 1, 2, 3, 4, 5);

        // Creating a new list with one element changed
        List<Integer> newList = new ArrayList<>(originalList);
        newList.set(2, 99);
    }
}
```

In the code above, a new ArrayList is instantiated to incorporate the change. For large lists, this would require significant memory because essentially the whole list is duplicated. Java ensures that immutable collections from libraries, such as Guava or Eclipse Collections, optimize memory usage by sharing structures where possible, but understanding the underlying implementation is crucial for managing performance.

Computation Overhead. Each creation of a new object requires not only memory but also computation time to initialize the new object. This overhead can be minimized using structural sharing, a common technique used in persistent data structures. Structural sharing ensures that unchanged parts of a data structure are shared between the old and new versions. For instance, elements of an immutable list that are not modified do not need to be copied.

```
import org.pcollections.ConsPStack;
import org.pcollections.PStack;

public class StructuralSharingExample {
    public static void main(String[] args) {
        PStack<Integer> originalStack = ConsPStack.empty();
        originalStack = originalStack.plus(1).plus(2).plus(3);

        // Changing the top element
        PStack<Integer> newStack = originalStack.plus(99);

        System.out.println("Original stack: " + originalStack);
        System.out.println("New stack: " + newStack);
    }
}
```

```
Original stack: [1, 2, 3]
New stack: [1, 2, 3, 99]
```

In this example, the new stack reuses the old stack and adds the new element only at the top, thus efficiently managing memory and computation time.

Garbage Collection. Immutability leads to frequent creation of new objects, which in turn increases the load on the garbage collector. While modern garbage collectors are highly optimized, excessive object creation and short-lived objects can still cause performance degradation. Monitoring and profiling the application can help identify and address such issues. Use of tools like Java Flight Recorder (JFR) and G1 Garbage Collector can be beneficial.

- **Java Flight Recorder (JFR)**: JFR is a performance monitoring tool that enables continuous monitoring and diagnostics of a running Java application with minimal overhead.
- **G1 Garbage Collector**: G1 is designed for applications with large heaps and offers predictable garbage collection pauses.

```
java -XX:+UnlockCommercialFeatures -XX:+FlightRecorder -jar YourApp.jar
```

Employing these tools can significantly help in analyzing the performance impact of immutability in the application.

Efficient Implementation Techniques. Adopting immutable data structures necessitates an efficient implementation to mitigate the performance costs. Here are a few techniques:

1. **Lazy Evaluation**: This technique delays the computation until it is absolutely necessary. This can be particularly useful in functional programming where constructing complex data transformations can be deferred to execution time.

2. **Memoization**: Storing the results of expensive function calls and reusing the cached result when the same inputs occur again can save computation time. This is particularly useful for recursive functions.

3. **Persistent data structures**: Libraries like PCollections provide efficient implementations of persistent data structures that utilize structural sharing to minimize duplication and memory overhead.

By integrating these techniques into the design and implementation of applications, developers can harness the benefits of immutability while mitigating potential performance issues. Practical understanding and profiling of applications allow better assessment and optimization, thus ensuring robust and efficient data management in functional programming contexts.

6.11 Common Patterns and Practices with Immutability

In functional programming, immutability is a fundamental concept that provides numerous advantages such as simplifying concurrent execution, reducing bugs related to state changes, and making it easier to reason about code behavior. Adopting a disciplined approach to immutability within Java entails adhering to certain patterns and practices that reinforce its principles.

A common pattern involves the use of factory methods to create immutable objects. Factory methods ensure that constructors remain private, thus preventing external modification. Here is an example illustrating how to create an immutable Person class using factory methods.

```
public final class Person {
    private final String name;
    private final int age;

    private Person(String name, int age) {
        this.name = name;
        this.age = age;
    }

    public static Person of(String name, int age) {
        return new Person(name, age);
    }

    public String getName() {
        return name;
    }

    public int getAge() {
        return age;
    }
}
```

By making the constructors private and providing a static factory method of(), we control object creation and ensure immutability. This pattern is especially useful for classes with complex initialization logic or multiple construction paths.

Another prevalent practice is the use of builder patterns for creating immutable objects, especially when such objects have many fields or optional parameters. The builder pattern encapsulates a construction process in a separate builder object, which accumulates the state and then constructs the immutable target object.

```
public final class ImmutableCar {
    private final String model;
    private final String color;
    private final int year;

    private ImmutableCar(Builder builder) {
        this.model = builder.model;
        this.color = builder.color;
        this.year = builder.year;
    }

    public static class Builder {
        private String model;
        private String color;
        private int year;

        public Builder withModel(String model) {
            this.model = model;
            return this;
        }

        public Builder withColor(String color) {
            this.color = color;
            return this;
```

```
        }

        public Builder withYear(int year) {
            this.year = year;
            return this;
        }

        public ImmutableCar build() {
            return new ImmutableCar(this);
        }
    }

    public String getModel() {
        return model;
    }

    public String getColor() {
        return color;
    }

    public int getYear() {
        return year;
    }
}
```

The builder pattern not only enhances readability and maintainability but also supports immutability by segregating the construction logic from the immutable object itself.

When dealing with collections, using immutable collections from libraries such as Guava or Java's own Collections.unmodifiableList() method is recommended. These immutable collections provide read-only access, thus preventing modifications after creation.

```
import com.google.common.collect.ImmutableList;

public class Course {
    private final ImmutableList<String> students;

    public Course(List<String> students) {
        this.students = ImmutableList.copyOf(students);
    }

    public ImmutableList<String> getStudents() {
        return students;
    }
}
```

In the above example, ImmutableList.copyOf() ensures that the list of students becomes immutable, preventing subsequent modifications.

Pattern matching is a functional programming feature that has seen some implementations and supports in Java through libraries like Vavr. Pattern matching facilitates the extraction of structure, values from immutable objects, and handling different types of data in a comprehensive manner.

```
import io.vavr.control.Option;

public class OptionPatternMatching {
    public static void main(String[] args) {
        Option<String> option = Option.of("hello");

        String result = option.map(value -> "Value: " + value)
                              .getOrElse("No value");
        System.out.println(result);
    }
}
```

In this case, Option.map() evidences immutability by returning a new Option instead of modifying the existing one.

Lastly, it is essential to embrace defensive copying when referencing objects containing mutable state. By making defensive copies of such objects, you ensure that external changes do not affect the internally maintained state.

```
import java.util.Date;

public final class Epoch {
    private final Date date;

    public Epoch(Date date) {
        this.date = new Date(date.getTime());
    }

    public Date getDate() {
        return new Date(this.date.getTime());
    }
}
```

Here, new Date(date.getTime()) ensures that the original date object remains unchanged, preserving immutability within the Epoch class.

Effective use of these patterns and practices solidifies an immutable design, fostering robust, predictable, and thread-safe applications. Integrating these methodologies into daily programming habits will instill best practices of immutability within Java development.

Chapter 7

Advanced Functional Techniques in Java

This chapter explores advanced functional programming techniques in Java. It covers currying, partial application, and memoization, along with function composition and pipelining. The chapter examines monads, functors, and applicative functors, providing a deeper insight into functional abstractions. Techniques to use Java Optional effectively, tail call optimization, advanced stream operations, custom collectors, and pattern matching are also discussed, equipping readers with sophisticated tools and strategies to implement complex functional solutions in Java.

7.1 Introduction to Advanced Techniques

Advanced functional programming techniques in Java build upon the foundations laid by basic functional concepts to introduce more powerful and expressive paradigms. Mastering these techniques enables developers to write cleaner, more modular, and highly reusable code. This section introduces several advanced concepts that will be elaborated upon throughout this chapter, focusing on their relevance and applicability in Java.

To achieve a comprehensive understanding, we will explore currying, partial application, memoization, function composition, pipelining, monads, functors, and applicative functors. Furthermore, we will delve into utilizing Optional effectively, implementing tail call optimization, advanced stream operations, creating custom collectors, and pattern matching and destructuring in Java.

The initial concepts of currying and partial application lay the groundwork for transforming functions into sets of smaller, more manageable functions. Currying is the process of converting a function that takes multiple arguments into a sequence of functions, each with a single argument. This technique is particularly useful in functional programming as it allows functions to be reused and composed more flexibly.

For example, consider a function that adds two numbers:

```
BiFunction<Integer, Integer, Integer> add = (a, b) -> a + b;
```

Currying this function in Java can be illustrated by using nested lambdas:

```
Function<Integer, Function<Integer, Integer>> curriedAdd = a -> b -> a + b;
```

Utilizing curriedAdd would look like:

```
Function<Integer, Integer> addFive = curriedAdd.apply(5);
int result = addFive.apply(3); // result is 8
```

Partial application is closely related, allowing a function to be called with fewer arguments than it expects, returning another function that takes the remaining arguments. This is highly beneficial in scenarios where certain parameters are fixed or context-dependent.

Memoization is another advanced technique that optimizes the performance of function calls by caching previously computed results. This approach can be particularly powerful in recursive functions or functions with expensive computations. Implementing memoization in Java typically involves utilizing a data structure, such as a Map, to store function output against its input.

Consider a simple memoization example for a factorial function:

```
Function<Integer, Integer> memoizedFactorial = memoize(n -> {
    if (n == 0) return 1;
    return n * factorial.apply(n - 1);
});
```

Memoization ensures that repetitive calls with the same input yield immediate results from the cache, significantly improving efficiency.

Function composition and pipelining enable the construction of intricate functions from simpler ones, following the principle of composing functions wherein the output of one function directly serves as the input to another. In Java, function composition can be implemented using the andThen and compose methods provided by the Function interface.

For instance, given functions f, g, and h:

```
Function<Integer, Integer> f = x -> x + 1;
Function<Integer, Integer> g = x -> x * 2;
Function<Integer, Integer> h = f.andThen(g);
```

Applying h to an input value produces a result by executing the composed functions sequentially.

Monads, functors, and applicative functors are advanced theoretical constructs that encapsulate behavior in functional programming, providing mechanisms to chain operations and manage side effects. While these abstractions are rooted in category theory, their practical applications in Java can be realized through constructs such as Optional, Stream, and custom implementations.

Effective usage of Optional is paramount in functional programming, ensuring null safety and representing potential absence of values without resorting to nulls. Tail call optimization, although not natively supported in the Java language, can be achieved via techniques like trampolining to prevent stack overflow errors in recursive functions.

Advanced stream operations and custom collectors in Java's Stream API facilitate complex data processing pipelines, while pattern matching and destructuring, albeit limited in current Java versions, can emulate functional pattern matching practices through creative use of features like the switch statement.

Through this chapter, we will develop a robust grasp of these advanced techniques, enhancing our functional programming prowess in Java and empowering us to solve intricate problems more effectively. Each concept will be dissected with ample examples and practical applications to ensure a thorough learning experience.

7.2 Currying and Partial Application

In the paradigm of functional programming, currying and partial application are indispensable techniques for transforming and simplifying functions. These concepts enable finer-grained control over function evaluation, manipulation of fixed arguments, and generation of new functions with pre-defined parameters.

Currying is the process of transforming a function that takes multiple arguments into a sequence of functions, each with a single argument. This allows the gradual application of arguments, facilitating more modular and reusable code. Consider the following example in Java:

```
import java.util.function.Function;

public class CurryingExample {
    public static void main(String[] args) {
        Function<Integer, Function<Integer, Integer>> curriedAdd = x -> y -> x + y;

        Function<Integer, Integer> addFive = curriedAdd.apply(5);
        int result = addFive.apply(10);

        System.out.println(result); // Output: 15
    }
}
```

In this snippet, curriedAdd is a curried function that takes an Integer x and returns another function that takes an Integer y. The result of applying x and then y is the sum of these two integers. By applying the first argument 5, we generate a new function, addFive, which incorporates this fixed argument. The subsequent application of 10 yields the final result 15.

Partial application, distinct yet related to currying, involves fixing some number of arguments to a function, producing a function with a reduced arity (number of arguments). This can be achieved seamlessly using Java's functional interfaces. Here is an illustration of partial application:

```
import java.util.function.BiFunction;
import java.util.function.Function;

public class PartialApplicationExample {
    public static void main(String[] args) {
        BiFunction<Integer, Integer, Integer> add = (a, b) -> a + b;

        Function<Integer, Integer> addThree = partialApply(add, 3);
        int result = addThree.apply(4);

        System.out.println(result); // Output: 7
    }

    public static <T, U, R> Function<U, R> partialApply(BiFunction<T, U, R>
            biFunction, T t) {
        return u -> biFunction.apply(t, u);
    }
}
```

In this case, addThree is a partially applied function derived from the BiFunction<Integer, Integer, Integer> add. By fixing the first argument of add to 3, the partialApply method returns a new function that requires only the second argument. Applying 4 to this new function produces the sum 7.

Currying allows a function with multiple arguments to be decomposed into a series of unary functions. The concept is closely related to partial application, where one or more arguments are fixed, resulting in a function with fewer arguments required. These techniques facilitate more flexible and reusable code by enabling higher-order functions and function composition. They are particularly useful in scenarios where functions must be manipulated extensively or where functions need to be generated dynamically with varying arguments.

7.3 Memoization

Memoization is an optimization technique used primarily to speed up computer programs by storing the results of expensive function calls and reusing the cached result when the same inputs occur again. This technique can help avoid redundant computations, making code more efficient and performant.

Memoization, in essence, is a specific form of caching. By storing the outcomes of function calls, it transforms a function that operates in an exponential time complexity into one that operates in linear time complexity for many cases. Memoization is particularly useful in the context of functional programming because it relies on the premise that functions are pure, i.e., their output depends only on their input and they produce no side effects.

In Java, memoization can be implemented using various techniques. For immutable and idempotent functions, it is particularly straightforward to apply memoization. The general approach involves the use of a map or dictionary to store previously computed function results.

Here's how memoization can be implemented in Java for a recursive function:

```
import java.util.HashMap;
import java.util.Map;

public class MemoizationExample {

    private Map<Integer, Integer> cache = new HashMap<>();

    public int fibonacci(int n) {
        if (n <= 1) {
            return n;
        }
```

```
        if (cache.containsKey(n)) {
            return cache.get(n);
        }

        int result = fibonacci(n - 1) + fibonacci(n - 2);
        cache.put(n, result);
        return result;
    }

    public static void main(String[] args) {
        MemoizationExample example = new MemoizationExample();
        System.out.println("Fibonacci of 10: " + example.fibonacci(10));
    }
}
```

In this example, fibonacci is a classical example of a function where the same values are computed multiple times without memoization, resulting in exponential time complexity. By using a HashMap to cache the computed values, each unique function call is stored and reused, improving the efficiency to linear time complexity, $\mathcal{O}(n)$.

Here's the output of the above program when executed:

```
Fibonacci of 10: 55
```

This output shows the computed value of the 10th Fibonacci number using the memoized function.

In a functional programming paradigm, you can further enhance your memoization logic by using functional interfaces and higher-order functions. Java 8's Function interface and method references provide more elegant and functional solutions. Let's look at a more functional approach:

```
import java.util.HashMap;
import java.util.Map;
import java.util.function.Function;

public class FunctionalMemoization {

    private static <T, R> Function<T, R> memoize(Function<T, R> function) {
        Map<T, R> cache = new HashMap<>();
        return input -> cache.computeIfAbsent(input, function);
    }

    private static Function<Integer, Integer> fibonacci = FunctionalMemoization.
        memoize(n -> {
        if (n <= 1) {
            return n;
        }
        return FunctionalMemoization.fibonacci.apply(n - 1) + FunctionalMemoization.
            fibonacci.apply(n - 2);
    });

    public static void main(String[] args) {
        System.out.println("Fibonacci of 10: " + fibonacci.apply(10));
    }
```

```
}
```

In this approach, the memoize method is a higher-order function that takes a Function<T, R> and returns a memoized version of it. This hides the caching mechanism behind a functional interface, making the code more declarative and developer-friendly. The fibonacci function uses this memoized function to compute values.

Here's the output of the functional memoization program:

```
Fibonacci of 10: 55
```

Memoization can also be applied to more complex problems, such as dynamic programming tasks, where intermediate results are stored and reused. A common example is the computation of combination values in Pascal's triangle, which can be optimized using memoization:

```
import java.util.HashMap;
import java.util.Map;

public class CombinationMemoization {
    private Map<String, Integer> cache = new HashMap<>();

    public int combination(int n, int k) {
        if (k == 0 || k == n) {
            return 1;
        }
        String key = n + "," + k;
        if (cache.containsKey(key)) {
            return cache.get(key);
        }

        int result = combination(n - 1, k - 1) + combination(n - 1, k);
        cache.put(key, result);
        return result;
    }

    public static void main(String[] args) {
        CombinationMemoization combMemo = new CombinationMemoization();
        System.out.println("Combination C(5, 2): " + combMemo.combination(5, 2));
    }
}
```

Executing this program would yield:

```
Combination C(5, 2): 10
```

In this context, memoization significantly enhances performance by avoiding redundant calculations of combinations. Each unique combination $C(n, k)$ is stored in the cache map, ensuring that once computed, it can be reused efficiently.

By integrating memoization into your computational tasks, you can substantially reduce time complexity, leveraging stored results for repeated function calls rather than resorting to expensive recomputation. This technique, combined with Java's functional capabilities, facilitates the implementation of performant and readable functional code.

7.4 Function Composition and Pipelining

Function composition and pipelining are fundamental techniques in functional programming that facilitate the construction of complex operations from simpler functions. These techniques enhance the modularity and readability of code by allowing developers to build sophisticated functionalities through the combination of smaller, well-defined functions.

Function composition refers to the process of combining two or more functions to produce a new function. In mathematical terms, if there are two functions f and g, their composition $f \circ g$ is defined such that for any input x, $(f \circ g)(x) = f(g(x))$. In Java, function composition can be achieved using the andThen and compose methods provided by the Function interface.

Consider the following example, where two functions are composed using andThen and compose:

```
import java.util.function.Function;

public class FunctionCompositionExample {
    public static void main(String[] args) {
        Function<Integer, Integer> multiplyByTwo = x -> x * 2;
        Function<Integer, Integer> addThree = x -> x + 3;

        // Compose functions using andThen
        Function<Integer, Integer> multiplyThenAdd = multiplyByTwo.andThen(
                addThree);
        System.out.println(multiplyThenAdd.apply(5)); // Output: 13

        // Compose functions using compose
        Function<Integer, Integer> addThenMultiply = multiplyByTwo.compose(
                addThree);
        System.out.println(addThenMultiply.apply(5)); // Output: 16
    }
}
```

In the example above, multiplyByTwo and addThree are two functions that are composed in different orders. When using the andThen method, the addThree function is applied after multiplyByTwo, whereas using the compose method applies addThree first, followed by multiplyByTwo. The results of executing the composed functions demonstrate the importance of the order of composition.

Function pipelining, on the other hand, involves passing the output of one function as the input to the next function in a sequence of operations. Pipelining is inherently similar to function composition but focuses more on the sequential nature of function execution. Consider the following example that demonstrates a pipeline of operations:

```
import java.util.function.Function;

public class FunctionPipeliningExample {
    public static void main(String[] args) {
        // Step 1: Define the initial function
        Function<Integer, Integer> multiplyByTwo = x -> x * 2;

        // Step 2: Chain additional functions using andThen
        Function<Integer, Integer> pipeline = multiplyByTwo
            .andThen(x -> x + 3)
            .andThen(x -> x - 1);

        System.out.println(pipeline.apply(5)); // Output: 12
    }
}
```

In this pipeline, the initial value is first multiplied by two, then three is added to the result, and finally, one is subtracted. This approach helps in creating a clear, maintainable chain of operations.

A special consideration in function composition and pipelining is the handling of potential exceptions. Java's Function interface does not allow checked exceptions, which means exceptions need to be handled within the lambda expressions or functions being composed. Here's an example demonstrating exception handling within a composed function:

```
import java.util.function.Function;

public class FunctionCompositionWithExceptionHandling {
    public static void main(String[] args) {
        Function<Integer, Integer> safeDivideByTwo = x -> {
            if (x == 0) {
                throw new ArithmeticException("Division by zero");
            }
            return x / 2;
        };

        Function<Integer, Integer> addThree = x -> x + 3;

        // Compose functions with exception handling
        Function<Integer, Integer> safePipeline = safeDivideByTwo.andThen(addThree
            );

        try {
            System.out.println(safePipeline.apply(10)); // Output: 8
            System.out.println(safePipeline.apply(0)); // Throws ArithmeticException
        } catch (ArithmeticException e) {
```

```
            System.out.println("Exception occurred: " + e.getMessage());
        }
    }
}
```

In this example, the safeDivideByTwo function checks for division by zero and throws an ArithmeticException if the input is zero. The exception is then caught and handled in the main method.

Function composition and pipelining in Java are powerful techniques that improve code modularity and clarity. By leveraging the Function interface and its compositional methods, developers can construct complex functionalities in a structured and maintainable manner.

7.5 Monads in Java

Monads are foundational constructs in functional programming, providing a way to handle side effects, encapsulate computations, and structure functional applications in a clean, modular way. Understanding monads is crucial for Java developers who want to harness the full power of functional programming in the language.

A monad can be thought of as a type that represents a computation, context, or effect. A monad provides two primary operations:

- unit (or return): This wraps a value into a monad.
- flatMap (or bind): This chains operations on the monadic value, allowing for the sequential processing of computations.

In Java, where immutability and higher-order functions are not first-class citizens, implementing monads requires a careful and idiomatic approach. Let's dive into an implementation using the Optional type, which is a monadic type in Java.

```
import java.util.Optional;

public class OptionalMonad {

    public static <T> Optional<T> unit(T value) {
        return Optional.ofNullable(value);
    }

    public static <T, R> Optional<R> flatMap(Optional<T> optional,
                                            Function<T, Optional<R>> mapper) {
        return optional.flatMap(mapper);
    }
```

```
    public static void main(String[] args) {
        Optional<Integer> optional = unit(5);

        Optional<Integer> result = flatMap(optional,
                                    x -> unit(x * 2));

        result.ifPresent(System.out::println); // Outputs: 10
    }
}
```

The unit method wraps a value into an Optional, while the flatMap method chains computations on the Optional value.

What Makes a Class Monadic?

For a class to be considered a monad, it must satisfy three laws:

- **Left identity**: Applying unit to a value v and then flatMap-ing over it with function f is the same as applying f to v.
  unit(v).flatMap(f) f(v)
- **Right identity**: Applying flatMap with unit over a monadic value m results in the original monadic value.
  m.flatMap(unit) m
- **Associativity**: Chaining flatMap operations should produce the same result regardless of grouping parentheses.
  m.flatMap(f).flatMap(g) m.flatMap(x -> f(x).flatMap(g))

A Practical Monad Example: The Try Monad

The Optional monad excels at handling nullability, but it doesn't handle exceptions. We'll implement a Try monad, which encapsulates computations that may throw exceptions.

The Try monad can have two states:

- Success: Contains a successfully computed value.
- Failure: Contains an exception that occurred during computation.

import java.util.function.Function; import java.util.function.Supplier;

public abstract class Try<T>

public static <T> Try<T> of(Supplier<T> supplier) try return new Success<>(supplier.get()); catch (Exception e) return new Failure<>(e);

public abstract <R> Try<R> flatMap(Function<T, Try<R» mapper);

public abstract T getOrElse(T other);

public static final class Success<T> extends Try<T> private final T value;

public Success(T value) this.value = value;

@Override public <R> Try<R> flatMap(Function<T, Try<R» mapper) try return mapper.apply(value); catch (Exception e) return new Failure<>(e);

@Override public T getOrElse(T other) return value;

public static final class Failure<T> extends Try<T> private final Exception exception;

public Failure(Exception exception) this.exception = exception;

@Override public <R> Try<R> flatMap(Function<T, Try<R» mapper) return new Failure<>(exception);

@Override public T getOrElse(T other) return other;

The Try class encapsulates a computation that may fail. The of method attempts to execute a Supplier and returns either a Success with the result or a Failure with the exception. The flatMap method allows sequential chaining of Try computations.

To use the Try monad:

public class TryExample

public static void main(String[] args) Try<Integer> tryDivide = Try.of(() -> divide(10, 2));

Try<Integer> result = tryDivide.flatMap(x -> Try.of(() -> x * 2));

System.out.println(result.getOrElse(0)); // Outputs: 10

public static int divide(int a, int b) return a / b;

In this example, Try captures any exceptions thrown during division and allows chaining operations while handling errors gracefully.

Conclusion

Understanding and implementing monads in Java provides a powerful toolset for managing side effects, structuring complex computations, and enhancing code readability and maintainability. The Optional and Try monads demonstrate how these concepts can be applied effectively within Java's type system.

7.6 Functor and Applicative Functors

Functional programming introduces various abstractions to manage effects, transformations, and computations. Functors and Applicative Functors are two such abstractions that provide powerful ways to handle operations in a functional paradigm seamlessly. These concepts are pivotal when leveraging Java's functional programming capabilities to create more expressive and flexible code.

The Functor is an abstraction that allows applying a function to values wrapped in a context. In Java, this context can be represented by various constructs such as collections or Optional. Formally, a Functor is any type that implements the Functor interface, which requires a single method, map.

Consider the following Functor interface:

```
public interface Functor<F, T> {
    <R> Functor<F, R> map(Function<T, R> f);
}
```

Here, F represents the context type, and T represents the type of the value contained within the context. The map method transforms a Functor<F, T> to a Functor<F, R> using the function f. This encapsulates the idea of applying f to the values inside the context without leaving the context.

Let's examine how Functor can be implemented for the Optional class:

```
public class OptionalFunctor<T> implements Functor<Optional<?>, T> {
    private final Optional<T> optional;

    public OptionalFunctor(Optional<T> optional) {
        this.optional = optional;
    }

    @Override
    public <R> Functor<Optional<?>, R> map(Function<T, R> f) {
        return new OptionalFunctor<>(optional.map(f));
    }
}
```

When using the above OptionalFunctor, we can apply functions to an Optional value easily:

```
OptionalFunctor<Integer> optionalInt = new OptionalFunctor<>(Optional.of(5));
OptionalFunctor<String> optionalStr = optionalInt.map(Object::toString);
```

On the output side:

optionalStr: OptionalFunctor{optional=Optional[5]}

The map method ensures that the transformation of the contained value happens within the context of Optional.

Moving to Applicative Functors, they extend the capabilities of Functors by allowing functions that themselves are within a context to be applied to values in another context. This is achieved through the ap (apply) method.

Consider the following Applicative interface:

```
public interface Applicative<F, T> extends Functor<F, T> {
    <R> Applicative<F, R> ap(Applicative<F, Function<T, R>> f);
    <R> Applicative<F, R> pure(R value);
}
```

The ap method applies a function wrapped in one context to a value wrapped in another context. The pure method lifts a value into the applicative context.

Let's implement Applicative for Optional:

```
public class OptionalApplicative<T> implements Applicative<Optional<?>, T> {
    private final Optional<T> optional;

    public OptionalApplicative(Optional<T> optional) {
        this.optional = optional;
    }

    @Override
    public <R> Applicative<Optional<?>, R> map(Function<T, R> f) {
        return new OptionalApplicative<>(optional.map(f));
    }

    @Override
    public <R> Applicative<Optional<?>, R> ap(Applicative<Optional<?>,
        Function<T, R>> f) {
        if (optional.isPresent() && ((OptionalApplicative<Function<T, R>>) f).
            optional.isPresent()) {
            Function<T, R> func = ((OptionalApplicative<Function<T, R>>) f).
                optional.get();
            return new OptionalApplicative<>(optional.map(func));
        }
        return new OptionalApplicative<>(Optional.empty());
    }

    @Override
    public <R> Applicative<Optional<?>, R> pure(R value) {
        return new OptionalApplicative<>(Optional.of(value));
    }
}
```

Usage of the OptionalApplicative is as follows:

```
OptionalApplicative<Integer> optionalInt = new OptionalApplicative<>(Optional.of
    (5));
```

```
OptionalApplicative<Function<Integer, String>> func = new OptionalApplicative<>(
    Optional.of(Object::toString));
OptionalApplicative<String> optionalStr = optionalInt.ap(func);
```

On the output side:

```
optionalStr: OptionalApplicative{optional=Optional[5]}
```

The ap method facilitates applying functions inside contexts to values in similar contexts, significantly enhancing the composability and flexibility in functional programming. The pure method ensures that any value can be brought into the applicative context.

The utilization of Functors and Applicative Functors offers remarkable abstraction for working with contextual operations. They provide a foundation to build more complex functional constructs, enabling developers to handle operations and transformations with greater precision and consistency.

7.7 Using Java Optional Effectively

Java's Optional class, introduced in Java 8, is a powerful tool for reducing null references and potential NullPointerExceptions. The Optional class provides a container that may or may not contain a non-null value, thus providing a more expressive way to deal with absent values. This section will provide a detailed examination of the effective use of Optional in your Java programs, focusing on best practices and idiomatic usage.

To begin, let's look at the creation of an Optional instance. The Optional class provides several methods to create an instance:

```
Optional<String> nonEmptyOptional = Optional.of("Hello, World!");
Optional<String> emptyOptional = Optional.empty();
Optional<String> nullableOptional = Optional.ofNullable(null);
```

In the first case, the Optional.of() method is used to create an Optional with a non-null value, and it will throw a NullPointerException if a null reference is passed. The second case demonstrates the Optional.empty() method, which returns an empty Optional. The third case, Optional.ofNullable(), allows for the creation of an Optional that can hold a null value without throwing an exception.

The primary use for Optional is to signal the potential absence of a value in a more structured manner than a null reference. This is particularly useful in APIs and method return types. Consider the following example:

```
public Optional<User> findUserById(String id) {
    User user = database.findById(id);
    return Optional.ofNullable(user);
}
```

Here, findUserById returns an Optional<User> instead of returning a potentially null User object. This signaling allows the caller to handle the absent case explicitly:

```
Optional<User> userOptional = userService.findUserById("12345");
userOptional.ifPresent(user -> System.out.println("User found: " + user.getName()));
```

The ifPresent method takes a Consumer and executes it if a value is present, providing an elegant way to handle the present case without explicit null checks. If the value is absent, the consumer is simply not executed.

For scenarios where an action should be performed regardless of whether a value is present, Optional provides the ifPresentOrElse method. This requires a Consumer for the present case and a Runnable for the absent case:

```
userOptional.ifPresentOrElse(
    user -> System.out.println("User found: " + user.getName()),
    () -> System.out.println("User not found.")
);
```

Handling default values with Optional can be achieved through the orElse and orElseGet methods. The orElse method returns the specified default value if the Optional is empty:

```
User user = userOptional.orElse(new User("default", "default@example.com"));
```

The orElseGet method is similar but takes a Supplier whose result is used only if the Optional is empty, which can be more efficient if the default value is expensive to create:

```
User user = userOptional.orElseGet(() -> createDefaultUser());
```

In cases where an absent value should lead to an exception, Optional provides the orElseThrow method. This method can be used to throw a custom exception if the value is not present:

```
User user = userOptional.orElseThrow(() -> new UserNotFoundException("User not
    found"));
```

Transforming the contained value of an Optional, if present, can be achieved using the map and flatMap methods. The map method applies a function to the value if present and returns a new Optional containing the transformed value:

```
Optional<String> userNameOptional = userOptional.map(User::getName);
```

The flatMap method is used when the transformation function itself returns an Optional, allowing for the chaining of Optional operations. It avoids nesting Optionals:

```
Optional<String> emailOptional = userOptional.flatMap(User::getEmailOptional);
```

Another powerful method is filter, which allows the retention of values that match a given predicate. This is useful for post-creation validation:

```
Optional<User> adultUserOptional = userOptional.filter(user -> user.getAge() >= 18)
    ;
```

When working with collections, the Optional class can be particularly useful. For instance, when attempting to find an element in a stream, findFirst and findAny return Optional instances:

```
Optional<User> userOptional = users.stream()
                                   .filter(user -> user.getId().equals("12345"))
                                   .findFirst();
```

To sum up, effectively using Optional involves understanding its methods and idiomatic use to avoid NullPointerExceptions and to express the intent of the possibility of absence in a cleaner, more manageable way. This approach enhances the readability and robustness of your code by employing Optional as a method return type and within collections, making code more explicit and reducing the potential for errors.

7.8 Tail Call Optimization

Tail Call Optimization (TCO) in functional programming languages is a crucial concept for optimizing recursive functions. When a function call is the last operation before the function returns a value, it is known as a "tail call." Optimization of tail calls allows recursive functions to execute in constant stack space, significantly improving performance and preventing stack overflow errors, which is particularly beneficial for deep or infinite recursion.

In Java, TCO is not natively supported due to its underlying stack frame management. However, developers can implement TCO manually by utilizing iterative approaches or coding patterns that simulate TCO. This section will examine how to convert typical recursive algorithms into their tail-recursive forms and demonstrate methods to manually achieve TCO in Java.

To comprehend the transition from a standard recursive function to a tail-recursive one, consider the following non-tail-recursive factorial function:

```
public static int factorial(int n) {
    if (n == 1) {
        return 1;
    } else {
        return n * factorial(n - 1);
    }
}
```

In this example, the multiplication operation occurs after the recursive call to factorial, preventing the function from being tail-recursive. For tail recursion, the operation must be part of the recursive call itself. Here's a tail-recursive version of the factorial function:

```
public static int tailRecursiveFactorial(int n, int accumulator) {
    if (n == 1) {
        return accumulator;
    } else {
        return tailRecursiveFactorial(n - 1, n * accumulator);
    }
}
```

In the tail-recursive version, tailRecursiveFactorial, the recursive call is in tail position. The intermediate result is passed along an additional parameter, accumulator. This technique transforms the function into a tail-recursive one.

To invoke this tail-recursive function, an initial call must supply the accumulator's initial value:

```
public static int factorial(int n) {
    return tailRecursiveFactorial(n, 1);
}
```

While Java does not directly optimize tail-recursive calls, converting them to iterative loops achieves a similar effect. Consider rewriting the tail-recursive factorial using a loop:

```
public static int iterativeFactorial(int n) {
    int accumulator = 1;
    while (n > 1) {
        accumulator *= n;
        n--;
```

```
    }
    return accumulator;
}
```

Instead of relying on the call stack for recursive calls, the iterativeFactorial implementation uses an iterative approach, preserving constant stack space usage.

Another application of TCO is in computing the Fibonacci sequence. The straightforward recursive approach has exponential time complexity and potential stack overflow issues:

```
public static int fibonacci(int n) {
    if (n == 0) return 0;
    if (n == 1) return 1;
    return fibonacci(n - 1) + fibonacci(n - 2);
}
```

By refactoring with TCO, we can improve the efficiency:

```
public static int tailRecursiveFibonacci(int n, int a, int b) {
    if (n == 0) return a;
    if (n == 1) return b;
    return tailRecursiveFibonacci(n - 1, b, a + b);
}

public static int fibonacci(int n) {
    return tailRecursiveFibonacci(n, 0, 1);
}
```

Here, tailRecursiveFibonacci converts the computation into a tail-recursive process, vastly improving the performance and eliminating the risk of stack overflow. An equivalent iterative version follows:

```
public static int iterativeFibonacci(int n) {
    int a = 0, b = 1;
    for (int i = 0; i < n; i++) {
        int temp = a;
        a = b;
        b = temp + b;
    }
    return a;
}
```

Implementing TCO manually in Java requires developers to restructure their recursive algorithms using accumulator variables and iterative constructs. This restructuring ensures that tail-recursive functions execute efficiently, with constant stack space usage, akin to a loop structure's behavior. While Java's lack of native TCO support presents challenges, with appropriate techniques and coding patterns, the benefits of recursion can be harnessed without sacrificing performance and reliability.

7.9 Advanced Stream Operations

Streams in Java provide powerful tools for processing sequences of elements. This section delves into advanced operations that elevate the utility of streams, presenting techniques such as custom collectors, flatMapping, and parallel stream operations. Understanding these advanced techniques will enhance your ability to write more efficient and expressive functional code in Java.

Custom Collectors: Custom collectors enable the aggregation of stream elements in ways not supported by the predefined collectors. To define a custom collector, implement the Collector interface, which consists of four key methods: supplier(), accumulator(), combiner(), and finisher(). These methods provide the building blocks to collect elements from a stream into a custom data structure or apply sophisticated transformation processes.

```
import java.util.stream.Collector;
import java.util.stream.Collectors;
import java.util.Set;
import java.util.HashSet;
import java.util.stream.Stream;

public class CustomCollectors {
  public static <T> Collector<T, Set<T>, Set<T>> toCustomSet() {
    return Collector.of(
      HashSet::new,
      Set::add,
      (left, right) -> { left.addAll(right); return left; }
    );
  }

  public static void main(String[] args) {
    Set<String> result = Stream.of("a", "b", "c", "a").collect(toCustomSet());
    System.out.println(result); // Output: [a, b, c]
  }
}
```

In the example above, the custom collector, toCustomSet(), aggregates elements into a HashSet, ensuring unique elements. This custom collector demonstrates flexibility in defining tailor-made collection strategies.

FlatMapping: flatMap() is an essential transformation operation that flattens nested structures, mapping each element to a stream and then flattening these into a single stream. This operation is vital when dealing with nested collections.

```
import java.util.Arrays;
import java.util.List;
import java.util.stream.Collectors;
```

```
public class FlatMapExample {
  public static void main(String[] args) {
    List<List<String>> nestedList = Arrays.asList(
      Arrays.asList("a", "b"),
      Arrays.asList("c", "d")
    );

    List<String> flatList = nestedList.stream()
      .flatMap(List::stream)
      .collect(Collectors.toList());
    System.out.println(flatList); // Output: [a, b, c, d]
  }
}
```

In this example, flatMap() is utilized to transform and flatten a list of lists into a single list. This technique is indispensable in scenarios such as processing hierarchical data structures or transforming streams within streams.

Parallel Streams: Parallel streams allow stream operations to be executed concurrently, leveraging multicore processors to improve performance for large datasets. Using parallel streams is straightforward, but it requires an understanding of potential pitfalls such as thread-safety and order of operations.

```
import java.util.stream.IntStream;

public class ParallelStreamExample {
  public static void main(String[] args) {
    int sum = IntStream.range(1, 1000000)
      .parallel()
      .filter(x -> x % 2 == 0)
      .sum();
    System.out.println(sum); // Output: Sum of all even numbers from 1 to 999999
  }
}
```

The use of .parallel() enables the stream to process its elements concurrently. This example sums all even numbers between 1 and 999999, illustrating how parallel streams can improve performance. However, developers must ensure that operations performed within parallel streams are stateless and associative to avoid unexpected results.

Reduction Operations: Reduction operations, such as reduce() and collect(), are pivotal in merging stream elements. While collect() is more flexible and often used for mutable reductions like accumulating elements into a collection, reduce() performs immutable reductions.

```
import java.util.Optional;
import java.util.stream.Stream;
```

```
public class ReduceExample {
  public static void main(String[] args) {
    Optional<Integer> sum = Stream.of(1, 2, 3, 4)
      .reduce((a, b) -> a + b);
    sum.ifPresent(System.out::println); // Output: 10
  }
}
```

This example demonstrates a reduction operation that calculates the sum of stream elements. The reduce() method applies a binary operator to merge the elements, providing a straightforward approach to aggregate results.

Advanced stream operations, as presented, empower developers to write succinct, expressive, and high-performance functional code. Leveraging custom collectors, flatMapping, parallel streams, and reduction operations offers comprehensive tools to handle complex data processing tasks proficiently.

7.10 Custom Collectors in Streams

In functional programming with Java, stream processing is a powerful tool that allows developers to write succinct, readable, and efficient data transformations. While Java provides a set of pre-defined collectors in the java.util.stream.Collectors class, there are scenarios where custom collectors are necessary to achieve specific processing goals. This section delves into the creation and usage of custom collectors within Java Streams.

Defining a Custom Collector

A collector in Java is an implementation of the Collector interface, encapsulating the strategies for accumulating elements into a target structure. The Collector interface has the following type signature:

```
public interface Collector<T, A, R> {
    Supplier<A> supplier();
    BiConsumer<A, T> accumulator();
    BinaryOperator<A> combiner();
    Function<A, R> finisher();
    Set<Characteristics> characteristics();
}
```

Here, T represents the type of elements to be collected, A represents the type of the accumulator for intermediate results, and R represents the type of the final result.

Example: Creating a Custom Collector

Consider the task of collecting elements from a stream into a custom data structure, such as a TreeMap which sorts elements by keys. The following example demonstrates how to implement such a collector.

```
import java.util.TreeMap;
import java.util.Map;
import java.util.stream.Collector;
import java.util.stream.Collectors;

public class CustomCollectors {

    public static <T, K, U> Collector<T, ?, Map<K, U>> toTreeMap(
            Function<? super T, ? extends K> keyMapper,
            Function<? super T, ? extends U> valueMapper) {

        return Collector.of(
            TreeMap::new, // supplier
            (map, element) -> map.put(keyMapper.apply(element), valueMapper.apply(
                element)), // accumulator
            (map1, map2) -> { map1.putAll(map2); return map1; }, // combiner
            Collector.Characteristics.IDENTITY_FINISH // characteristics
        );
    }
}
```

Here, toTreeMap is a static method that returns a custom collector which can be used to accumulate stream elements into a TreeMap. Below is an example of how to use the toTreeMap collector:

```
import java.util.List;
import java.util.Map;
import java.util.TreeMap;
import java.util.stream.Collectors;

public class Main {
    public static void main(String[] args) {
        List<String> names = List.of("Charlie", "Alice", "Bob", "David");

        Map<String, Integer> nameLengthMap = names.stream()
            .collect(CustomCollectors.toTreeMap(
                name -> name,
                name -> name.length()
            ));

        System.out.println(nameLengthMap);
    }
}
```

This code produces the following output:

```
{Alice=5, Bob=3, Charlie=7, David=5}
```

Characteristics of Collectors

The characteristics of a collector, represented by the Collector.Characteristics enumeration, influence how the collector behaves in parallel stream operations. Some of the critical characteristics are:

- CONCURRENT: Indicates that the accumulator function can be called concurrently.
- UNORDERED: Indicates that the collection operation does not commit to preserving the encounter order of the stream elements.
- IDENTITY_FINISH: Indicates that the finisher function is the identity function and can be skipped.

In our example, we used Collector.Characteristics.IDENTITY_FINISH because the finisher function is an identity function, meaning the accumulator directly represents the final result.

More Complex Custom Collectors

For more complex scenarios, custom collectors may require non-trivial state management and combination logic. Consider the following example where we create a collector to group elements by their string lengths and collect the results in a TreeMap.

```
public static <T> Collector<T, ?, Map<Integer, List<T>>> groupingByLength() {
    return Collector.of(
        TreeMap<Integer, List<T>>::new, // supplier
        (map, element) -> {
            int length = element.length();
            map.computeIfAbsent(length, k -> new ArrayList<>()).add(element);
        }, // accumulator
        (map1, map2) -> {
            map2.forEach((key, value) -> {
                map1.merge(key, value, (v1, v2) -> { v1.addAll(v2); return v1; });
            });
            return map1;
        }, // combiner
        Collector.Characteristics.IDENTITY_FINISH // characteristics
    );
}
```

In this example, we use computeIfAbsent and merge methods from Map to handle possible null values and merge lists efficiently. This ensures that the collector operates correctly both in sequential and parallel stream contexts.

```
import java.util.List;
import java.util.Map;
import java.util.TreeMap;
import java.util.stream.Collectors;

public class Main {
    public static void main(String[] args) {
        List<String> names = List.of("Charlie", "Alice", "Bob", "David", "Zoey");

        Map<Integer, List<String>> groupedByLength = names.stream()
            .collect(CustomCollectors.groupingByLength());

        System.out.println(groupedByLength);
    }
}
```

This produces:

```
{3=[Bob], 4=[Zoey], 5=[Alice, David], 7=[Charlie]}
```

Understanding how to construct custom collectors opens up vast possibilities for managing complex data transformations with robustness and efficiency.

7.11 Pattern Matching and Destructuring

Pattern matching and destructuring are powerful techniques in functional programming that enable concise and expressive code. Although Java does not natively support pattern matching in the same way as languages like Haskell or Scala, upcoming versions of Java and certain libraries provide tools that can approximate these techniques. This section explores how to implement pattern matching and destructuring in Java, leveraging current language features and external libraries.

Consider the need for a construct that can inspect and decompose complex data structures based on their shapes. Pattern matching gives us this ability by allowing checks against a specific structure and extracting the relevant parts of the data. Destructuring works hand-in-hand with pattern matching by effectively unpacking data structures into individual elements.

Pattern Matching with Instanceof: Java 16 introduced pattern matching for instanceof which streamlines type checking and casting. Consider the following example where we match a type and immediately extract the variable:

```
public void processShape(Object shape) {
```

```
    if (shape instanceof Circle c) {
        // handle Circle case
        System.out.println("Circle with radius: " + c.getRadius());
    } else if (shape instanceof Rectangle r) {
        // handle Rectangle case
        System.out.println("Rectangle with width: " + r.getWidth()
                           + " and height: " + r.getHeight());
    } else {
        System.out.println("Unknown shape");
    }
}
```

In this example, we avoid the need for redundant casting after the instanceof check. The variable is immediately available within the appropriate scope.

Destructuring Tuples: Java doesn't have built-in syntax for tuples or destructuring, but we can simulate this behavior for specific cases. Libraries like javatuples provide tuple classes, enabling more readable and flexible code.

```
import org.javatuples.Pair;

public class TupleExample {
    public static Pair<Integer, String> getPair() {
        return new Pair<>(1, "one");
    }

    public static void main(String[] args) {
        Pair<Integer, String> pair = getPair();
        Integer number = pair.getValue0();
        String text = pair.getValue1();

        System.out.println("Number: " + number);
        System.out.println("Text: " + text);
    }
}
```

Here, Pair from javatuples is used to return and destructure values. The values can be accessed using getValue0 and getValue1 methods, representing a simple form of destructuring.

Advanced Pattern Matching with Libraries: Several third-party libraries provide extensive pattern matching capabilities. VAVR is a popular library that brings functional programming constructs and pattern matching to Java.

Let's consider how to utilize VAVR for pattern matching:

```
import io.vavr.API;
import io.vavr.Predicates;
import static io.vavr.API.*;
import static io.vavr.Predicates.*;

public class VavrPatternMatching {
```

```
    public static void main(String[] args) {
        Object object = 42;

        String result = Match(object).of(
            Case($(instanceOf(Integer.class)), i -> "Integer: " + i),
            Case($(instanceOf(String.class)), s -> "String: " + s),
            Case($(), "Unknown")
        );

        System.out.println(result);
    }
}
```

In this example, Match from VAVR is used for pattern matching. It allows checking against different data types and executing corresponding actions. The case clauses use the $ operator for pattern matching, with instanceOf predicates to identify the type of the object.

Destructuring Data Classes: With the advent of records in Java 14, creating immutable data classes becomes more straightforward. Records also make destructuring more convenient. Consider the following record definition and usage:

```
public record Point(int x, int y) {}

public class RecordExample {
    public static void main(String[] args) {
        Point p = new Point(3, 4);

        int xCoordinate = p.x();
        int yCoordinate = p.y();

        System.out.println("x: " + xCoordinate + ", y: " + yCoordinate);
    }
}
```

Here, the Point record simplifies the creation of an immutable class with positional parameters x and y. Accessor methods x() and y() provide an easy way to destructure the record.

Another Example using Pattern Matching for Switch Expressions: Java 17 further enhances pattern matching with switch expressions:

```
public class PatternMatchingSwitch {
    public static void main(String[] args) {
        Object obj = "Hello";

        String result = switch (obj) {
            case Integer i -> "Integer: " + i;
            case String s -> "String: " + s;
            default -> "Unknown type";
        };

        System.out.println(result);
    }
}
```

This example leverages the pattern matching feature in switch expressions to match and destructure based on type, simplifying the control flow.

Understanding and utilizing pattern matching and destructuring in Java enhances code readability and maintainability. These constructs provide a functional approach to handling complex data structures and conditional logic, aligning Java more closely with paradigms found in other functional programming languages.

Chapter 8

Error Handling in Functional Programming

This chapter addresses error handling within the context of functional programming. It compares traditional error handling in Java with functional approaches, focusing on the use of Java Optional, Try, and Either classes. The chapter explains lifting functions to handle errors, composing error handlers, and managing checked exceptions in a functional style. Best practices and patterns for robust error handling are discussed, along with an overview of error handling techniques in popular functional libraries.

8.1 Introduction to Error Handling

Error handling is an essential aspect of software development. It ensures that programs can manage unexpected conditions gracefully and maintain a stable and predictable behavior even under adverse circumstances. In functional programming, error handling takes a different approach from traditional programming paradigms, emphasizing immutability, declarative constructs, and the use of higher-order functions to manage errors in a more compositional and predictable way.

In Java, traditional error handling predominantly relies on exceptions. Exceptions are objects that encapsulate information about an error. They provide a mechanism for signaling the occurrence of an unexpected event and can be caught and handled appropriately. Traditional Java error handling typically uses try-catch blocks. For example:

```
public void readFile(String filePath) {
    try {
        BufferedReader reader = new BufferedReader(new FileReader(filePath));
        String firstLine = reader.readLine();
        System.out.println(firstLine);
    } catch (FileNotFoundException e) {
        System.err.println("File not found: " + filePath);
    } catch (IOException e) {
        System.err.println("Error reading file: " + filePath);
    }
}
```

In this example, the readFile method attempts to read the first line of a given file. If the file does not exist, a FileNotFoundException is thrown and caught, printing an error message to the console. If an IOException occurs during the read operation, it is similarly handled. This approach has several limitations, particularly evident when scaling error handling across complex systems.

Functional programming introduces concepts that aim to handle errors more declaratively and compositionally. Instead of relying on side effects and mutable states, functional programming encourages the use of types such as Optional, Try, and Either to represent computations that may fail. These types encapsulate the result of a computation along with the possibility of an error, allowing developers to compose functions that handle errors in a more predictable and concise manner.

Optional is a container object that may or may not contain a value. It is used to represent the presence or absence of a value without resorting to null references. Using Optional can reduce the risk of NullPointerExceptions and make the absence of a value explicit. An example of using Optional is as follows:

```
public Optional<String> readFirstLine(String filePath) {
    try {
        BufferedReader reader = new BufferedReader(new FileReader(filePath));
        return Optional.ofNullable(reader.readLine());
    } catch (FileNotFoundException e) {
        return Optional.empty();
    } catch (IOException e) {
        return Optional.empty();
    }
}
```

In this example, the readFirstLine method returns an Optional<String>. If the file cannot be found or an I/O error occurs, the method returns an empty Optional, clearly signaling the absence of a result.

Try is another type used in functional programming to capture the concept of computations that may fail. Try can either be a Success, encapsulating a successful result, or a Failure, encapsulating an exception. This type allows for the construction of error-handling workflows that are more expressive and composable.

```
import io.vavr.control.Try;

public Try<String> readFirstLine(String filePath) {
    return Try.of(() -> {
        BufferedReader reader = new BufferedReader(new FileReader(filePath));
        return reader.readLine();
    });
}

public static void main(String[] args) {
    Try<String> result = new Example().readFirstLine("somefile.txt");
    result.onSuccess(line -> System.out.println("First line: " + line))
          .onFailure(ex -> System.err.println("Error: " + ex.getMessage()));
}
```

In this example, the readFirstLine method returns a Try<String>, encapsulating the possibility of both success and failure. The main method demonstrates how to handle the result by specifying actions to perform in the case of success or failure.

Finally, Either is a type that represents a value of one of two possible types (a disjoint union). An Either instance can be either a Left or a Right, typically used to represent an error or a successful result, respectively. This type allows developers to distinguish between success and failure cases and handle them appropriately.

```
import io.vavr.control.Either;

public Either<Exception, String> readFirstLine(String filePath) {
    try {
        BufferedReader reader = new BufferedReader(new FileReader(filePath));
        return Either.right(reader.readLine());
    } catch (Exception e) {
        return Either.left(e);
    }
}

public static void main(String[] args) {
    Either<Exception, String> result = new Example().readFirstLine("somefile.txt");
    if (result.isRight()) {
        System.out.println("First line: " + result.get());
    } else {
        System.err.println("Error: " + result.getLeft().getMessage());
    }
}
```

In this example, the readFirstLine method returns an Either<Exception, String>, encapsulating the dual possibility of a successful result or an encountered exception. The main method illustrates how to process both cases.

Understanding these essential concepts and types—Optional, Try, and Either—is crucial for mastering error handling in functional programming. These constructs enable developers to build more robust, maintainable, and predictable error-handling mechanisms while adhering to the core principles of functional programming.

8.2 Traditional Error Handling in Java

Traditional error handling in Java relies heavily on the use of exceptions. Exceptions represent conditions that a reasonable application might want to catch and deal with. They provide a mechanism for propagating errors up the call stack and enabling deliberate error-handling strategies. There are several types of exceptions within the Java programming language, including checked exceptions, unchecked exceptions, and errors. Each category of exception serves different purposes in error handling and robustness of a Java application.

Checked Exceptions are exceptions that are checked at compile time. A method that can throw a checked exception must declare it using the throws keyword in its method signature.

```
public void readFile(String path) throws IOException {
    // Method body
}
```

In the above example, any code that calls the readFile method must either handle the IOException using a try-catch block or declare that it throws the exception further up the call stack.

Unchecked exceptions, on the other hand, are not checked at compile time. They are descendants of RuntimeException. Unchecked exceptions do not require explicit handling in the method signatures and are usually indicative of programming errors, such as NullPointerException or IndexOutOfBoundsException.

```
public int divide(int numerator, int denominator) {
    if (denominator == 0) {
        throw new ArithmeticException("Cannot divide by zero");
    }
    return numerator / denominator;
}
```

Errors represent serious issues that a program should not attempt to catch. These are typically problems outside the control of the application code, such as OutOfMemoryError.

```
try {
    int[] hugeArray = new int[Integer.MAX_VALUE];
} catch (OutOfMemoryError e) {
    System.err.println("Out of memory!");
}
```

To handle exceptions, traditional Java programs use try-catch blocks. In these blocks, the code likely to throw an exception is placed inside the try block, and the exception handling code is written in one or more catch blocks.

```
public void processFile(String path) {
    try {
        readFile(path);
    } catch (IOException e) {
        System.err.println("An error occurred while reading the file: " + e.getMessage())
            ;
    }
}
```

In this example, if the readFile method throws an IOException, the catch block will handle the exception by printing an error message. Traditional error handling in Java provides mechanisms for both catching exceptions locally and propagating them up the call stack using the throws keyword.

Beyond try-catch, Java also supports the use of finally blocks, which always execute after the try block and the relevant catch blocks, whether an exception was thrown or not. The finally block is often used to release resources such as closing a file or database connection.

```
public void processFile(String path) {
    BufferedReader reader = null;
    try {
        reader = new BufferedReader(new FileReader(path));
        // Process the file
    } catch (IOException e) {
        System.err.println("An error occurred while processing the file: " + e.
            getMessage());
    } finally {
        if (reader != null) {
            try {
                reader.close();
            } catch (IOException e) {
                System.err.println("Failed to close the reader: " + e.getMessage());
            }
        }
    }
}
```

Although the traditional approach to error handling in Java provides robust mechanisms to handle various exceptional conditions, it has several drawbacks. The error-handling code often pollutes the main logic, leading to reduced readability and maintainability of the program. The scourge of nested try-catch-finally blocks can also be a source of redundant and error-prone code.

Another critical drawback includes the potential for improper exception handling. Exception swallowing, where exceptions are caught and ignored without proper handling or logging, poses significant risks. Additionally, checked exceptions force every caller to handle the exception, which can sometimes lead to burdensome and boilerplate code.

```
public void processFiles(List<String> paths) {
    for (String path : paths) {
        try {
            processFile(path);
        } catch (IOException e) {
            // Exception is caught and ignored
        }
    }
}
```

Finally, translating exceptions across different layers of an application can be cumbersome and requires careful design to prevent the leakage of implementation details through exceptions. This verbosity and potential for error make traditional error handling in Java a good candidate for enhancement through functional programming techniques, as explored in the subsequent sections.

8.3 Functional Error Handling Basics

Functional error handling is an integral part of writing robust functional programs. Unlike traditional imperative programming, which often uses exceptions and error codes, functional programming aims to manage errors seamlessly within the type system. This section delves into the basics of functional error handling, presenting fundamental concepts and illustrating them with examples in Java.

In functional programming, the primary goal is to transform functions that might fail into functions that explicitly return their success or failure state. This approach enables more predictable and easier-to-understand code without relying on exceptions that disrupt the normal control flow.

A commonly used construct for handling possible absence of a value is

Java's Optional. Optional is a container object which may or may not contain a value. When a value is present, the Optional is considered non-empty, and when no value is present, it is considered empty. The following example illustrates the use of Optional:

```
import java.util.Optional;

public class UserService {
    public Optional<User> findUserByName(String name) {
        // Assume userRepo is an instance of UserRepository
        User user = userRepo.findByName(name);
        return Optional.ofNullable(user);
    }

    public void printUserEmail(String name) {
        Optional<User> userOpt = findUserByName(name);
        userOpt.ifPresent(user -> System.out.println(user.getEmail()));
    }
}
```

In this example, the findUserByName method returns an Optional<User>. This approach explicitly states that the result may be absent, encouraging the caller to handle both the presence and absence of a value.

Next, we consider the Try class for representing computations that may fail. The Try class in functional programming often encapsulates a computation that can either result in a success or a failure (commonly known as a Success or a Failure). Below is an example of how you might implement and use Try in Java:

```
import java.util.function.Supplier;

public abstract class Try<T> {

    public abstract <U> Try<U> map(Function<? super T, ? extends U> mapper);
    public abstract <U> Try<U> flatMap(Function<? super T, Try<U>> flatMapper
        );

    public static <T> Try<T> of(Supplier<T> supplier) {
        try {
            return new Success<>(supplier.get());
        } catch (Exception e) {
            return new Failure<>(e);
        }
    }

    public static final class Success<T> extends Try<T> {
        private final T value;

        public Success(T value) {
            this.value = value;
        }

        @Override
        public <U> Try<U> map(Function<? super T, ? extends U> mapper) {
            return Try.of(() -> mapper.apply(value));
```

```
        }

        @Override
        public <U> Try<U> flatMap(Function<? super T, Try<U>> flatMapper) {
            return flatMapper.apply(value);
        }
    }

    public static final class Failure<T> extends Try<T> {
        private final Throwable exception;

        public Failure(Throwable exception) {
            this.exception = exception;
        }

        @Override
        public <U> Try<U> map(Function<? super T, ? extends U> mapper) {
            return new Failure<>(exception);
        }

        @Override
        public <U> Try<U> flatMap(Function<? super T, Try<U>> flatMapper) {
            return new Failure<>(exception);
        }
    }
}
```

This Try implementation involves two subclasses, Success and Failure, which represent the two possible outcomes of a computation. The of method is a factory method that performs a safe computation and wraps the result in a Success or Failure.

Using the Try construct provides a more functional approach for error handling. Here is an example of using Try to handle a scenario where file reading might fail:

```
import java.nio.file.Files;
import java.nio.file.Paths;
import java.util.List;

public class FileService {
    public Try<List<String>> readFile(String path) {
        return Try.of(() -> Files.readAllLines(Paths.get(path)));
    }

    public void printFileContent(String path) {
        Try<List<String>> contentTry = readFile(path);
        contentTry.map(lines -> {
            lines.forEach(System.out::println);
            return lines;
        });
    }
}
```

In the printFileContent method, we attempt to read a file using the readFile method. Try encapsulates any IO exceptions, avoiding the need to handle them directly within the method, making the code cleaner and more focused on the business logic.

Another essential construct in functional error handling is the Either class, which represents a value of two possible types, typically denoted as Left or Right. By convention, Left is used for an error or failure, and Right is used for a successful computation.

```
public abstract class Either<L, R> {
    public abstract <T> Either<L, T> map(Function<? super R, ? extends T>
        mapper);
    public abstract <T> Either<T, R> mapLeft(Function<? super L, ? extends T>
        mapper);

    public static <L, R> Either<L, R> right(R value) {
        return new Right<>(value);
    }

    public static <L, R> Either<L, R> left(L value) {
        return new Left<>(value);
    }

    public static final class Right<L, R> extends Either<L, R> {
        private final R value;

        public Right(R value) {
            this.value = value;
        }

        @Override
        public <T> Either<L, T> map(Function<? super R, ? extends T> mapper) {
            return new Right<>(mapper.apply(value));
        }

        @Override
        public <T> Either<T, R> mapLeft(Function<? super L, ? extends T> mapper
            ) {
            return new Right<>(value);
        }
    }

    public static final class Left<L, R> extends Either<L, R> {
        private final L value;

        public Left(L value) {
            this.value = value;
        }

        @Override
        public <T> Either<L, T> map(Function<? super R, ? extends T> mapper) {
            return new Left<>(value);
        }

        @Override
        public <T> Either<T, R> mapLeft(Function<? super L, ? extends T> mapper
            ) {
            return new Left<>(mapper.apply(value));
        }
    }
}
```

The Either construct provides the ability to handle different types of errors or values elegantly. Here's an example demonstrating how we might use Either to handle parsing of integers:

```
public class ParserService {
    public Either<String, Integer> parseInt(String input) {
        try {
            int result = Integer.parseInt(input);
            return Either.right(result);
        } catch (NumberFormatException e) {
            return Either.left("Invalid number format: " + input);
        }
    }

    public void processInput(String input) {
        Either<String, Integer> result = parseInt(input);
        result.map(value -> {
            System.out.println("Parsed value: " + value);
            return value;
        }).mapLeft(error -> {
            System.err.println("Error: " + error);
            return error;
        });
    }
}
```

In this scenario, the parseInt method uses Either to return either a successfully parsed integer (Right) or an error message (Left). When processing the input, different behaviors are applied using the map and mapLeft functions accordingly.

These foundational concepts and constructs provide a robust framework for handling errors and exceptions in functional programming. They allow developers to handle success and failure explicitly and gracefully, leading to code that is more expressive, safe, and easy to reason about.

8.4 Using Java Optional for Error Handling

The Optional class, introduced in Java 8, offers a more expressive way to handle possible absence of values, thus addressing the frequent occurrence of NullPointerExceptions in Java applications. The Optional type is essentially a container that may or may not hold a non-null value. This concept aligns closely with the principles of functional programming by promoting composability and immutable types.

To illustrate the fundamental concepts of using Optional for error handling, consider the following example involving a method that retrieves a user by their username. In a traditional approach, this might return null if the user is not found:

```
// Traditional Approach
public User findUserByUsername(String username) {
    // Assume this method interacts with a data source
    User user = dataSource.getUser(username);
    return user; // May return null if user is not found
}
```

Utilizing Optional, the method signature and handling logic are modified to return an Optional<User> instead of a potentially null user.

```
// Functional Approach
public Optional<User> findUserByUsername(String username) {
    // Assume this method interacts with a data source
    User user = dataSource.getUser(username);
    return Optional.ofNullable(user); // Wraps the user in an Optional
}
```

Here, Optional.ofNullable(user) ensures that a non-null value is wrapped in an Optional, whereas a null value results in Optional.empty().

The consumer of this method must now handle the possibility of the absence of a value, typically done using methods provided by the Optional class:

```
Optional<User> optionalUser = findUserByUsername("john_doe");

optionalUser.ifPresentOrElse(
    user -> System.out.println("User found: " + user.getName()),
    () -> System.out.println("User not found")
);
```

In this example, ifPresentOrElse accepts a Consumer to execute if the value is present and a Runnable if it is not. This approach explicitly handles both scenarios, thus increasing code readability and robustness.

The Optional class also provides several other methods for dealing with the presence or absence of values, enhancing error handling:

- orElse(T other): Returns the contained value if present, otherwise returns the specified value.
- orElseGet(Supplier<? extends T> other): Returns the contained value if present, otherwise invokes the specified Supplier and returns its result.
- orElseThrow(Supplier<? extends X> exceptionSupplier): Returns the contained value if present, otherwise throws an exception created by the specified Supplier.

- map(Function<? super T,? extends U> mapper): If a value is present, applies the provided mapping function.
- flatMap(Function<? super T,Optional<U» mapper): Similar to map, but the mapping function must return an Optional.

Consider a scenario where we want to transform the user object only if it exists, using the map or flatMap methods:

```
optionalUser
    .map(User::getName)
    .ifPresent(name -> System.out.println("User name: " + name));
```

In this instance, map is used to transform the User object to its name property if it exists, and ifPresent is subsequently used to handle the result.

For cases requiring throwing exceptions when the optional value is not present, orElseThrow can be utilized to maintain a functional style that avoids early returns and enhances flow control:

```
User user = optionalUser.orElseThrow(() -> new UserNotFoundException("User not
      found"));
```

By incorporating Optional in error handling, developers adhere to a pattern that visibly enforces presence validation at compile-time, reducing the risk of null-related errors. Embracing this approach aligns with functional programming principles, facilitating more predictable and maintainable code and allowing error handling to be seamlessly integrated within the functional compositional paradigm.

8.5 Try Class and Its Usage

The Try class is a robust alternative for handling errors in a functional programming paradigm. It addresses the limitations of checked exceptions in Java's traditional error-handling mechanisms. Unlike the Optional class, which handles the presence or absence of a value, Try can capture both successful outcomes and failures.

The Try class can be either Success or Failure. When a computation completes successfully, a Success instance is returned. If an error occurs, a Failure containing the exception is returned. This dual nature mitigates the need for try-catch blocks, propagating the error handling downstream.

To demonstrate the usage of Try, let's consider a function that may throw an exception. We will use the Vavr library, which provides an implementation of Try:

```
import io.vavr.control.Try;

public class TryExample {
    public static void main(String[] args) {
        Try<Integer> result = divide(4, 0);

        result.onSuccess(value -> System.out.println("Result: " + value))
              .onFailure(exception -> System.out.println("Error: " + exception.
                    getMessage()));
    }

    public static Try<Integer> divide(int dividend, int divisor) {
        return Try.of(() -> dividend / divisor);
    }
}
```

In this example, the divide method performs a division and may throw an ArithmeticException if the divisor is zero. The call to Try.of wraps this computation and handles any exception, encapsulating it within a Failure.

The method onSuccess processes the successful outcome, and onFailure handles the potential error. Running the above code yields:

```
Error: / by zero
```

Thus, Try allows seamless handling of errors without disrupting the code flow with try-catch blocks.

For more complex scenarios, such as chaining operations that might fail, Try provides methods like map, flatMap, and recover. These methods facilitate the composition of operations while propogating errors correctly.

Consider an example that includes chained operations:

```
import io.vavr.control.Try;

public class TryChainedExample {
    public static void main(String[] args) {
        Try<Integer> result = Try.of(() -> "1234")
                                 .map(Integer::valueOf)
                                 .map(n -> n / 0)
                                 .recover(exception -> 0);

        System.out.println("Result: " + result.get());
    }
}
```

In this case, the operations are chained: converting a string to an integer and then performing a division. The division by zero will cause an exception, caught and managed internally by the Try construct. The recover method provides a way to supply a default value if an error occurs. The output is:

```
Result: 0
```

Leveraging the Try class also enhances readability and maintainability by reducing boilerplate code. Functions like filter, transform, and peek further expand its utilization.

```
import io.vavr.control.Try;

public class TryAdvancedHandling {
    public static void main(String[] args) {
        Try<Integer> result = Try.of(() -> "abcd")
                                 .map(Integer::valueOf)
                                 .recoverWith(exception -> Try.success(-1))
                                 .filter(value -> value > 0)
                                 .getOrElseGet(exception -> 0);

        System.out.println("Result: " + result); // Prints: Result: -1
    }
}
```

Here, an attempt is made to convert a non-numeric string to an integer, resulting in a NumberFormatException. The recoverWith method allows us to return a fallback Try in case of an error. The filter method is then used to check if the captured value satisfies a predicate. If not, the computation falls back to the default value provided by getOrElseGet.

The Try class's adaptability makes it invaluable for managing computations that can fail. It effectively bridges the gap between functional programming and Java's traditional imperative error-handling constructs.

8.6 Either Class for Handling Errors

The Either class in functional programming is a powerful tool for error handling, offering a robust alternative to traditional exception-based methods. Unlike Optional and Try, the Either class can encapsulate two distinct types of values, providing a clear distinction between successful and erroneous computations. This dual capability makes Either particularly useful for scenarios where functions can return more than one type of outcome.

Either typically holds one of two types: Left (representing an error or unexpected case) and Right (signifying a successful result). In functional programming, it is customary to reserve Right for the standard return type and Left for error scenarios. This convention aids in maintaining consistency across different functions and codebases.

```
import io.vavr.control.Either;

public class EitherExample {
    public static Either<String, Integer> parseInteger(String input) {
        try {
            return Either.right(Integer.parseInt(input));
        } catch (NumberFormatException e) {
            return Either.left("Invalid number: " + input);
        }
    }

    public static void main(String[] args) {
        Either<String, Integer> result1 = parseInteger("123");
        Either<String, Integer> result2 = parseInteger("abc");

        System.out.println(result1); // prints: Right(123)
        System.out.println(result2); // prints: Left(Invalid number: abc)
    }
}
```

In this example, the parseInteger method attempts to parse a string into an integer. If the parsing succeeds, it returns a Right containing the integer value. If a NumberFormatException is thrown, it returns a Left with an error message. When executed, the main method demonstrates how to distinguish between successful and failed outcomes.

Either also provides various methods to manipulate and transform its content. For instance, isRight and isLeft methods can check the type of value contained in the Either, facilitating conditional processing.

```
if (result1.isRight()) {
    System.out.println("Parsed value: " + result1.get());
} else {
    System.out.println("Error: " + result1.getLeft());
}

if (result2.isLeft()) {
    System.out.println("Error: " + result2.getLeft());
}
```

In the above snippet, isRight and isLeft methods are used to check whether the Either contains a Right or Left value, respectively. Depending on the check outcome, the appropriate value or error message is printed.

Transformation operations are also supported by Either. The map method allows transformation of the Right value, while the mapLeft method is used for transforming the Left value.

```
Either<String, Integer> rightExample = Either.right(5);
Either<String, Integer> leftExample = Either.left("Error");
```

```
Either<String, Integer> incremented = rightExample.map(i -> i + 1);
Either<String, String> upperCasedError = leftExample.mapLeft(String::toUpperCase);

System.out.println(incremented); // prints: Right(6)
System.out.println(upperCasedError); // prints: Left(ERROR)
```

Here, the map method increments the integer contained in a Right value, while mapLeft method converts the Left error message to uppercase.

The chaining of operations is streamlined with flatMap, facilitating more complex transformations without deep nesting of code. This method applies a function to the Right value if present, and returns a new Either.

```
Either<String, Integer> divided = rightExample.flatMap(i -> {
    if (i != 0) {
        return Either.right(10 / i);
    } else {
        return Either.left("Division by zero");
    }
});

System.out.println(divided); // prints: Right(2)
```

In this example, flatMap applies a function that performs a division if the value is not zero, wrapping the result in a new Right. If division by zero is attempted, it returns a Left with an error message.

Either can be effectively utilized in handling complex error scenarios that involve multiple error types or require detailed error information. Its structure inherently ensures a clear and explicit method of managing both successes and failures, thus enhancing code readability and maintainability.

8.7 Lifting Functions to Handle Errors

In functional programming, enabling functions to handle errors seamlessly is crucial to ensuring robust and maintainable code. One of the fundamental techniques in this regard is lifting functions. Lifting refers to the process of transforming a function that operates on plain values into a function that operates within a context, such as Optional, Try, or Either in Java. This section explores the concept of lifting in detail and demonstrates how it can be applied to different error-handling paradigms in Java.

Consider a simple function that divides two integers and might throw an ArithmeticException if there is an attempt to divide by zero:

```
public int divide(int numerator, int denominator) {
    return numerator / denominator;
}
```

This function assumes the inputs are always valid, but in practice, this is not always the case. Using functional programming principles, we can lift this function to safely handle potential errors without throwing exceptions.

Optional is a well-known Java class in the java.util package, used to represent a value that might be absent. A lifted version of the divide function using Optional can handle the error case of dividing by zero and return an Optional.empty() instead of throwing an exception:

```
public Optional<Integer> divideWithOptional(int numerator, int denominator) {
    if (denominator == 0) {
        return Optional.empty();
    }
    return Optional.of(numerator / denominator);
}
```

Using the lifted function, we handle error cases gracefully without corrupting the program flow with exceptions. However, Optional tends to be limited in scenarios where providing error messages or handling specific error types is necessary.

To overcome these limitations, we can utilize the Try class from the Vavr library. Try represents a computation that may either result in a value or fail with an exception. Here's how we can lift the divide function using Try:

```
import io.vavr.control.Try;

public Try<Integer> divideWithTry(int numerator, int denominator) {
    return Try.of(() -> divide(numerator, denominator));
}
```

The Try class is particularly useful because it encapsulates both successful and failed computations. This approach ensures that even if an exception occurs, it's captured within the Try context. The function can then be used as follows:

```
Try<Integer> result = divideWithTry(10, 0);
if (result.isSuccess()) {
    System.out.println("Result: " + result.get());
} else {
    System.out.println("Error: " + result.getCause());
}
```

The third lifting mechanism involves the Either class, which is often used to represent a value of one of two possible types (a disjoint union). Either is a more general form of error handling and can be useful when the error information needs to be more descriptive:

```
import io.vavr.control.Either;

public Either<String, Integer> divideWithEither(int numerator, int denominator) {
    if (denominator == 0) {
        return Either.left("Denominator cannot be zero.");
    }
    return Either.right(numerator / denominator);
}
```

The Either class carries a value of type Left (for errors) or Right (for successful results). When dividing zero, it returns an appropriate message instead of an exception. This offers better error reporting as it provides specific error messages:

```
Either<String, Integer> result = divideWithEither(10, 0);
if (result.isRight()) {
    System.out.println("Result: " + result.get());
} else {
    System.out.println("Error: " + result.getLeft());
}
```

Lifting functions form a powerful technique to handle errors in a clean, functional style, enabling the chaining and composition of computations without exception handling clutter. By lifting functions into Optional, Try, or Either, we can achieve a more functional and declarative style of error management, leveraging the capabilities of functional programming to construct resilient and readable code.

Lifted functions facilitate composing higher-order functions, promoting reusability and maintainability. They ensure that our code conveys a clear and concise intent, decoupling error handling from core logic, paving the way toward robust functional programming paradigms.

8.8 Composing Error Handlers

When developing robust applications in a functional programming style, it is essential to compose error handlers effectively. This technique facilitates the creation of resilient and maintainable code. In this section, the concept of composing error handlers will be explored in detail, emphasizing how they integrate into previously discussed functional paradigms.

Error composition primarily revolves around the ability to combine multiple error handling strategies to produce a single, cohesive mechanism for responding to errors. This approach allows for modular and reusable error handling logic, aligning with the principles of functional programming.

1. Error Composing Using Optional

The java.util.Optional class provides a streamlined method for handling absent values. When composing error handlers with Optional, we can chain multiple operations that may produce Optional values seamlessly.

Consider an example where we have two methods that may return an empty Optional:

```
public Optional<String> fetchUserName(int userId) {
    if (userId > 0) {
        return Optional.of("User" + userId);
    } else {
        return Optional.empty();
    }
}
public Optional<String> fetchUserEmail(int userId) {
    if (userId > 0) {
        return Optional.of("user" + userId + "@example.com");
    } else {
        return Optional.empty();
    }
}
```

To compose error handling logic where both methods are called and their results are combined only if both return non-empty Optionals, streams can be utilized:

```
public String composeUserDetails(int userId) {
    return fetchUserName(userId)
        .flatMap(name -> fetchUserEmail(userId)
            .map(email -> name + " (" + email + ")"))
        .orElse("Unknown User");
}
```

In this code, if either fetchUserName or fetchUserEmail return an empty Optional, the composed handler results in "Unknown User". This demonstrates compositionality where the handling logic is encapsulated, making the code easy to read and maintain.

2. Error Composing Using Try

The Try class, often used in functional libraries like Vavr, provides another powerful tool for error handling composition. The Try class encapsulates computations that might fail with an exception. Similar to Optional, it supports chaining operations.

Assume we have methods that might throw an exception:

```
public Try<String> parseInt(String value) {
    return Try.of(() -> Integer.parseInt(value));
}

public Try<Integer> divideBy(int dividend, int divisor) {
    return Try.of(() -> {
        if (divisor == 0) throw new ArithmeticException("Division by zero");
        return dividend / divisor;
    });
}
```

To compose these Try operations, where parsing and division are chained, we utilize the flatMap method:

```
public Try<Integer> parseAndDivide(String dividendStr, String divisorStr) {
    return parseInt(dividendStr)
        .flatMap(dividend -> parseInt(divisorStr)
            .flatMap(divisor -> divideBy(dividend, divisor)));
}
```

In this composition, each successive operation depends on the success of the previous one. If any step fails, the entire computation fails gracefully, preserving the error information.

3. Composing Error Handlers with Either

The Either class represents a value of two possible types, Left or Right. Typically, Left represents an error, while Right represents a success. This class is powerful for error composition because it captures both successful and erroneous results.

Consider methods returning Either:

```
public Either<String, Integer> parseSafe(String value) {
    try {
        return Either.right(Integer.parseInt(value));
    } catch (NumberFormatException e) {
        return Either.left("Invalid number format: " + value);
    }
}

public Either<String, Integer> safeDivide(int dividend, int divisor) {
    if (divisor == 0) {
        return Either.left("Division by zero");
    } else {
        return Either.right(dividend / divisor);
    }
}
```

To compose these Either operations, use the flatMap method:

```
public Either<String, Integer> parseAndSafeDivide(String dividendStr, String
    divisorStr) {
    return parseSafe(dividendStr)
```

```
        .flatMap(dividend -> parseSafe(divisorStr)
            .flatMap(divisor -> safeDivide(dividend, divisor)));
}
```

This allows each operation to proceed only if the previous was successful, consolidating error messages at each step, thus providing a robust error handling pipeline.

Algorithmic Composition of Error Handlers

The following algorithm illustrates the general structure for composing error handlers using monadic types like Optional, Try, and Either:

Data: Inputs requiring transformation and validation
Result: Chained computation handling errors gracefully
1 Initialize the first operation O_1;
2 **foreach** *subsequent operation* O_i **do**
3   Apply O_i using flatMap to the result of O_{i-1};
4   Propagate errors if any ;
5 Return the final result or the accumulated error ;

Effective error handling in functional programming requires the thoughtful composition of error handlers. By leveraging constructs like Optional, Try, and Either, and through the use of functions such as flatMap, developers can build extensive yet comprehensible error management workflows. This facilitates writing code that not only performs its intended task but also remains clear and maintainable amidst the inevitable emergence of runtime anomalies.

8.9 Handling Checked Exceptions in Functional Style

Handling checked exceptions in a functional style necessitates a shift from conventional error handling mechanisms and necessitates the use of higher-order functions and monadic constructs. Traditional Java mandates the use of try-catch blocks to manage exceptions, which often leads to boilerplate code that interrupts the flow of logic. Functional programming offers an alternative by treating functions as first-class citizens and leveraging the power of high-order functions.

Checked exceptions are those that must be either caught or declared in the method signature. They serve to enforce error handling in Java.

However, this enforcement can fragment code and hamper composability, a core principle in functional programming. To maintain composability, we must encapsulate these exceptions in a way that aligns with functional idioms.

Consider a function that performs file reading and may throw an IOException:

```
public String readFile(String path) throws IOException {
    return new String(Files.readAllBytes(Paths.get(path)));
}
```

Traditionally, you would handle the IOException using a try-catch block:

```
try {
    String content = readFile("path/to/file");
} catch (IOException e) {
    e.printStackTrace();
}
```

To handle checked exceptions functionally, you can use wrappers like Try from functional libraries, such as Vavr.

```
import io.vavr.control.Try;

public Try<String> readFile(String path) {
    return Try.of(() -> new String(Files.readAllBytes(Paths.get(path))));
}
```

In this functional style, readFile returns a Try object that encapsulates both the successful result and the potential exception. This approach harmonizes with functional programming principles by making exception handling an explicit part of the function's interface.

To further explore functional composition with Try, consider chaining operations that may each throw an exception. Instead of nested try-catch blocks, you can compose operations fluently:

```
public Try<Integer> readFileAndParseLength(String path) {
    return readFile(path)
            .map(String::length)
            .mapTry(len -> len / 0); // This will throw ArithmeticException
}
```

With this structure, if any step fails, Try short-circuits and propagates the error, providing an elegant way to manage multiple potential failure points without sacrificing code readability. To handle the exceptions, Try offers mechanisms like recover and recoverWith:

```
Try<Integer> result = readFileAndParseLength("path/to/file")
        .recover(IOException.class, -1)
        .recover(ArithmeticException.class, -2);
```

```
System.out.println(result.getOrElse(-3)); // Outputs the appropriate recovery value
```

In scenarios requiring more specific control or additional checks, Either can be employed to model computations that might fail. Unlike Try, Either explicitly distinguishes between the success and failure cases using Right and Left, respectively.

```
import io.vavr.control.Either;

public Either<Exception, String> readFileEither(String path) {
    try {
        return Either.right(new String(Files.readAllBytes(Paths.get(path))));
    } catch (IOException e) {
        return Either.left(e);
    }
}
```

This structure clearly differentiates success from failure, allowing better pattern matching and more granular error handling:

```
Either<Exception, String> result = readFileEither("path/to/file");

String output = result.fold(
    ex -> "Error: " + ex.getMessage(),
    content -> content
);

System.out.println(output);
```

Incorporating these concepts into existing or larger applications necessitates seamless integration of these error-handling constructs. Utility methods can aid in converting functions that throw exceptions into forms compatible with functional programming. An example utility method to create a checked function:

```
@FunctionalInterface
public interface CheckedFunction<T, R> {
    R apply(T t) throws Exception;

    static <T, R> Function<T, Try<R>> lift(CheckedFunction<T, R> function) {
        return t -> Try.of(() -> function.apply(t));
    }
}
```

Utilizing the above utility method, you can convert a traditional function that might throw an exception into a Try wrapped function:

```
CheckedFunction<String, String> checkedReadFile = this::readFile;
Function<String, Try<String>> liftedReadFile = CheckedFunction.lift(
        checkedReadFile);
```

Such methods help bridge the imperative and functional paradigms by encapsulating checked exceptions within function compositions, thus preserving flow and compositionality.

This functional approach to handling checked exceptions aligns with the core tenets of functional programming: immutability, composability, and declarative constructs, ultimately fostering more resilient and maintainable code structures.

8.10 Best Practices in Functional Error Handling

Functional error handling in Java follows distinct patterns that shift emphasis from imperative control flows like try-catch blocks, towards more declarative and expressive constructs. This section elucidates several best practices to adopt when handling errors in a functional programming paradigm, helping ensure that your code remains robust, clean, and maintainable.

Consider using the Optional, Try, and Either classes to handle error scenarios without propagating null references or unchecked exceptions. These classes encapsulate the notion of operations that may fail, thereby encouraging developers to account for failure scenarios explicitly and systemically.

- **Prefer Functional Interfaces and Lambda Expressions:** Functional interfaces such as Function<T, R>, Supplier<T>, and Consumer<T> can be leveraged to create error-handling constructs. For example, functions that would traditionally throw exceptions can be wrapped to return Optional<T> or Try<T>.

```
import java.util.function.Function;
import java.util.Optional;

Function<String, Optional<Integer>> parseInt = s -> {
    try {
        return Optional.of(Integer.parseInt(s));
    } catch (NumberFormatException e) {
        return Optional.empty();
    }
};
```

- **Monadic Error Handling:** Using monadic types such as Optional and Try provides a structured way to propagate error states. Chaining operations via map, flatMap, or filter methods allows for concise yet readable error management.

```
import io.vavr.control.Try;

Function<String, Try<Integer>> parseIntTry = s -> Try.of(() -> Integer.
      parseInt(s));

Try.of(() -> "123")
   .flatMap(parseIntTry)
   .onSuccess(System.out::println)
   .onFailure(Throwable::printStackTrace);
```

- **Use** Either **for Detailed Error Information:** Either<L, R> bifurcates logic into two possibilities: one for success and another for failure. With left and right projections, it becomes easier to trace exact error causes without ambiguity.

```
import io.vavr.control.Either;

Function<String, Either<String, Integer>> parseIntEither = s -> {
    try {
        return Either.right(Integer.parseInt(s));
    } catch (NumberFormatException e) {
        return Either.left("Invalid number format: " + s);
    }
};
```

- **Avoid Side-Effects in Error Handling:** Functional programming emphasizes immutability and predictability. Ensure that methods handling errors do not produce side-effects. Instead, encapsulate side-effects in safe constructs.

```
Optional<Integer> safeMethod(Optional<Integer> input) {
    return input.filter(i -> i > 0).map(i -> i * 2);
}
```

- **Leverage Composition to Simplify Error Flows:** Composing multiple functions can streamline complex error-handling logic. Use combinators to chain function executions, effectively managing intermediate states and errors.

```
import io.vavr.control.Try;

Function<String, Try<Long>> parseAndAddTen = s ->
    Try.of(() -> Long.parseLong(s)).map(i -> i + 10);
```

- **Fallback Mechanisms:** Plan for fallback scenarios when a certain operation fails. Utilizing orElse, orElseGet, or recover methods, for example, can ensure continuity of execution in the face of failures.

```
Try<Integer> safeDivide = Try.of(() -> divide(10, 0)).recover(
      ArithmeticException.class, 1);
```

```
System.out.println(safeDivide.get()); // Outputs: 1
```

- **Proper Exception Translation:** Convert checked exceptions into unchecked exceptions or functional constructs. This practice exempts clients from handling low-level exceptions directly and adheres to functional principles.

```
<T> Try<T> toTry(Callable<T> callable) {
    try {
        return Try.successful(callable.call());
    } catch (Exception e) {
        return Try.failure(e);
    }
}
```

- **Logging and Monitoring:** Ensure that errors are logged appropriately without disrupting the functional flow. Use monitoring tools to track patterns of failure for analysis and mitigation.

```
Optional<String> fetchConfig(String key) {
    Optional<String> config = configService.get(key);
    if (!config.isPresent()) {
        logger.warn("Configuration key not found: " + key);
    }
    return config;
}
```

By implementing these best practices, developers can harness the true power of functional programming for error handling, ensuring that their applications are both resilient and easy to understand.

8.11 Error Handling in Functional Libraries

Functional programming libraries provide various mechanisms and abstractions for error handling, enabling developers to write more predictable and maintainable code. These libraries often offer richer and more expressive ways to handle errors compared to traditional approaches. This section explores error handling techniques provided by popular functional programming libraries, such as Vavr and Arrow, and demonstrates how they can be effectively utilized to manage errors.

Error Handling with Vavr

Vavr is a functional programming library for Java that extends the standard Java library with persistent collections, functional data structures, and control structures. Vavr offers several constructs for error handling, including Option, Try, and Either.

The Try class is one of the primary constructs for handling errors. It represents a computation that may result in a success (yielding a value) or a failure (throwing an exception).

```
import io.vavr.control.Try;

public class Example {
    public static void main(String[] args) {
        Try<Integer> result = Try.of(() -> compute());
        result.onSuccess(value -> System.out.println("Success: " + value))
              .onFailure(ex -> System.err.println("Error: " + ex.getMessage()));
    }

    private static Integer compute() throws Exception {
        // Some computation that may throw an exception
    }
}
```

In this example, Try.of takes a lambda expression that represents a computation. If the computation is successful, onSuccess is invoked with the result. If the computation fails, onFailure handles the exception.

The Try class provides several useful methods for composing and transforming Try instances, such as map, flatMap, and recover:

```
Try<Integer> result = Try.of(() -> compute())
                         .map(value -> value * 2)
                         .recover(ex -> handleException(ex));
```

Here, map transforms the successful result, and recover handles the exception by providing an alternative value.

Error Handling with Arrow

Arrow is a functional programming library for Kotlin that provides numerous type classes and data types for handling errors. Arrow's Either and Validated are commonly used for error handling.

The Either type represents a value of one of two possible types: Left for errors and Right for successful results. This encapsulation allows for clear and concise error handling.

```
import arrow.core.Either
```

```
import arrow.core.right
import arrow.core.left

fun compute(value: Int): Either<String, Int> =
    if (value < 0) "Negative value".left()
    else value.right()

fun main() {
    val result = compute(4)
    result.fold(
        { error -> println("Error: $error") },
        { success -> println("Success: $success") }
    )
}
```

In this example, the compute function returns an Either. If the input is negative, it returns a Left with an error message. Otherwise, it returns a Right with the computed result. The fold function is used to handle both cases.

Arrow's Validated type is suited for validating multiple conditions and collecting errors. It can be useful when validating complex objects with multiple fields.

```
import arrow.core.Validated
import arrow.core.valid
import arrow.core.invalid

data class Person(val name: String, val age: Int)

fun validateName(name: String): Validated<String, String> =
    if (name.isNotBlank()) name.valid()
    else "Name cannot be blank".invalid()

fun validateAge(age: Int): Validated<String, Int> =
    if (age >= 0) age.valid()
    else "Age must be positive".invalid()

fun main() {
    val nameValidation = validateName("John")
    val ageValidation = validateAge(30)

    val personValidation = nameValidation.combine(ageValidation) { name, age ->
        Person(name, age)
    }

    when (personValidation) {
        is Validated.Valid -> println("Valid: ${personValidation.value}")
        is Validated.Invalid -> println("Invalid: ${personValidation.errors}")
    }
}
```

In this example, validateName and validateAge return Validated instances. combine is used to aggregate the validation results and construct the Person object if all validations succeed.

The use of Try, Either, and Validated forms robust patterns in error handling within functional programming libraries. These abstractions foster immutability, a clear separation between successful outcomes and errors, and compositionality, enabling developers to construct predictable and manageable error handling workflows.

Chapter 9

Concurrency and Parallelism in Functional Programming

This chapter explores concurrency and parallelism from a functional programming perspective. It distinguishes between concurrency and parallelism and examines how functional programming principles like immutability enhance thread safety. The chapter covers leveraging Java Streams for parallel processing, using CompletableFuture for asynchronous programming, and introduces reactive programming with Project Reactor and the Akka actor model. It also discusses Java's concurrency utilities and best practices for achieving functional concurrency, providing a comprehensive understanding of concurrent and parallel programming techniques in Java.

9.1 Introduction to Concurrency and Parallelism

Concurrency and parallelism are essential concepts in computer science, particularly when optimizing and efficiently utilizing computational resources. Understanding these concepts is vital for leveraging multi-core processors and distributed architectures, which are ubiquitous in modern computing environments.

Concurrency is the ability of a system to handle multiple tasks seemingly simultaneously. In a concurrent system, tasks are typically interleaved during execution; they share resources and execute in overlapping time periods, but not necessarily at the same instant. Concurrency is essential in situations like handling multiple user inputs, managing I/O operations, or running multiple applications simultaneously on a single processor.

Parallelism, on the other hand, involves performing multiple tasks simultaneously, leveraging multiple processing units. This can remarkably speed up computational tasks by dividing the work into smaller subtasks executed in parallel. Parallelism is a subset of concurrency but specifically instances where tasks actually run at the same time. Multicore CPUs and distributed computing systems exemplify environments designed to take advantage of parallel processes.

Functional programming inherently offers advantages in concurrent and parallel execution due to principles like immutability and lack of side effects. Immutability ensures that data cannot be modified after it is created, leading to thread-safe operations without the need for locks or other synchronization mechanisms. This reduces common pitfalls encountered in concurrent programming, such as race conditions and deadlocks.

Below is a concise example illustrating the difference between sequential and parallel processing using Java Streams.

```
List<Integer> numbers = Arrays.asList(1, 2, 3, 4, 5, 6, 7, 8, 9, 10);
List<Integer> squaredNumbers = numbers.stream()
                                      .map(n -> n * n)
                                      .collect(Collectors.toList());
```

The above code snippet demonstrates a sequential stream where each element is processed one after the other.

To achieve parallelism, we utilize the parallelStream method:

```
List<Integer> squaredNumbers = numbers.parallelStream()
                                      .map(n -> n * n)
                                      .collect(Collectors.toList());
```

In the parallel processing example, the stream is divided into multiple sub-streams, which are processed in parallel on different threads, leading to potential speedup on multi-core systems.

Understanding the difference between concurrency and parallelism helps in identifying the appropriate tools and methods for writing efficient and reliable concurrent programs. Concurrent executions allow handling of high-throughput tasks without blocking, while parallel executions optimize computational tasks by reducing execution time through simultaneous processing.

```
Output:
[1, 4, 9, 16, 25, 36, 49, 64, 81, 100]
```

Functional programming languages like Java, leveraging constructs such as streams, lambdas, and functional interfaces, simplify working with concurrent and parallel executions. Throughout this chapter, we will delve deeper into these concepts, exploring various constructs and frameworks that aid in writing functional concurrent and parallel programs.

The seamless integration of concurrency and parallelism is paramount in achieving scalable and performance-efficient programs. It is crucial to blend functional programming principles with robust concurrency and parallel techniques to exploit the full computational power of modern hardware.

9.2 Concurrency vs Parallelism

Concurrency and parallelism, though often used interchangeably, refer to distinct concepts in the realm of computing. Concurrency involves the management of multiple tasks at the same time, where these tasks can make progress independently or may wait for each other at certain points. Parallelism, on the other hand, is the execution of multiple tasks simultaneously, typically on different processors or cores. Understanding the distinction between these concepts is crucial for designing and implementing efficient functional programs that effectively utilize hardware resources.

Concurrency is concerned with decomposing a problem into various components and managing their execution. This often involves coordinating access to resources to ensure no conflicts occur. For instance, consider a web server handling multiple client requests. Here, concurrency comes into play as the server must manage multiple connections by allocating time slices to each request, potentially switching between them as needed. The essence of concurrency is achieving perceived simultaneity through context switching, even if there is only one processing unit available.

```
public class ConcurrentWebServer {
    private static ExecutorService executor = Executors.newFixedThreadPool(10);

    public static void main(String[] args) throws IOException {
        ServerSocket serverSocket = new ServerSocket(8080);
        while (true) {
            Socket clientSocket = serverSocket.accept();
            executor.submit(() -> handleRequest(clientSocket));
        }
    }

    private static void handleRequest(Socket socket) {
        // Handle the request
    }
}
```

In the ConcurrentWebServer example, the ExecutorService manages a pool of threads to handle incoming socket connections concurrently. Each thread handles an individual client request, allowing the server to process multiple connections cohesively. This abstraction simplifies the design by decoupling the request handling from the underlying threading mechanism.

Parallelism, by contrast, entails the simultaneous execution of multiple operations to leverage multi-core processors or distributed computing environments. Consider a data-processing task where a large dataset needs to be processed in chunks. By dividing the dataset and processing each chunk in parallel across multiple cores, substantial performance gains can be achieved.

```
public class ParallelDataProcessor {
    public static void main(String[] args) {
        List<Integer> data = Arrays.asList(1, 2, 3, 4, 5, 6, 7, 8, 9, 10);
        ForkJoinPool forkJoinPool = new ForkJoinPool(4);
        forkJoinPool.submit(() -> data.parallelStream().forEach(ParallelDataProcessor::
                process)).join();
    }

    private static void process(Integer item) {
        // Process item
    }
}
```

The ParallelDataProcessor example employs Java's parallel streams, which internally use the ForkJoinPool framework to process data in parallel. This leverages the multiple CPU cores, executing the process method on different items concurrently, thereby reducing the overall processing time.

A critical distinction lies in their usage scenarios. Concurrency is vital when there are multiple independent tasks that require interleaving, whereas parallelism is leveraged to expedite computationally intensive operations by distributing them across multiple processing units.

Algorithm 4 illustrates the conceptual difference between concurrency and parallelism.

Algorithm 4: Concurrency vs Parallelism

Data: Set of Tasks $T = \{T_1, T_2, T_3, ..., T_n\}$
Result: Execution Plan
// Concurrent Execution
foreach $T_i \in T$ **do**
  Assign T_i to next available time slice;
  Execute T_i for assigned time slice;
  if T_i *is not completed* **then**
    Save T_i's state and re-queue;
  end
end
// Parallel Execution
foreach $T_i \in T$ **do**
  Assign T_i to an available processor core;
  Execute T_i simultaneously;
end

Concurrency maximizes CPU utilization by managing the execution of multiple tasks over time, while parallelism maximizes throughput by dividing tasks across available processing units. Both paradigms often entwine to create robust, high-performance programs, especially in functional programming where immutability and pure functions (deterministic outputs without side-effects) enhance the safety and correctness of concurrent and parallel operations.

It is essential to consider the suitability of concurrency and parallelism based on the problem requirements and available hardware resources. Employing concurrency can enhance responsiveness in I/O-bound applications, while parallelism is advantageous in CPU-bound tasks requiring heavy computations. Understanding when and how to use each approach is a fundamental skill in achieving efficient functional programming in Java.

9.3 Functional Programming and Concurrency

Functional programming (FP) inherently promotes the establishment of concurrent systems. The immutable data structures, pure functions, and lack of side effects cleanly align with the principles of safe concurrent execution. In imperative programming, concurrency often necessitates complex mechanisms for synchronization and state management, leading to potential pitfalls such as deadlocks, race conditions, and other concurrency-related bugs. Conversely, functional programming minimizes these issues through its core tenets.

First, we analyze how immutability contributes to thread safety in FP. When data is immutable, once created, it can't be modified. This means that multiple threads can read the same data without colliquing or needing locks to coordinate changes. Consider the following example:

```
// Java Example: Creating an Immutable Class
public final class Point {
    private final int x;
    private final int y;

    public Point(int x, int y) {
        this.x = x;
        this.y = y;
    }

    public int getX() { return x; }
    public int getY() { return y; }
}
```

In this code, Point is an immutable class. Both x and y are declared as final, ensuring that once they are initialized through the constructor, their values cannot be modified. This immutability means instances of Point can be shared across threads safely without additional synchronization.

Pure functions in FP also align well with concurrent execution. A pure function is deterministic: it always produces the same output given the same input, without any observable side effects. This determinism implies that pure functions can be executed in parallel without dependency conflicts. Consider a function that computes the square of a number:

```
public static int square(int x) {
    return x * x;
}
```

This square function is pure, meaning multiple invocations can be parallelized safely, as shown:

```
// Java Example: Parallel Execution of Pure Functions
import java.util.Arrays;
import java.util.List;

public class ParallelSquares {
    public static void main(String[] args) {
        List<Integer> numbers = Arrays.asList(1, 2, 3, 4, 5);
        numbers.parallelStream()
               .map(ParallelSquares::square)
               .forEach(System.out::println);
    }

    public static int square(int x) {
        return x * x;
    }
}
```

In this example, the numbers list is processed in parallel using parallelStream(). Java Streams API, with its functional-style operations and abstraction, caters to parallel execution models efficiently while maintaining thread safety.

Higher-order functions, which take other functions as arguments or return them as results, further empower concurrency. They allow the composition of small, pure functions into complex operations cleanly and safely. For instance, consider the use of Function interfaces to create more complex transformations:

```
// Java Example: Using Higher-Order Functions
import java.util.function.Function;

public class HigherOrder {
    public static void main(String[] args) {
        Function<Integer, Integer> square = x -> x * x;
        Function<Integer, Integer> increment = x -> x + 1;
        Function<Integer, Integer> squareThenIncrement = square.andThen(increment)
            ;

        System.out.println(squareThenIncrement.apply(2)); // Outputs 5
    }
}
```

The square.then(increment) illustrates function composition, enabling complex operations by chaining simpler, independently testable functions. This functional composition aligns seamlessly with concurrent execution paradigms, where each function can be executed in an isolated and thread-safe context.

Another aspect of FP that supports concurrency is the use of monads for handling state and side effects in a controlled manner. A monad, in its essence, is a design pattern that allows composable computations about pure function context. For example, CompletableFuture in Java offers a monadic way to handle asynchronous computation:

```
// Java Example: Using CompletableFuture for Asynchronous Programming
import java.util.concurrent.CompletableFuture;

public class AsyncDemo {
    public static void main(String[] args) {
        CompletableFuture<Void> future = CompletableFuture.supplyAsync(() -> {
            // Simulate a long-running task
            return "Hello, World!";
        }).thenAccept(System.out::println);

        // Continue with other computations...
        future.join(); // Wait for the completion
    }
}
```

In this example, CompletableFuture.supplyAsync() offloads a task to be executed asynchronously. The subsequent thenAccept(System.out::println) runs a function upon the task's completion, maintaining the operation's purity and immutability.

Through these examples, it is evident that functional programming constructs provide robust foundations for developing concurrent applications. The paradigmatic shift towards immutability, pure functions, higher-order functions, and controlled side effects through monads like CompletableFuture ensures a more deterministic, maintainable, and safer concurrent computing environment in Java.

9.4 Immutability and Thread Safety

Immutability and thread safety are central tenets in concurrent programming, particularly within the realm of functional programming. By understanding and applying immutability, we can simplify the development of thread-safe applications—this section delves into these concepts and their significance.

Immutability refers to objects whose state cannot be modified after their creation. In Java, this can be enforced by using the final keyword. An immutable object ensures that its state remains constant throughout its lifetime, thereby providing stable and predictable behavior in concurrent environments.

For instance, consider the following immutable class in Java:

```
public final class ImmutablePoint {
```

```
    private final int x;
    private final int y;

    public ImmutablePoint(int x, int y) {
        this.x = x;
        this.y = y;
    }

    public int getX() {
        return x;
    }

    public int getY() {
        return y;
    }

    // No set methods provided
}
```

In this class, ImmutablePoint, the x and y coordinates are set during construction and cannot be altered afterward, thus ensuring immutability. The final keyword ensures that these fields are assigned only once, preserving their initial state.

Immutability inherently addresses several concurrency challenges:

- **Thread Safety:** Immutable objects are intrinsically thread-safe. Multiple threads can freely access immutable objects concurrently without the risk of data races, as there are no state changes to cause inconsistent views of the object.
- **Simplicity:** With no state changes to manage, writing and reasoning about concurrent code becomes simpler and less error-prone. This eliminates the need for complex synchronization mechanisms.
- **Caching and Sharing:** Since the state does not change, immutable objects can be safely cached and shared across threads. This can significantly enhance performance by avoiding redundant object creation and minimizing synchronization overhead.

Java's functional programming constructs, such as lambda expressions and Streams, naturally complement immutable designs. When processing collections in parallel, immutable data structures prevent inadvertent side-effects. Consider a scenario where we use Java Streams for parallel processing:

```
List<Integer> numbers = Arrays.asList(1, 2, 3, 4, 5);

int sum = numbers.parallelStream()
```

```
            .mapToInt(Integer::intValue)
            .sum();
```

In this example, the sum of elements within the list numbers is computed in parallel. Since the elements of numbers are immutable Integer objects, there is no risk of modifying shared state, hence thread safety is guaranteed.

Moreover, the immutability principle fits seamlessly with functional programming predicates:

- **Referential Transparency:** Given the immutable nature of objects within functional programming, functions that operate on these objects are referentially transparent, meaning any expression can be replaced by its value without affecting the program's behavior.

- **Pure Functions:** Functions that produce new immutable objects rather than modifying existing ones are pure—yielding the same output for identical input, free from side-effects.

Functional programming's emphasis on immutability and pure functions enhances the predictability and reliability of concurrent and parallel operations. The following example demonstrates a pure function that produces an immutable result:

```
public static List<Integer> incrementAll(List<Integer> numbers) {
    return numbers.stream()
                 .map(n -> n + 1)
                 .collect(Collectors.toList());
}
```

In the function incrementAll, the original list numbers remains unmodified. Instead, a new list containing incremented values is constructed. This practice of creating new immutable objects rather than modifying existing ones aligns well with functional paradigms, facilitating safer concurrent code.

Algorithm 5: Pure Function Example to Increment List Elements

Data: Immutable list of integers
Result: New immutable list with each element incremented by one

```
incrementAll(numbers):
begin
    return numbers.stream().map(n -> n +
      1).collect(Collectors.toList());
end
```

To further reinforce immutability within concurrent programming, Java's standard library provides numerous constructs such as java.util.Collections.unmodifiableList, unmodifiableSet, and unmodifiableMap, which create immutable views over existing collections. These constructs ensure that the underlying data structure cannot be altered through these views.

```
List<String> modifiableList = new ArrayList<>(Arrays.asList("A", "B", "C"));
List<String> immutableList = Collections.unmodifiableList(modifiableList);

// Attempting to modify the immutable list will result in
    UnsupportedOperationException
immutableList.add("D"); // This line will throw an exception
```

While immutability is a powerful concept to enhance thread safety, developers should be mindful of the performance implications it might entail, especially if applied indiscriminately. Creating too many transient immutable objects can lead to increased garbage collection overhead. Therefore, a balanced approach, combined with effective use of concurrent collections and careful profiling, is recommended to optimize both safety and performance.

Understanding and applying immutability is fundamental to achieving thread safety in functional programming. Through consistent use of immutable objects, developers can create robust, predictable, and maintainable concurrent applications in Java.

9.5 Leveraging Java Streams for Parallel Processing

Java Streams provide a powerful mechanism to perform bulk operations on data sequences in both sequential and parallel modes. Leveraging these streams for parallel processing can significantly enhance performance by distributing tasks across multiple threads.

A Stream in Java represents a sequence of elements supporting sequential and parallel aggregate operations. Parallel streams divide the data stream into multiple substreams that are processed in parallel, leveraging the capabilities of modern multi-core processors. To efficiently utilize parallel streams, it is crucial to understand their workings and the underlying principles.

Creating Parallel Streams:

Parallel streams are created from an existing sequential stream using the parallel() method. Alternatively, streams can be created in parallel from collections.

```
List<Integer> numbers = Arrays.asList(1, 2, 3, 4, 5, 6, 7, 8, 9, 10);

// Create a sequential stream
Stream<Integer> sequentialStream = numbers.stream();

// Convert to a parallel stream
Stream<Integer> parallelStream = sequentialStream.parallel();
```

Using Parallel Streams:

Parallel streams can significantly reduce the execution time of aggregate operations such as map, filter, reduce, and others by utilizing multiple threads.

```
List<Integer> numbers = Arrays.asList(1, 2, 3, 4, 5, 6, 7, 8, 9, 10);

// Process elements in parallel
List<Integer> doubledNumbers = numbers.parallelStream()
                                      .map(n -> n * 2)
                                      .collect(Collectors.toList());

System.out.println(doubledNumbers);
```

```
[2, 4, 6, 8, 10, 12, 14, 16, 18, 20]
```

Performance Considerations:

When using parallel streams, certain factors must be considered to maximize performance and avoid pitfalls:

- Splitting: Java parallel streams internally use the ForkJoinPool to split the task into smaller sub-tasks, processed in parallel. Efficient splitting of data significantly influences performance.

- Overhead: Parallelism introduces overhead due to task coordination, thread management, and merging results. For small datasets or simple operations, the overhead of parallelism may outweigh the benefits.

- Mutability: Avoid using mutable data structures within parallel streams to prevent race conditions and data corruption. Preferably, operations should be stateless and free of side effects.

Controlled Parallelism:

The default parallelism level is equal to the number of available processors, but it can be adjusted by configuring the ForkJoinPool.commonPool() or using a custom ForkJoinPool.

```
ForkJoinPool customThreadPool = new ForkJoinPool(4);

customThreadPool.submit(() -> {
    List<Integer> numbers = Arrays.asList(1, 2, 3, 4, 5, 6, 7, 8, 9, 10);
    List<Integer> processedNumbers = numbers.parallelStream()
                                            .map(n -> n * 2)
                                            .collect(Collectors.toList());
    System.out.println(processedNumbers);
}).join();
```

```
[2, 4, 6, 8, 10, 12, 14, 16, 18, 20]
```

Best Practices:

- Benchmarking: Conduct performance benchmarking to evaluate the effectiveness of parallel streams for specific use cases.

- Stream Size: Prefer parallel streams for large collections where the potential performance gains outweigh the overhead.

- Task Complexity: Ensure tasks being parallelized have substantial computational complexity to benefit from multi-threading.

- Effect-Free Functions: Implement functions within streams to be stateless and without side effects for thread safety.

Parallel streams can leverage the full power of multicore architectures, providing significant speedup in appropriate scenarios. Understanding the nuances of their implementation and optimal usage is crucial to unlocking their full potential.

9.6 CompletableFuture and Asynchronous Programming

The CompletableFuture class, introduced in Java 8, is a robust tool for asynchronous programming and represents a *promise* to return a result in the future. Unlike traditional synchronous programming, asynchronous programming allows us to execute tasks concurrently without blocking the main execution flow.

CompletableFuture supports a wide range of applications due to its ability to chain actions and handle results or exceptions once computations are completed. We can use it in a functional programming context to write non-blocking, readable, and maintainable asynchronous code.

```
CompletableFuture<String> future = CompletableFuture.supplyAsync(() -> {
    // Simulate a long-running task
    try {
        Thread.sleep(2000);
    } catch (InterruptedException e) {
        throw new IllegalStateException(e);
    }
    return "Result";
});

future.thenAccept(result -> System.out.println("The result is: " + result));
```

The above code snippet demonstrates creating a CompletableFuture that runs a task asynchronously using supplyAsync. The lambda expression inside supplyAsync simulates a long-running task. Upon completion, the result is processed using thenAccept, which consumes the result without returning a new CompletableFuture.

CompletableFuture provides several methods to combine multiple futures, handle errors, and apply transformations. Here, we enumerate some commonly used methods:

- thenApply: Transforms the result upon completion.
- thenAccept: Consumes the result without returning anything.
- thenCompose: Chains another CompletableFuture.
- exceptionally: Handles exceptions if they occur.
- join: Waits for the completion and retrieves the result.

Chaining Futures: One of the powerful features is chaining multiple asynchronous operations. Consider the following example:

```
CompletableFuture<String> future1 = CompletableFuture.supplyAsync(() -> {
    return "Hello";
});

CompletableFuture<String> future2 = future1.thenApply(result -> {
    return result + " World";
});

future2.thenAccept(result -> System.out.println(result)); // Prints "Hello World"
```

This code initially completes future1 with "Hello", then applies a transformation to append " World" and completes future2. The thenAccept method is used to print the final result.

Combining Futures: We can combine multiple futures to execute tasks in parallel and wait for their completion. The CompletableFuture.allOf and CompletableFuture.anyOf static methods are useful for such scenarios.

```
CompletableFuture<String> future1 = CompletableFuture.supplyAsync(() -> {
    return "Task 1";
});

CompletableFuture<String> future2 = CompletableFuture.supplyAsync(() -> {
    return "Task 2";
});

CompletableFuture<Void> combinedFuture = CompletableFuture.allOf(future1,
      future2);
combinedFuture.thenRun(() -> {
    try {
        System.out.println("Result from future1: " + future1.get());
        System.out.println("Result from future2: " + future2.get());
    } catch (InterruptedException | ExecutionException e) {
        e.printStackTrace();
    }
});
```

Here, CompletableFuture.allOf is used to wait for both future1 and future2 to complete before running the final task that prints their results.

Error Handling: Handling errors in asynchronous workflows is crucial. The exceptionally method allows specifying fallback logic in case of errors:

```
CompletableFuture<String> future = CompletableFuture.supplyAsync(() -> {
    if (Math.random() > 0.5) {
        throw new RuntimeException("Something went wrong!");
    }
    return "Success";
});

future.exceptionally(ex -> {
    System.out.println("Error occurred: " + ex.getMessage());
    return "Failure";
```

```
}).thenAccept(result -> System.out.println(result));
```

In this example, if an exception occurs during the execution, it is handled by exceptionally, which logs the error and returns "Failure". The final thenAccept processes the resolved value of the future, whether it is "Success" or "Failure".

Combining Synchronous and Asynchronous Code: It's possible to mix synchronous and asynchronous code by joining futures synchronously if needed. The join method blocks until the future is complete, returning the result directly:

```
CompletableFuture<String> future = CompletableFuture.supplyAsync(() -> {
    try {
        Thread.sleep(1000);
    } catch (InterruptedException e) {
        throw new IllegalStateException(e);
    }
    return "Completed Future";
});

System.out.println(future.join()); // Blocks and prints "Completed Future"
```

join should be used cautiously as it blocks the calling thread, countering the benefits of asynchronous programming.

Understanding and leveraging CompletableFuture enhances our ability to create responsive and efficient applications, especially when combined with functional programming principles.

9.7 Reactive Programming Basics

Reactive programming is an essential paradigm for building robust, scalable, and efficient applications, especially when dealing with asynchronous data streams and event-driven architectures. It focuses on the propagation of changes and the monitoring of data flows in a non-blocking manner. This section delves into the fundamental concepts and principles of reactive programming, setting the stage for its application in Java.

Observables and Observers: At the heart of reactive programming lies the Observable pattern, which is based on two primary entities: Observable and Observer. An Observable represents a data source or event stream, while an Observer subscribes to this Observable to receive notifications about data changes or events.

```
import io.reactivex.Observable;
```

```
import io.reactivex.Observer;
import io.reactivex.disposables.Disposable;

public class ReactiveExample {
    public static void main(String[] args) {
        Observable<String> observable = Observable.just("Hello", "Reactive", "World")
            ;

        Observer<String> observer = new Observer<String>() {
            @Override
            public void onSubscribe(Disposable d) {
                System.out.println("Subscribed");
            }

            @Override
            public void onNext(String s) {
                System.out.println("Received: " + s);
            }

            @Override
            public void onError(Throwable e) {
                System.out.println("Error: " + e.getMessage());
            }

            @Override
            public void onComplete() {
                System.out.println("Completed");
            }
        };

        observable.subscribe(observer);
    }
}
```

The example above demonstrates the creation of an Observable emitting a sequence of strings and an Observer that reacts to these emissions. The onSubscribe, onNext, onError, and onComplete methods define how the observer handles the subscription, incoming data, errors, and the completion of the data stream, respectively.

Reactive Streams API: The Reactive Streams API in Java provides a standard for asynchronous stream processing with non-blocking backpressure. Backpressure is a mechanism to handle situations where data is produced faster than it can be consumed. The core interfaces of the Reactive Streams API are Publisher, Subscriber, Subscription, and Processor.

```
import org.reactivestreams.Publisher;
import org.reactivestreams.Subscriber;
import org.reactivestreams.Subscription;

public class SimplePublisher implements Publisher<String> {
    @Override
    public void subscribe(Subscriber<? super String> subscriber) {
        subscriber.onSubscribe(new Subscription() {
            @Override
            public void request(long n) {
```

```
                for (int i = 0; i < n; i++) {
                    subscriber.onNext("Message " + i);
                }
                subscriber.onComplete();
            }

            @Override
            public void cancel() {
                // Handle cancellation
            }
        });
    }
}

public class SimpleSubscriber implements Subscriber<String> {
    @Override
    public void onSubscribe(Subscription s) {
        System.out.println("Subscribed");
        s.request(5); // Request 5 items
    }

    @Override
    public void onNext(String s) {
        System.out.println("Received: " + s);
    }

    @Override
    public void onError(Throwable t) {
        System.out.println("Error: " + t.getMessage());
    }

    @Override
    public void onComplete() {
        System.out.println("Completed");
    }
}

public class ReactiveStreamsExample {
    public static void main(String[] args) {
        SimplePublisher publisher = new SimplePublisher();
        SimpleSubscriber subscriber = new SimpleSubscriber();
        publisher.subscribe(subscriber);
    }
}
```

In the above code snippet, the SimplePublisher class implements the Publisher interface and generates a specified number of messages on request. The SimpleSubscriber class subscribes to the publisher and handles the received messages accordingly.

Operators: Operators are functions that allow the transformation, filtering, and combination of data streams. They are the building blocks of reactive programming, enabling complex data flow manipulations with ease.

```
import io.reactivex.Observable;

public class OperatorsExample {
```

```
    public static void main(String[] args) {
        Observable<Integer> observable = Observable.range(1, 10);

        observable
            .filter(i -> i % 2 == 0) // Only even numbers
            .map(i -> "Number: " + i) // Transform each number
            .subscribe(System.out::println);
    }
}
```

In this example, the filter operator is used to allow only even numbers through the stream, and the map operator transforms each number to a string by prefixing it with "Number: ".

Schedulers: Schedulers control the threading model in which the operations are executed. Commonly used schedulers include Schedulers.io(), Schedulers.computation(), and Schedulers.newThread(). They provide flexibility for managing concurrency and parallelism in reactive programming.

```
import io.reactivex.Observable;
import io.reactivex.schedulers.Schedulers;

public class SchedulersExample {
    public static void main(String[] args) throws InterruptedException {
        Observable<Integer> observable = Observable.range(1, 5);

        observable
            .subscribeOn(Schedulers.io())
            .observeOn(Schedulers.computation())
            .subscribe(i -> {
                System.out.println("Received: " + i + " on thread: " + Thread.
                        currentThread().getName());
            });

        // Sleep to allow time for completion
        Thread.sleep(1000);
    }
}
```

This code demonstrates the use of Schedulers.io() to perform work on an I/O thread and Schedulers.computation() for handling computational tasks. The use of subscribeOn and observeOn influences where the subscription and observation of the data stream occur.

Reactive programming enables developers to create responsive, resilient, and scalable applications by leveraging asynchronous data streams, backpressure, operators, and schedulers. These fundamental concepts form the foundation upon which more advanced reactive programming techniques and frameworks are built.

9.8 Using Project Reactor

Project Reactor is a highly efficient and resilient library for building non-blocking applications on the JVM. Built on the Reactive Streams specification, Project Reactor provides a powerful API for composing asynchronous event-driven applications. In this section, we will explore how to utilize Project Reactor effectively in Java, taking advantage of its flux and mono types, schedulers, and advanced operators to handle complex data flows and asynchronous tasks.

Project Reactor introduces two main types to represent asynchronous sequences: Flux and Mono. A Flux represents a stream of 0 to N elements, whereas a Mono represents a stream of 0 to 1 element. These types form the cornerstone of Reactor's API, allowing developers to build efficient and scalable applications.

```
Flux<String> stringFlux = Flux.just("Hello", "Reactive", "World");
```

The example above demonstrates the creation of a Flux that emits a sequence of three strings. The just method is a convenient way to create a Flux from a finite sequence of elements.

For more dynamic data flows, Reactor offers a plethora of operators to transform, combine, filter, and process sequences.

```
Flux<Integer> numberFlux = Flux.range(1, 10)
    .filter(number -> number % 2 == 0)
    .map(number -> number * number);
```

Here, Flux.range generates a sequence of integers from 1 to 10. The filter operator retains only even numbers, and the map operator transforms these numbers by squaring them. Operators are chained to form a seamless data processing pipeline.

For handling scenarios involving a single data item or an empty state, the Mono type is appropriate.

```
Mono<String> helloMono = Mono.just("Hello Mono");
```

Project Reactor facilitates the orchestration of asynchronous tasks through its Schedulers. A Scheduler represents an execution context such as a bounded elastic thread pool, a single thread, or an immediate execution.

```
Flux<String> asyncFlux = Flux.just("Task1", "Task2", "Task3")
    .delayElements(Duration.ofSeconds(1))
    .publishOn(Schedulers.boundedElastic());
```

The example uses delayElements to introduce a delay between emissions, and publishOn to shift the execution context to a bounded elastic scheduler. This approach enables non-blocking operations by offloading work to a pool of worker threads.

Advanced compositions involving Flux and Mono types can be achieved using zip, merge, combineLatest, and other combinator operators.

```
Flux<String> flux1 = Flux.just("A", "B", "C");
Flux<String> flux2 = Flux.just("1", "2", "3");

Flux<String> zippedFlux = Flux.zip(flux1, flux2, (a, b) -> a + b);
// Result: A1, B2, C3
```

In the example, Flux.zip combines two Flux instances, emitting paired values as tuples, which are transformed as specified in the provided BiFunction.

For error handling, Reactor provides operators such as onErrorResume, onErrorReturn, and retry.

```
Flux<String> fluxWithError = Flux.just("A", "B")
    .concatWith(Flux.error(new RuntimeException("Error occurred")))
    .onErrorResume(e -> Flux.just("Recovered"));
```

onErrorResume allows the sequence to continue with a fallback Flux in case of an error, ensuring fault tolerance in reactive pipelines.

Project Reactor integrates seamlessly with existing Java concurrency utilities, providing a comprehensive toolkit for building reactive applications. Conformance to the Reactive Streams specification ensures interoperability with other reactive libraries and frameworks.

A thorough grasp of Project Reactor's abstractions and operators empowers developers to create responsive and resilient systems. Understanding the interplay of Flux, Mono, and Schedulers, along with effective error handling and composition techniques, is crucial for harnessing the full potential of reactive programming in Java.

9.9 Akka and Actor Model in Java

The Actor Model is a conceptual framework for handling concurrent computation. In this model, "actors" are the fundamental units of computation that encapsulate state and behavior. Actors communicate exclusively by sending and receiving messages, ensuring that state is not shared between actors, thus avoiding the pitfalls of synchronization.

Akka is a popular toolkit for building concurrent and distributed applications on the Java Virtual Machine (JVM). It leverages the Actor Model to provide a higher level of abstraction for writing concurrent code. Akka ensures that developers can build robust, scalable, and resilient systems without delving deeply into the complexities of thread management.

To understand Akka in the context of Java, we will cover essential concepts including actor creation, message passing, actor lifecycle, actor supervision, and remote actors.

Actor Creation:

In Akka, actors are created using the ActorSystem and ActorRef classes. Each actor has an associated ActorRef that acts as a reference to communicate with the actor.

```
import akka.actor.ActorSystem;
import akka.actor.AbstractActor;
import akka.actor.Props;
import akka.actor.ActorRef;

public class MyActor extends AbstractActor {
    @Override
    public Receive createReceive() {
        return receiveBuilder()
                .match(String.class, message -> {
                    System.out.println("Received String message: " + message);
                })
                .build();
    }

    public static void main(String[] args) {
        ActorSystem system = ActorSystem.create("mySystem");
        ActorRef myActor = system.actorOf(Props.create(MyActor.class), "myActor");

        myActor.tell("Hello Actor", ActorRef.noSender());
    }
}
```

In the example above, MyActor extends AbstractActor and overrides the createReceive method to define the behavior when a message is received. The ActorSystem named mySystem is instantiated, and an actor of type MyActor is created with the name myActor.

Message Passing:

Actors communicate by sending messages to each other. This can be done through the tell and ask methods.

```
myActor.tell("Another message", ActorRef.noSender());
```

The tell method sends a message asynchronously, without expecting a response. The ask method, on the other hand, expects a response and returns a Future.

```
import akka.pattern.Patterns;
import scala.concurrent.Future;
import scala.concurrent.Await;
import scala.concurrent.duration.Duration;

Future<Object> future = Patterns.ask(myActor, "What's the time?", 1000);
String result = (String) Await.result(future, Duration.create(1, "seconds"));
System.out.println("Response: " + result);
```

Actor Lifecycle:

Actors have a lifecycle that includes stages such as creation, running, and termination. Akka provides hooks to manage actions at different stages using the preStart and postStop methods.

```
@Override
public void preStart() {
    System.out.println("Actor is starting up!");
}

@Override
public void postStop() {
    System.out.println("Actor has stopped!");
}
```

The actor's lifecycle is crucial for ensuring clean resource management and predictable behavior in a concurrent system.

Actor Supervision:

Supervision in Akka follows the "let it crash" philosophy, where actors are supervised by their parents. Supervisors manage the lifecycle and failure handling of child actors.

Algorithm 6: Supervision Strategy in Akka

```
Input: Supervised child actor
Output: Decision to restart, stop, resume, or escalate
if child actor fails then
    Analyze the type of failure;
    if failure is recoverable then
        Restart the child actor;
    else
        Stop the child actor;
    if parent cannot handle then
        Escalate the failure to the parent;
```

```
import akka.actor.OneForOneStrategy;
import akka.actor.SupervisorStrategy;
import akka.actor.Actor;
import akka.actor.Props;
import static akka.actor.SupervisorStrategy.restart;
import static akka.actor.SupervisorStrategy.stop;

public class Supervisor extends AbstractActor {
    private static SupervisorStrategy strategy =
        new OneForOneStrategy(10, Duration.create("1 minute"),
        DeciderBuilder.match(Exception.class, e -> restart())
                    .match(RuntimeException.class, e -> stop())
                    .build());

    @Override
    public SupervisorStrategy supervisorStrategy() {
        return strategy;
    }

    @Override
    public Receive createReceive() {
        return receiveBuilder().build();
    }

    public static void main(String[] args) {
        ActorSystem system = ActorSystem.create("supervisionSystem");
        ActorRef supervisor = system.actorOf(Props.create(Supervisor.class), "
              supervisor");
        ActorRef child = system.actorOf(Props.create(MyActor.class), "child");

        child.tell(new RuntimeException(), ActorRef.noSender()); // This will stop the
              child actor
    }
}
```

Remote Actors:

Akka allows actors to communicate across different JVMs through Akka Remote. This capability is essential for building distributed systems.

```
akka {
  actor {
    provider = remote
  }

  remote {
    artery {
      enabled = on
      transport = tcp
      canonical.hostname = "127.0.0.1"
      canonical.port = 2552
    }
  }
}
```

Akka and the Actor Model in Java provide a powerful abstraction for building concurrent and distributed systems. By encapsulating state within actors and using message passing for communication, Akka ensures that developers can write scalable and resilient code without dealing with the intricacies of low-level concurrency constructs.

9.10 Concurrency Utilities in Java

Java provides a rich set of utilities within the java.util.concurrent package to facilitate the development of concurrent programs. These utilities offer various mechanisms to handle threads, tasks, synchronization, and coordination. This section delves into several of these utilities and their applications in functional programming.

Executor Framework

The Executor framework is a key component for managing threads in a scalable and efficient manner. It abstracts the creation, management, and scheduling of threads from the application's business logic. The core interface in this framework is Executor, which provides a simple interface for launching new tasks:

```
Executor executor = Executors.newFixedThreadPool(10);
executor.execute(() -> System.out.println("Task executed"));
```

Executors is a factory class that provides various methods to create thread pools, such as newFixedThreadPool, newCachedThreadPool, and newSingleThreadExecutor. These methods are designed for different use cases, offering different performance and resource usage characteristics.

Future and Callable

To retrieve results from concurrent tasks, Java provides the Future interface and the Callable interface. While Runnable does not return any result, Callable can return a result and throw a checked exception.

Here is an example of submitting a Callable task to an ExecutorService and retrieving the result using a Future:

```
ExecutorService executorService = Executors.newFixedThreadPool(10);
Callable<String> task = () -> {
    Thread.sleep(1000);
    return "Task completed";
};
Future<String> future = executorService.submit(task);
```

```
if (future.isDone()) {
    String result = future.get(); // Can throw InterruptedException or
        ExecutionException
    System.out.println(result);
}
```

CompletionService

The CompletionService interface combines the functionalities of an Executor and a BlockingQueue to manage the tasks' completion order. The ExecutorCompletionService is a concrete implementation of this interface.

```
ExecutorService executorService = Executors.newFixedThreadPool(10);
CompletionService<String> completionService = new ExecutorCompletionService<>(
    executorService);

for (int i = 0; i < 5; i++) {
    final int taskId = i;
    completionService.submit(() -> {
        Thread.sleep(1000);
        return "Task " + taskId + " completed";
    });
}

for (int i = 0; i < 5; i++) {
    Future<String> future = completionService.take();
    System.out.println(future.get());
}
```

ForkJoinPool and RecursiveTask

For divide-and-conquer algorithms, ForkJoinPool is a suitable executor service. It implements work-stealing, allowing idle threads to take tasks from busy threads. The RecursiveTask and RecursiveAction classes are designed for tasks that can be recursively broken down into smaller tasks.

Here is an example of a simple recursive task using ForkJoinPool to calculate the sum of an array segment:

```
class SumTask extends RecursiveTask<Integer> {
    private final int[] array;
    private final int start;
    private final int end;

    public SumTask(int[] array, int start, int end) {
        this.array = array;
        this.start = start;
        this.end = end;
```

```
    }

    @Override
    protected Integer compute() {
        if (end - start <= 10) { // Threshold for sequential computation
            int sum = 0;
            for (int i = start; i < end; i++) {
                sum += array[i];
            }
            return sum;
        } else {
            int mid = (start + end) / 2;
            SumTask leftTask = new SumTask(array, start, mid);
            SumTask rightTask = new SumTask(array, mid, end);
            invokeAll(leftTask, rightTask);
            return leftTask.join() + rightTask.join();
        }
    }
}

ForkJoinPool forkJoinPool = new ForkJoinPool();
int[] array = {1, 2, 3, 4, 5, 6, 7, 8, 9, 10};
SumTask task = new SumTask(array, 0, array.length);
int result = forkJoinPool.invoke(task);
System.out.println("Sum: " + result);
```

Synchronizers

Java provides various synchronizers that help in controlling the interaction between threads. This section focuses on CountDownLatch, CyclicBarrier, and Semaphore.

CountDownLatch allows one or more threads to wait until a set of operations in other threads completes:

```
CountDownLatch latch = new CountDownLatch(3);

for (int i = 0; i < 3; i++) {
    new Thread(() -> {
        System.out.println("Thread " + Thread.currentThread().getId() + " started");
        latch.countDown();
        System.out.println("Thread " + Thread.currentThread().getId() + " ended");
    }).start();
}
latch.await();
System.out.println("All threads completed");
```

CyclicBarrier is used to make threads wait at a predefined execution point until a given number of threads have reached that point:

```
CyclicBarrier barrier = new CyclicBarrier(3, () -> System.out.println("Barrier Reached
    "));

for (int i = 0; i < 3; i++) {
    new Thread(() -> {
```

```
        System.out.println("Thread " + Thread.currentThread().getId() + " started");
        barrier.await();
        System.out.println("Thread " + Thread.currentThread().getId() + " crossed
            barrier");
    }).start();
}
```

Semaphore controls access to a shared resource with a set number of permits:

```
Semaphore semaphore = new Semaphore(2);

for (int i = 0; i < 5; i++) {
    new Thread(() -> {
        try {
            semaphore.acquire();
            System.out.println("Thread " + Thread.currentThread().getId() + "
                acquired permit");
            Thread.sleep(1000);
        } catch (InterruptedException e) {
            Thread.currentThread().interrupt();
        } finally {
            semaphore.release();
            System.out.println("Thread " + Thread.currentThread().getId() + " released
                permit");
        }
    }).start();
}
```

These utilities are instrumental in handling various concurrency scenarios efficiently. By leveraging these robust mechanisms, programmers can create more responsive and stable multi-threaded applications. Their effective use is essential for achieving functional concurrency and ensuring thread safety and performance in Java applications.

9.11 Best Practices for Functional Concurrency

Designing and implementing concurrent systems in a functional programming paradigm requires adherence to certain best practices to ensure efficiency, maintainability, and correctness. The following practices are essential in utilizing Java's concurrency mechanisms while adhering to functional programming principles.

Embrace Immutability: Immutability is a cornerstone of functional programming and plays a crucial role in concurrent systems. Since immutable objects cannot change state once created, there are no consistency issues when multiple threads access the same data. In Java, use final keyword extensively to define immutable fields.

```
public class ImmutablePoint {
    private final int x;
    private final int y;

    public ImmutablePoint(int x, int y) {
        this.x = x;
        this.y = y;
    }

    public int getX() {
        return x;
    }

    public int getY() {
        return y;
    }
}
```

Minimize Shared State: Shared mutable state is the primary cause of concurrency issues. Whenever possible, avoid sharing state between threads. Employ local variables that are confined to the method scope or use thread-safe data structures such as ConcurrentHashMap.

```
ConcurrentMap<String, Integer> concurrentMap = new ConcurrentHashMap<>();

public void incrementValue(String key) {
    concurrentMap.merge(key, 1, Integer::sum);
}
```

Leverage Pure Functions: Pure functions help avoid side effects, making them inherently thread-safe. When functions do not rely on or alter shared state, the risk of race conditions and other concurrency problems is minimized.

```
public int add(int a, int b) {
    return a + b;
}
```

Utilize Higher-Order Functions: Functions that take other functions as parameters or return them can help abstract control structures and minimize direct handling of threads and synchronization.

```
public static <T, R> List<R> map(List<T> list, Function<T, R> function) {
    return list.stream().map(function).collect(Collectors.toList());
}
```

Prefer ForkJoinPool for Parallel Tasks: ForkJoinPool is a specialized implementation of the ExecutorService interface designed to work well with computation-intensive parallelism. Use it in combination with Java streams for parallel processing.

```
int sum = Arrays.asList(1, 2, 3, 4, 5)
    .parallelStream()
    .reduce(0, Integer::sum);
```

Apply Functional Data Structures: Functional data structures like PersistentList or PersistentMap are inherently thread-safe and can be used in concurrent scenarios without explicit synchronization.

```
PersistentMap<String, Integer> persistentMap = new PersistentHashMap<>();
persistentMap = persistentMap.plus("key", 1);
```

Use CompletableFuture for Async Operations: Utilize CompletableFuture for non-blocking asynchronous computations. This can lead to more responsive applications without the complexity of manually managing threads.

```
CompletableFuture.supplyAsync(() -> calculateResult())
    .thenAccept(result -> System.out.println("Result: " + result));
```

Implement Reactive Programming Using Project Reactor: Project Reactor provides a powerful API for building reactive applications in Java. Non-blocking, backpressure-aware streams help manage asynchronous data streams effectively.

```
Flux<Integer> numbers = Flux.range(1, 10)
    .map(i -> i * 2)
    .filter(i -> i % 3 == 0);
numbers.subscribe(System.out::println);
```

Prefer Actors for Stateful Concurrency: The Actor model, as implemented by Akka, encapsulates state within actors. Actors process messages asynchronously, reducing the complexity of thread management and synchronization.

```
public class CounterActor extends AbstractActor {
    private int counter = 0;

    @Override
    public Receive createReceive() {
        return receiveBuilder()
            .match(Integer.class, i -> {
                counter += i;
                getSender().tell(counter, getSelf());
            })
            .build();
    }
}
```

Monitor and Profile Concurrency Performance: Employ tools like Java Mission Control and VisualVM to profile and monitor the performance of concurrent applications. Identifying bottlenecks and contention points early can help in optimizing the concurrency aspects of the application.

```
ThreadMXBean threadMXBean = ManagementFactory.getThreadMXBean();
long[] threadIds = threadMXBean.findDeadlockedThreads();
if (threadIds != null) {
    ThreadInfo[] threadInfos = threadMXBean.getThreadInfo(threadIds);
    for (ThreadInfo threadInfo : threadInfos) {
        System.out.println("Deadlocked Thread: " + threadInfo.getThreadName());
    }
}
```

Adhering to these practices fosters the development of robust, maintainable, and efficient concurrent systems in Java while staying true to the principles of functional programming.

Chapter 10

Practical Applications of Functional Programming in Java

This chapter demonstrates real-world applications of functional programming in Java. It covers functional data transformation, building domain-specific languages, and implementing business rules engines. The chapter also explores event-driven systems, data validation, configuration management, and querying collections using functional techniques. Additionally, practical examples include web services, REST APIs, and handling JSON and XML in a functional style, providing actionable insights and case studies to illustrate the benefits and practical implementation of functional programming in various domains.

10.1 Introduction to Practical Applications

Functional programming in Java offers numerous advantages for developing robust, maintainable, and scalable software systems. While the theoretical underpinnings of functional programming are essential for understanding its principles, this section focuses on its practical applications in real-world scenarios. The principles covered in this chapter can be employed to solve a wide range of problems, from data transformation and querying through modern web service design, to implementing sophisticated domain-specific languages (DSLs) and business rules engines.

A focal point of functional programming is the use of higher-order functions, which are functions that can take other functions as arguments or return them as results. This concept, combined with immutability and referential transparency, underpins many practical applications discussed here. Java 8 and later versions facilitate functional programming via the java.util.function package and the Stream API. These tools enable developers to write concise and expressive code while maintaining high levels of abstraction.

One of the practical applications of functional programming is functional data transformation. By leveraging Streams and lambda expressions, data can be processed in a clean and modular fashion. Consider a scenario where we need to filter, transform, and collect a list of objects:

```
List<String> names = Arrays.asList("Alice", "Bob", "Charlie", "Dave");
List<String> result = names.stream()
    .filter(name -> name.startsWith("A") || name.startsWith("B"))
    .map(String::toUpperCase)
    .collect(Collectors.toList());
System.out.println(result);
```

This snippet demonstrates transforming a stream of names by filtering those starting with 'A' or 'B', mapping each name to uppercase, and collecting the results into a list:

```
[Alice, Bob]
```

Building domain-specific languages (DSLs) is another powerful application of functional programming in Java. DSLs allow developers to write code in a language tailored to a specific problem domain, improving readability and expressiveness. By using functional programming constructs, it's possible to implement lightweight DSLs efficiently. For instance, consider a mini-DSL for constructing SQL queries:

```
public interface SQL {
    SQL select(String columns);
    SQL from(String table);
    SQL where(String condition);
    String build();
}

public class SQLBuilder implements SQL {
    private StringBuilder query = new StringBuilder();

    public SQL select(String columns) {
        query.append("SELECT ").append(columns).append(" ");
        return this;
    }
```

```
    public SQL from(String table) {
        query.append("FROM ").append(table).append(" ");
        return this;
    }

    public SQL where(String condition) {
        query.append("WHERE ").append(condition).append(" ");
        return this;
    }

    public String build() {
        return query.toString().trim();
    }
}

public class Main {
    public static void main(String[] args) {
        SQL sql = new SQLBuilder();
        String query = sql.select("*")
                          .from("users")
                          .where("age > 30")
                          .build();
        System.out.println(query);
    }
}
```

This example illustrates a fluent interface for query construction where each method returns an instance of SQL, enabling method chaining:

```
SELECT * FROM users WHERE age > 30
```

Implementing business rules engines is another significant application of functional programming. Business rules engines separate business logic from application code, enabling non-developers to modify business rules without changing the source code. Functional programming can aid in creating these engines by using function composition and higher-order functions. Consider an engine that processes orders based on different discount strategies:

```
interface DiscountStrategy {
    double apply(double totalPrice);
}

public class OrderProcessor {
    public double processOrder(double totalPrice, DiscountStrategy strategy) {
        return strategy.apply(totalPrice);
    }
}

public class Main {
    public static void main(String[] args) {
        DiscountStrategy christmasDiscount = price -> price * 0.9;
        DiscountStrategy newYearDiscount = price -> price * 0.85;

        OrderProcessor processor = new OrderProcessor();
        double price = 100.0;
```

```
        System.out.println("Christmas Discount: " + processor.processOrder(price,
            christmasDiscount));
        System.out.println("New Year Discount: " + processor.processOrder(price,
            newYearDiscount));
    }
}
```

This approach separates discount rules from the order processing logic, making it easy to add new strategies or modify existing ones:

```
Christmas Discount: 90.0
New Year Discount: 85.0
```

Event-driven systems rely heavily on functional programming paradigms. Events can be processed and handled using higher-order functions and event listeners, ensuring that the logic is modular and easily extendable. The Observer pattern, frequently used in event-driven systems, fits naturally with functional programming. Java's java.util.Observer and java.util.Observable can be utilized, but functional constructs like streams or reactive libraries such as RxJava provide more expressive alternatives.

```
import io.reactivex.Observable;

public class EventDrivenSystem {
    public static void main(String[] args) {
        Observable<String> eventStream = Observable.just("Event1", "Event2", "
            Event3");

        eventStream.subscribe(event -> System.out.println("Received: " + event));
    }
}
```

The event stream is observed, and each event is processed as it is emitted:

```
Received: Event1
Received: Event2
Received: Event3
```

Each of these practical applications showcases the versatility and power of functional programming in Java. By increasing the abstraction level and enhancing code reusability and readability, functional programming equips developers with tools to tackle a variety of software development challenges efficiently and effectively.

10.2 Functional Data Transformation

Functional programming facilitates the transformation of data through the use of higher-order functions, immutability, and pure functions.

Java, since the advent of Java 8, has incorporated numerous functional constructs, allowing developers to apply functional programming paradigms to solve various data transformation problems effectively. This section delves into the mechanisms and paradigms that drive functional data transformation in Java and provides practical examples to elucidate these concepts.

Higher-Order Functions Higher-order functions are functions that either take other functions as parameters, return functions, or both. In Java, java.util.function package provides several functional interfaces, such as Function, Predicate, and Consumer, which are pivotal for functional data transformation.

```
List<Integer> numbers = Arrays.asList(1, 2, 3, 4, 5);

List<Integer> squaredNumbers = numbers.stream()
    .map(x -> x * x)
    .collect(Collectors.toList());

System.out.println(squaredNumbers);
```

```
[1, 4, 9, 16, 25]
```

In the above code, we use the Stream.map() method, which applies a given function to each element of the stream, producing a new stream of transformed elements. By employing a lambda expression, x -> x * x, we succinctly define the transformation logic required to compute the squares of the integers in the list.

Function<T, R> interface represents a function that accepts one argument of type T and produces a result of type R. The use of Stream API and function composition principles allow for elegant and concise data transformations.

Filtering Data with Predicate Filtering is a fundamental operation in data transformation, enabling the selection of specific elements based on predefined criteria. Predicate<T> is a functional interface that represents a predicate (boolean-valued function) of one argument. The Stream.filter() method utilizes a predicate to filter elements.

```
List<Integer> evenNumbers = numbers.stream()
    .filter(x -> x % 2 == 0)
    .collect(Collectors.toList());

System.out.println(evenNumbers);
```

```
[2, 4]
```

In this example, the lambda expression x -> x % 2 == 0 serves as the filtering criterion, yielding a new list consisting solely of even numbers.

Combining multiple operations, such as mapping and filtering, can yield powerful and flexible data transformation pipelines.

```
List<Integer> squaredEvenNumbers = numbers.stream()
    .filter(x -> x % 2 == 0)
    .map(x -> x * x)
    .collect(Collectors.toList());

System.out.println(squaredEvenNumbers);
```

```
[4, 16]
```

This combined approach first filters the input list to retain even numbers and subsequently maps these filtered elements to their squares.

Using Optional for Safe Transformations Functional programming emphasizes the avoidance of null values, and Java provides the Optional<T> class to encapsulate optional values, which may or may not be present. This approach ensures safer transformations.

```
Optional<String> optionalString = Optional.ofNullable("hello");

Optional<Integer> stringLength = optionalString.map(String::length);

stringLength.ifPresent(System.out::println);
```

```
5
```

In this example, Optional.ofNullable() initializes an Optional object, and the map() method is used to transform the encapsulated value if it is present, thus avoiding potential NullPointerExceptions.

Grouping and Partitioning Data Complex data transformations often require grouping or partitioning of data based on certain characteristics. Java's Collectors utility provides the groupingBy() and partitioningBy() methods to achieve this.

```
Map<Boolean, List<Integer>> groupedNumbers = numbers.stream()
    .collect(Collectors.groupingBy(x -> x % 2 == 0));

System.out.println(groupedNumbers);
```

```
{false=[1, 3, 5], true=[2, 4]}
```

The groupingBy() method partitions the list into two groups, one for even and one for odd numbers. Similarly, the partitioningBy() method can be used to directly create a map of boolean values.

```
Map<Boolean, List<Integer>> partitionedNumbers = numbers.stream()
    .collect(Collectors.partitioningBy(x -> x % 2 == 0));

System.out.println(partitionedNumbers);
```

```
{false=[1, 3, 5], true=[2, 4]}
```

Both methods offer powerful mechanisms for categorizing data, pivotal for constructing complex datasets that cater to specific business logic requirements. Functional programming paradigms, coupled with Java's rich API features, provide an extensive toolkit for transforming data in precise and effective manners, facilitating the development of robust and maintainable software systems.

10.3 Building Domain-Specific Languages (DSL)

When constructing Domain-Specific Languages (DSLs) within Java, functional programming techniques provide a versatile and expressive toolkit. DSLs are specialized mini-languages designed for a specific aspect of an application. They enable domain experts to express solutions directly in the domain semantics, improving readability and maintainability.

Create a Fluent Interface: Java's lambda expressions and method references can craft a fluent interface for a DSL. A fluent interface uses method chaining to create more readable code. Here is an example of a DSL for constructing SQL queries:

```
public class SQLQuery {
    private String table;
    private List<String> columns;
    private String condition;

    public SQLQuery select(String... columns) {
        this.columns = Arrays.asList(columns);
        return this;
    }

    public SQLQuery from(String table) {
        this.table = table;
        return this;
    }

    public SQLQuery where(String condition) {
        this.condition = condition;
        return this;
    }

    @Override
    public String toString() {
        return "SELECT " + String.join(", ", columns) +
               " FROM " + table +
               (condition != null ? " WHERE " + condition : "");
    }
```

```
}

// Usage Example
SQLQuery query = new SQLQuery()
                    .select("id", "name", "age")
                    .from("users")
                    .where("age > 18");
System.out.println(query);
```

SELECT id, name, age FROM users WHERE age > 18

Leveraging Functional Interfaces: When implementing DSLs, Java's functional interfaces (e.g., Function, Predicate) can create more powerful and reusable abstractions within the DSL. Here's an example that uses higher-order functions to build a DSL for filtering collections:

```
@FunctionalInterface
interface Predicate<T> {
    boolean test(T t);
}

public class FilterDSL<T> {
    private Predicate<T> predicate;

    public FilterDSL<T> where(Predicate<T> predicate) {
        this.predicate = predicate;
        return this;
    }

    public List<T> apply(List<T> items) {
        return items.stream()
                    .filter(predicate::test)
                    .collect(Collectors.toList());
    }
}

// Usage Example
FilterDSL<Integer> filter = new FilterDSL<Integer>()
                                .where(x -> x > 10);

List<Integer> numbers = Arrays.asList(5, 15, 20, 25);
List<Integer> filtered = filter.apply(numbers);

System.out.println(filtered);
```

[15, 20, 25]

Defining Grammar with Enums and Builder Patterns: Using enums and builder patterns can define the grammar of a DSL, ensuring the syntax rules are adhered to. Below is an example of a DSL for constructing arithmetic expressions:

```
public enum Operator {
    ADD, SUBTRACT, MULTIPLY, DIVIDE
}

public class Expression {
```

```
    private final int leftOperand;
    private final int rightOperand;
    private final Operator operator;

    private Expression(int leftOperand, int rightOperand, Operator operator) {
        this.leftOperand = leftOperand;
        this.rightOperand = rightOperand;
        this.operator = operator;
    }

    public static class Builder {
        private int leftOperand;
        private int rightOperand;
        private Operator operator;

        public Builder left(int leftOperand) {
            this.leftOperand = leftOperand;
            return this;
        }

        public Builder right(int rightOperand) {
            this.rightOperand = rightOperand;
            return this;
        }

        public Builder operator(Operator operator) {
            this.operator = operator;
            return this;
        }

        public Expression build() {
            return new Expression(leftOperand, rightOperand, operator);
        }
    }

    @Override
    public String toString() {
        return leftOperand + " " + operator + " " + rightOperand;
    }

    public int evaluate() {
        switch (operator) {
            case ADD: return leftOperand + rightOperand;
            case SUBTRACT: return leftOperand - rightOperand;
            case MULTIPLY: return leftOperand * rightOperand;
            case DIVIDE: return leftOperand / rightOperand;
            default: throw new IllegalArgumentException("Unknown operator: " +
                    operator);
        }
    }
}
// Usage Example
Expression exp = new Expression.Builder()
                .left(10)
                .right(5)
                .operator(Operator.ADD)
                .build();

System.out.println(exp + " = " + exp.evaluate());
```

```
10 ADD 5 = 15
```

Combining Functional Programming with DSLs: Functional programming's declarative style simplifies constructing and chaining operations within DSLs. Consider a domain-specific language for configuration:

```
public class ConfigDSL {
    private Map<String, String> settings = new HashMap<>();

    public ConfigDSL set(String key, String value) {
        settings.put(key, value);
        return this;
    }

    public ConfigDSL loadFrom(Properties properties) {
        properties.forEach((key, value) -> settings.put((String) key, (String) value));
        return this;
    }

    public ConfigDSL apply(Consumer<Map<String, String>> configFunction) {
        configFunction.accept(settings);
        return this;
    }

    public Map<String, String> getSettings() {
        return settings;
    }
}

// Usage Example
Properties props = new Properties();
props.setProperty("db.url", "jdbc:mysql://localhost:3306/mydb");
props.setProperty("db.user", "admin");
props.setProperty("db.password", "password");

ConfigDSL config = new ConfigDSL()
                    .set("app.name", "MyApp")
                    .loadFrom(props)
                    .apply(settings -> settings.put("app.version", "1.0.0"));

System.out.println(config.getSettings());
```

```
{app.name=MyApp, db.url=jdbc:mysql://localhost:3306/mydb, db.user=admin,
 db.password=password, app.version=1.0.0}
```

These examples illustrate designing DSLs using Java's functional programming capabilities to achieve both expressiveness and flexibility. Employing fluent interfaces, functional interfaces, builder patterns, and declarative constructs contributes to creating robust and maintainable domain-specific languages.

10.4 Implementing Business Rules Engine

In this section, we delve into the construction of a Business Rules Engine (BRE) using functional programming concepts in Java. The primary objective of a BRE is to separate business logic from the core application code, enhancing maintainability and scalability. By leveraging functional programming paradigms, we can ensure the Business Rules Engine is both flexible and efficient.

To begin with, let's conceptualize a Business Rule. In our context, a business rule is a specification that describes how certain business operations should be conducted. Typically, business rules are represented as conditional statements that execute certain actions when specific conditions are met. The declarative nature of functional programming is well-suited to expressing such logic, allowing us to articulate rules succinctly and clearly.

We start by considering a basic representation of a business rule. Each rule consists of a predicate (a test condition) and an action (the behavior to execute if the predicate holds true).

```
@FunctionalInterface
interface Rule {
    boolean condition(Object context);

    default void action(Object context) {
        // Default action implementation (if any)
    }
}
```

In the above code snippet, Rule is a functional interface representing a business rule. It contains a method condition, which evaluates to true or false based on the given context. The context is represented as a generic Object here, but in practical applications, it would be a more specific type corresponding to the application's data model.

The next step is to define specific rules by implementing the Rule interface.

```
class AgeRule implements Rule {
    @Override
    public boolean condition(Object context) {
        User user = (User) context;
        return user.getAge() > 18;
    }

    @Override
    public void action(Object context) {
        User user = (User) context;
        user.setExecutedRules("AgeRule");
```

```
    }
}

class AccountActiveRule implements Rule {
    @Override
    public boolean condition(Object context) {
        User user = (User) context;
        return user.isActive();
    }

    @Override
    public void action(Object context) {
        User user = (User) context;
        user.setExecutedRules("AccountActiveRule");
    }
}
```

Here, we define two rules: AgeRule and AccountActiveRule. Each has its condition logic encapsulated within the condition method. If a condition evaluates to true, the corresponding action method will be executed, which marks the rule as executed in the User object.

To manage and apply these rules, we will create a RuleEngine.

```
class RuleEngine {
    private final List<Rule> rules;

    public RuleEngine(List<Rule> rules) {
        this.rules = rules;
    }

    public void process(Object context) {
        for (Rule rule : rules) {
            if (rule.condition(context)) {
                rule.action(context);
            }
        }
    }
}
```

The RuleEngine class accepts a list of rules upon instantiation. The process method iterates through each rule and executes it if the condition is satisfied. The context represents the state of the application (e.g., a User object).

We can now bring it all together to see the Business Rules Engine in action.

```
public class BREExample {
    public static void main(String[] args) {
        User user = new User(20, true);

        List<Rule> rules = Arrays.asList(new AgeRule(), new AccountActiveRule());

        RuleEngine engine = new RuleEngine(rules);
        engine.process(user);
```

```
        System.out.println("Executed Rules: " + user.getExecutedRules());
    }
}
```

```
Executed Rules: [AgeRule, AccountActiveRule]
```

In the above example, we instantiate a User object and a list of rules. The RuleEngine processes these rules against the User context. As both conditions are met (user age is greater than 18 and account is active), the actions associated with the AgeRule and AccountActiveRule are executed, and the executed rules are printed.

Functional programming excels at handling business rules due to higher-order functions and lambda expressions.

```
Rule ageRule = (context) -> ((User) context).getAge() > 18;
Rule activeRule = (context) -> ((User) context).isActive();

List<Rule> lambdaRules = Arrays.asList(ageRule, activeRule);

RuleEngine lambdaEngine = new RuleEngine(lambdaRules);
lambdaEngine.process(user);
```

Lambda expressions simplify rule definitions, making the rules more concise. Functional programming constructs enhance the modularity of business rule definitions, promoting reuse and reducing redundancy.

Implementing a Business Rules Engine using functional programming paradigms in Java brings about several benefits: clearer rule definitions, decoupled business logic, and enhanced code maintainability. Each rule is self-contained, promoting better organization and testability.

10.5 Event-Driven Systems

Event-driven systems are a core architectural pattern in modern software development, where the flow of the program is determined by events - actions or occurrences recognized by software, generated by the user, other programs, or the system itself. This section delves into how functional programming paradigms in Java can be effectively utilized to engineer robust event-driven systems.

A fundamental principle of event-driven systems is the decoupling of event producers and event consumers. Producers generate events that are consumed by handlers or listeners. This design promotes a loose coupling and enhances the scalability and maintainability of the system.

In Java, the functional programming approach can be leveraged to handle events in a declarative manner. One commonly used library for facilitating event-driven programming in Java is the Project Reactor, which is part of the Reactive Streams initiative. It offers a powerful API for working with asynchronous sequences of data.

Let's start by defining a simple event class in Java:

```
public class Event {
    private final String type;
    private final String payload;

    public Event(String type, String payload) {
        this.type = type;
        this.payload = payload;
    }

    public String getType() {
        return type;
    }

    public String getPayload() {
        return payload;
    }
}
```

In this example, Event consists of a type and a payload, where type is a string representing the kind of event, and payload contains the event data.

Using Project Reactor, we can define a simple event handler functionally. Event publishers can emit events into a Flux, and subscribers can respond to these events:

```
import reactor.core.publisher.Flux;
import reactor.core.publisher.Sinks;

import java.util.function.Consumer;

public class EventDrivenSystem {
    private final Sinks.Many<Event> sink = Sinks.many().multicast().
        onBackpressureBuffer();

    public void publish(Event event) {
        sink.tryEmitNext(event);
    }

    public Flux<Event> getEvents() {
        return sink.asFlux();
    }

    public void subscribe(Consumer<Event> consumer) {
        getEvents().subscribe(consumer);
    }
```

```
    public static void main(String[] args) {
        EventDrivenSystem system = new EventDrivenSystem();

        // Adding a subscriber
        system.subscribe(event -> System.out.println("Received event: " + event.
            getType() + " with payload: " + event.getPayload()));

        // Publishing an event
        system.publish(new Event("exampleEvent", "payloadData"));
    }
}
```

In this implementation: - Sinks.Many is used to create a multicast sink capable of buffering events. - The publish method emits events to the sink. - The getEvents method returns a Flux stream to which subscribers can listen. - The subscribe method accepts a Consumer<Event> and subscribes it to the events stream. - In main, we instantiate the event-driven system, add a subscriber that prints received events, and publish an example event.

When this code is run, the output will be:

```
Received event: exampleEvent with payload: payloadData
```

This pattern scales well with the complexity of event-driven systems. Each component can be encapsulated into more sophisticated modules, and event handlers can incorporate complex event-processing logic, including filtering, transforming, and reacting to events based on sophisticated business rules.

For instance, filtering events based on their type can be seamlessly managed by using the rich operators available in the Reactor library:

```
system.getEvents()
    .filter(event -> "specificType".equals(event.getType()))
    .subscribe(event -> System.out.println("Processing specific type event with
        payload: " + event.getPayload()));
```

This filter operation ensures that only events of type "specificType" are processed by the subscribed consumer, providing a flexible mechanism to enact fine-grained control over event handling.

Additionally, one might want to aggregate event data over time, apply backpressure strategies, or combine multiple event sources. Reactor's Flux API supports a plethora of operations to this end:

```
system.getEvents()
    .window(Duration.ofSeconds(10))
    .flatMap(window -> window.collectList())
    .subscribe(events -> System.out.println("Collected events within 10 seconds: " +
        events.size()));

Flux<Event> anotherEventSource = Flux.just(new Event("otherType", "otherPayload"
```

```
    ));

Flux.merge(system.getEvents(), anotherEventSource)
    .subscribe(event -> System.out.println("Received event from merged sources: " +
        event.getPayload()));
```

Here, the window operation groups events into batches based on time intervals (e.g., every 10 seconds), and collectList accumulates events in these windows into lists. The merge operation combines event streams from multiple sources, allowing the system to react to a diverse array of events.

The combined use of these functional programming techniques in an event-driven architecture empowers developers to build extensible, maintainable, and scalable systems adept at handling dynamic and asynchronous workflows, providing significant advantages in reactive system design and implementation.

10.6 Data Validation and Sanitization

Data validation and sanitization are crucial steps in ensuring the integrity and security of applications. Functional programming in Java provides powerful tools to streamline these processes by leveraging the expressive nature of functional constructs. The principles of immutability, higher-order functions, and function composition afford a robust mechanism to validate and sanitize data efficiently.

Validators are functions designed to check whether a piece of data meets certain criteria. Sanitizers, on the other hand, transform the data into a standardized or safe format. In functional programming, these operations can be elegantly represented as pure functions—functions that do not cause side effects and always produce the same output for the same set of inputs.

To implement data validation, we can employ higher-order functions that take validation rules (predicates) as parameters. These predicates can then be applied to the data to confirm its validity.

Consider a simple example where we need to validate whether a string is a valid email address. We can define an email validator function as follows:

```
import java.util.function.Predicate;
import java.util.regex.Pattern;

public class Validator {
```

```
    private static final Pattern emailPattern = Pattern.compile(
        "^[a-zA-Z0-9._%+-]+@[a-zA-Z0-9.-]+\\.[a-zA-Z]{2,6}$");

    public static Predicate<String> isEmailValid() {
        return email -> emailPattern.matcher(email).matches();
    }
}
```

The isEmailValid method returns a Predicate<String> that checks if an input string matches the specified email pattern. Using the Validator class, we can validate email addresses within our application.

```
public class Application {
    public static void main(String[] args) {
        String email = "user@example.com";
        boolean isValid = Validator.isEmailValid().test(email);
        System.out.println("Is email valid? " + isValid);
    }
}
```

```
Is email valid? true
```

Functional composition allows combining multiple validators into a single compound validator. For instance, if the requirement is to validate both the format and the domain of the email, we can compose these two predicates:

```
public class CompositeValidator {
    public static Predicate<String> isEmailDomainValid() {
        return email -> email.endsWith("@example.com");
    }

    public static Predicate<String> isCompositeEmailValid() {
        return Validator.isEmailValid().and(isEmailDomainValid());
    }
}
```

```
public class CompositeApp {
    public static void main(String[] args) {
        String email = "user@example.com";
        boolean isValid = CompositeValidator.isCompositeEmailValid().test(email);
        System.out.println("Is composite email valid? " + isValid);
    }
}
```

```
Is composite email valid? true
```

Sanitizers can be implemented as unary functions that take an input and return a sanitized output. A common use case is trimming whitespace from user inputs.

```
import java.util.function.Function;

public class Sanitizer {
    public static Function<String, String> trimWhitespace() {
```

```
        return input -> input == null ? null : input.trim();
    }
}
```

The trimWhitespace sanitizer removes leading and trailing white spaces from the input string:

```
public class SanitizeApp {
    public static void main(String[] args) {
        String input = " user@example.com ";
        String sanitizedInput = Sanitizer.trimWhitespace().apply(input);
        System.out.println("Sanitized Input: \"" + sanitizedInput + "\"");
    }
}
```

```
Sanitized Input: "user@example.com"
```

Combining validation and sanitization into a single pipeline increases the reliability and readability of your code. By chaining these operations, you ensure that data is validated and sanitized in a sequential and predictable manner.

```
public class Pipeline {
    public static void main(String[] args) {
        String input = " user@example.com ";

        boolean isValid = CompositeValidator.isCompositeEmailValid()
            .and(email -> email.equals(Sanitizer.trimWhitespace().apply(email)))
            .test(input.trim());

        System.out.println("Is input valid after sanitization? " + isValid);
    }
}
```

```
Is input valid after sanitization? true
```

By utilizing higher-order functions and functional composition, functional programming in Java supports robust, maintainable, and efficient data validation and sanitation processes.

10.7 Configuration Management

Configuration management involves the maintenance and administration of configurations across software systems, ensuring that each system behaves as intended under varying conditions. In functional programming, Java's approach to configuration management can be streamlined by leveraging immutable data structures, higher-order functions, and declarative expressions. This section explores the functional techniques and tools available in Java to manage configurations efficiently.

Configurations are typically read from external files such as properties files, YAML, JSON, or XML. The handling of these files within a functional paradigm enhances readability and maintainability, allowing for easier versioning and testing.

java.util.Properties is a commonly used class for handling configurations within Java. The following example demonstrates reading from a properties file using a functional approach. Assume a properties file named config.properties with the content:

```
app.name=FunctionalJavaApp
app.version=1.0.0
app.debug=true
```

The following functional code reads the properties from this file:

```java
import java.io.IOException;
import java.io.InputStream;
import java.util.Properties;
import java.util.function.Function;
import java.util.function.Supplier;

public class ConfigManager {

    public static Properties loadProperties(String fileName) {
        Properties properties = new Properties();
        try (InputStream input = ConfigManager.class.getClassLoader().
                getResourceAsStream(fileName)) {
            if (input == null) {
                throw new IOException("Unable to find " + fileName);
            }
            properties.load(input);
        } catch (IOException ex) {
            ex.printStackTrace();
        }
        return properties;
    }

    public static <T> T getProperty(String key, Function<String, T> converter,
          Properties properties) {
        return converter.apply(properties.getProperty(key));
    }

    public static void main(String[] args) {
        Properties properties = loadProperties("config.properties");

        // Using functional interfaces to convert property types
        String appName = getProperty("app.name", Function.identity(), properties);
        String appVersion = getProperty("app.version", Function.identity(), properties);
        Boolean appDebug = getProperty("app.debug", Boolean::parseBoolean,
                properties);

        System.out.println("App Name: " + appName);
        System.out.println("App Version: " + appVersion);
        System.out.println("App Debug: " + appDebug);
    }
}
```

In this code, loadProperties is a method that reads and loads properties from a file. The getProperty method is a generic function that converts property values to the desired type using higher-order functions. This approach allows for reuse without converting each property individually.

Using JSON for configuration is also common, particularly in environments where configurations are more complex. Java libraries such as Jackson or Gson facilitate JSON parsing in a functional style. Consider the following JSON configuration file, config.json:

```
{
  "app": {
    "name": "FunctionalJavaApp",
    "version": "1.0.0",
    "debug": true
  }
}
```

The following Java code demonstrates loading and parsing JSON configuration using the Jackson library:

```
import com.fasterxml.jackson.databind.JsonNode;
import com.fasterxml.jackson.databind.ObjectMapper;

import java.io.IOException;
import java.io.InputStream;
import java.util.function.Function;

public class JsonConfigManager {

    public static JsonNode loadJsonConfig(String fileName) {
        ObjectMapper mapper = new ObjectMapper();
        JsonNode jsonNode = null;
        try (InputStream input = JsonConfigManager.class.getClassLoader().
                getResourceAsStream(fileName)) {
            if (input == null) {
                throw new IOException("Unable to find " + fileName);
            }
            jsonNode = mapper.readTree(input);
        } catch (IOException ex) {
            ex.printStackTrace();
        }
        return jsonNode;
    }

    public static <T> T getJsonProperty(JsonNode node, Function<JsonNode, T>
            converter) {
        return converter.apply(node);
    }

    public static void main(String[] args) {
        JsonNode config = loadJsonConfig("config.json");

        // Using functional interfaces to convert JSON properties
        String appName = getJsonProperty(config.path("app").path("name"), JsonNode
                ::asText);
        String appVersion = getJsonProperty(config.path("app").path("version"),
                JsonNode::asText);
        Boolean appDebug = getJsonProperty(config.path("app").path("debug"),
```

```
            JsonNode::asBoolean);

        System.out.println("App Name: " + appName);
        System.out.println("App Version: " + appVersion);
        System.out.println("App Debug: " + appDebug);
    }
}
```

This example leverages Jackson for JSON parsing. The loadJsonConfig method reads and parses the JSON file, while getJsonProperty uses a higher-order function to convert the JsonNode properties to the desired types. Such implementations can enhance the configuration management process by maintaining immutability and simplicity in handling diverse data sources.

Functional programming also encourages declarative configuration management, which can be achieved using libraries like Lightbend Config (Typesafe Config). This library supports HOCON (Human-Optimized Config Object Notation) and provides an immutable, thread-safe model for configurations.

Consider a HOCON configuration file, application.conf:

```
app {
  name = "FunctionalJavaApp"
  version = "1.0.0"
  debug = true
}
```

Loading this configuration using Typesafe Config:

```
import com.typesafe.config.Config;
import com.typesafe.config.ConfigFactory;

import java.util.function.Function;

public class HoconConfigManager {

    public static Config loadConfig(String fileName) {
        return ConfigFactory.load(fileName);
    }

    public static <T> T getConfigProperty(Config config, String path, Function<
            Config, T> converter) {
        return converter.apply(config.getConfig(path));
    }

    public static void main(String[] args) {
        Config config = loadConfig("application");

        // Using functional interfaces to convert HOCON properties
        String appName = config.getString("app.name");
        String appVersion = config.getString("app.version");
        Boolean appDebug = config.getBoolean("app.debug");

        System.out.println("App Name: " + appName);
        System.out.println("App Version: " + appVersion);
```

```
        System.out.println("App Debug: " + appDebug);
    }
}
```

By using the Typesafe Config library, configurations are more structured and declarative. The functional approach to reading and processing configurations ensures consistency and predictability in application behavior.

This section highlights the importance of functional techniques in managing configurations in Java. Leveraging immutability, higher-order functions, and declarative data structures can simplify configuration management, making the system more robust and easier to maintain.

10.8 Querying Collections with Functional Techniques

Functional programming provides powerful techniques for manipulating and querying collections of data in a concise, expressive, and productive manner. In Java, the java.util.stream package provides a natural way to apply functional programming principles to collections. This section explores various functional techniques for querying collections, illustrating these concepts with practical examples.

Basic Stream Operations

At the core of functional programming in Java are streams. Streams allow for in-memory operations over collections with a fluent and flexible API. The primary stream operations fall into three categories: intermediate operations, terminal operations, and short-circuiting operations.

Intermediate operations process elements of a stream and return another stream. Common intermediate operations include map, filter, and flatMap. Terminal operations mark the end of a stream's processing and produce a result or side-effect such as collect, forEach, and reduce. Short-circuiting operations are a subset of terminal operations that may terminate stream processing early, such as findFirst, findAny, anyMatch, and allMatch.

An initial example demonstrates a simple query using streams:

```
// List of integers
List<Integer> numbers = Arrays.asList(1, 2, 3, 4, 5, 6, 7, 8, 9, 10);
```

```
// Filter and collect even numbers
List<Integer> evenNumbers = numbers.stream()
    .filter(n -> n % 2 == 0)
    .collect(Collectors.toList());

System.out.println(evenNumbers);
```

The output is:

```
[2, 4, 6, 8, 10]
```

Here, the filter method is used to retain only even numbers, and the collect method gathers the results into a list.

Mapping and Reducing Collections

The map operation transforms each element of a collection. For example, you can apply a function to square each number in a list:

```
// Square each number in the list
List<Integer> squaredNumbers = numbers.stream()
    .map(n -> n * n)
    .collect(Collectors.toList());

System.out.println(squaredNumbers);
```

Output:

```
[1, 4, 9, 16, 25, 36, 49, 64, 81, 100]
```

A more complex operation can combine map and reduce. The reduce method performs a reduction on the elements of the stream to produce a single result, such as summing all elements.

```
// Sum of squares of even numbers
int sumOfSquaresEven = numbers.stream()
    .filter(n -> n % 2 == 0)
    .map(n -> n * n)
    .reduce(0, Integer::sum);

System.out.println(sumOfSquaresEven);
```

Output:

```
220
```

Here, the stream is first filtered for even numbers, then each number is squared, and finally, reduce sums the squares.

Advanced Functional Queries

For more complex queries, intermediate operations can be chained. Consider employees with attributes like name, role, and salary. To find the average salary of developers, you can chain multiple operations:

```
// Employee class
class Employee {
    String name;
    String role;
    double salary;

    Employee(String name, String role, double salary) {
        this.name = name;
        this.role = role;
        this.salary = salary;
    }

    public String getRole() {
        return role;
    }

    public double getSalary() {
        return salary;
    }
}

// List of employees
List<Employee> employees = Arrays.asList(
    new Employee("Alice", "Developer", 100000),
    new Employee("Bob", "Developer", 110000),
    new Employee("Charlie", "Manager", 120000)
);

// Average salary of developers
double averageSalary = employees.stream()
    .filter(e -> e.getRole().equals("Developer"))
    .mapToDouble(Employee::getSalary)
    .average()
    .orElse(0);

System.out.println(averageSalary);
```

Output:

```
105000.0
```

This query filters for employees with the role Developer, maps to their salaries, and computes the average salary, using mapToDouble and average.

Grouping and Partitioning

Grouping elements in a collection based on a classifier function is a common need. The Collectors.groupingBy method can be used to group data. For instance, grouping employees by role:

```
Map<String, List<Employee>> employeesByRole = employees.stream()
    .collect(Collectors.groupingBy(Employee::getRole));

System.out.println(employeesByRole);
```

Output:

```
{Developer=[Employee@1, Employee@2], Manager=[Employee@3]}
```

Partitioning is a special case of grouping, where the partitioning function returns a boolean. This divides elements into two groups:

```
Map<Boolean, List<Employee>> partitionedBySalary = employees.stream()
    .collect(Collectors.partitioningBy(e -> e.getSalary() > 105000));

System.out.println(partitionedBySalary);
```

Output:

```
{false=[Employee@1], true=[Employee@2, Employee@3]}
```

Grouping and partitioning can be further combined with other collectors for complex operations, such as counting:

```
Map<String, Long> countByRole = employees.stream()
    .collect(Collectors.groupingBy(Employee::getRole, Collectors.counting()));
System.out.println(countByRole);
```

Output:

```
{Developer=2, Manager=1}
```

This collects the number of employees for each role by pairing groupingBy with counting.

Concurrent Processing

Streams can be processed in parallel to leverage multi-core processors for performance gains using the parallelStream method or stream.parallel() construct. This switches the stream into a parallel mode:

```
// Parallel processing example
List<Integer> largeList = IntStream.rangeClosed(1, 1000000)
    .boxed()
    .collect(Collectors.toList());

long count = largeList.parallelStream()
    .filter(n -> n % 2 == 0)
    .count();
```

```
System.out.println(count);
```

Output:

```
500000
```

This example demonstrates parallel filtering and counting over a large list, employing all available processors.

Functional techniques for querying collections not only offer concise and direct methods for manipulating large data sets but also improve readability and maintainability of the code. The power of these functional operations lies in their composability, enabling complex queries through a chain of simple transformations.

10.9 Web Services and REST APIs

Web services and REST APIs (Representational State Transfer Application Programming Interfaces) are foundational to modern distributed systems. They enable communication and data exchange between different services and applications. Leveraging functional programming techniques in Java for these services can lead to more readable, maintainable, and efficient code.

Functional programming emphasizes immutability and side-effect-free functions, fitting naturally into the stateless nature of RESTful services. We'll explore how to build web services and REST APIs using functional programming principles in Java.

First, consider a foundational example of a simple REST API using functional programming constructs with the popular Java library, Spring Boot.

```
import org.springframework.boot.SpringApplication;
import org.springframework.boot.autoconfigure.SpringBootApplication;
import org.springframework.web.bind.annotation.GetMapping;
import org.springframework.web.bind.annotation.RequestParam;
import org.springframework.web.bind.annotation.RestController;

@SpringBootApplication
public class WebServiceApplication {

    public static void main(String[] args) {
        SpringApplication.run(WebServiceApplication.class, args);
    }
}

@RestController
```

```
class GreetingController {

    @GetMapping("/greeting")
    public Greeting greet(@RequestParam(value = "name", defaultValue = "World")
            String name) {
        return new Greeting(String.format("Hello, %s!", name));
    }
}

class Greeting {
    private final String message;

    public Greeting(String message) {
        this.message = message;
    }

    public String getMessage() {
        return message;
    }
}
```

The above code sets up a basic RESTful web service with a single endpoint, '/greeting'. This endpoint is mapped to the GreetingController class's greet method. The method uses functional programming principles:

- **Immutability**: The Greeting class is immutable; once an instance is created, its state cannot change.
- **Pure Function**: The greet method produces the same output given the same input, without side effects.

Next, let's consider a more complex example involving data transformation and error handling—a common necessity in web services.

```
import org.springframework.web.bind.annotation.ExceptionHandler;
import org.springframework.http.ResponseEntity;

@RestController
class UserController {

    private final UserService userService;

    public UserController(UserService userService) {
        this.userService = userService;
    }

    @GetMapping("/user")
    public ResponseEntity<UserDTO> getUser(@RequestParam("id") String id) {
        return userService.getUser(id)
            .map(user -> ResponseEntity.ok(new UserDTO(user)))
            .orElseGet(() -> ResponseEntity.notFound().build());
    }

    @ExceptionHandler(IllegalArgumentException.class)
```

```
    public ResponseEntity<String> handleIllegalArgumentException(
            IllegalArgumentException e) {
        return ResponseEntity.badRequest().body(e.getMessage());
    }
}

class UserDTO {
    private final String id;
    private final String name;

    public UserDTO(User user) {
        this.id = user.getId();
        this.name = user.getName();
    }

    // Getters omitted for brevity
}

@Service
class UserService {

    private final Map<String, User> userRepository = Map.of(
        "1", new User("1", "Alice"),
        "2", new User("2", "Bob")
    );

    public Optional<User> getUser(String id) {
        return Optional.ofNullable(userRepository.get(id));
    }
}

class User {
    private final String id;
    private final String name;

    public User(String id, String name) {
        this.id = id;
        this.name = name;
    }

    public String getId() {
        return id;
    }

    public String getName() {
        return name;
    }
}
```

This code introduces several functional programming and API concepts:

- **Optional**: The getUser method in UserService returns an Optional<User>, a functional approach to handle the possibility of missing values.
- **Map and OrElseGet**: The getUser method in UserController uses Optional's map to transform a User to a UserDTO and orElseGet

to handle the case where the user is not found.

- **Exception Handler**: The handleIllegalArgumentException method demonstrates a clean and functional way of dealing with exceptions, mapping exceptions to appropriate HTTP responses.

Another functional aspect of building REST APIs involves stream processing—powerful for handling large datasets efficiently.

```
@RestController
class ProductController {

    private final ProductService productService;

    public ProductController(ProductService productService) {
        this.productService = productService;
    }

    @GetMapping("/products")
    public ResponseEntity<List<ProductDTO>> getProducts(@RequestParam("
        category") Optional<String> category) {
        List<ProductDTO> products = productService.getProducts()
            .stream()
            .filter(product -> category.map(c -> product.getCategory().equals(c)).orElse
                (true))
            .map(ProductDTO::new)
            .collect(Collectors.toList());
        return ResponseEntity.ok(products);
    }
}

@Service
class ProductService {

    private final List<Product> productRepository = List.of(
        new Product("1", "Laptop", "Electronics"),
        new Product("2", "Shirt", "Apparel")
    );

    public List<Product> getProducts() {
        return productRepository;
    }
}

class Product {
    private final String id;
    private final String name;
    private final String category;

    public Product(String id, String name, String category) {
        this.id = id;
        this.name = name;
        this.category = category;
    }

    public String getId() {
        return id;
    }
```

```
    public String getName() {
        return name;
    }

    public String getCategory() {
        return category;
    }
}

class ProductDTO {
    private final String id;
    private final String name;

    public ProductDTO(Product product) {
        this.id = product.getId();
        this.name = product.getName();
    }

    // Getters omitted for brevity
}
```

This example showcases the following functional programming techniques:

- **Streams API**: Java Streams API allows for functional-style operations on collections of objects. In this case, filtering and mapping the list of products.
- **Lambda Expressions**: Used extensively within the stream pipeline to filter and map products.
- **Optional Parameters**: The category parameter is wrapped in an Optional, demonstrating a functional approach to handle optional query parameters.

Functional programming in Java enhances the development of RESTful APIs by promoting immutability, reducing side effects, and providing expressive and declarative constructs for handling data. This approach improves code maintainability, readability, and robustness, making it a valuable paradigm for modern API development.

10.10 Handling JSON and XML Functional Style

Handling JSON and XML data is a fundamental aspect of modern application development, given its ubiquity in web services, configuration files, and data interchange formats. Leveraging functional programming techniques in Java can streamline these processes, making the code more concise, expressive, and easier to maintain. This section will delve into manipulating JSON and XML using functional constructs, showcasing the benefits through practical examples.

To parse and transform JSON and XML in a functional style, we will utilize popular libraries like Jackson for JSON and JAXB for XML, combined with Java's functional programming features such as Streams, Optional, and lambda expressions.

```
import com.fasterxml.jackson.databind.JsonNode;
import com.fasterxml.jackson.databind.ObjectMapper;
import javax.xml.bind.JAXBContext;
import javax.xml.bind.JAXBException;
import javax.xml.bind.Unmarshaller;
import java.io.StringReader;
import java.util.Optional;
import java.util.stream.Stream;
```

We begin by defining some JSON and XML data structures and corresponding parsing functions.

```
class Person {
    private String name;
    private int age;

    // Getters and setters
    public String getName() { return name; }
    public void setName(String name) { this.name = name; }

    public int getAge() { return age; }
    public void setAge(int age) { this.age = age; }
}
```

Parsing JSON

To parse JSON data, we will use the Jackson library. Jackson's ObjectMapper class can read JSON into a tree model that consists of JsonNode objects.

```
ObjectMapper objectMapper = new ObjectMapper();
String jsonString = "{\"name\":\"John Doe\",\"age\":30}";
JsonNode jsonNode = objectMapper.readTree(jsonString);
```

Once we have the JsonNode, extracting and transforming data using functional constructs becomes straightforward.

```
Optional<String> name = Optional.ofNullable(jsonNode.get("name"))
    .map(JsonNode::asText);

Optional<Integer> age = Optional.ofNullable(jsonNode.get("age"))
    .map(JsonNode::asInt);
```

```
name.ifPresent(n -> System.out.println("Name: " + n));
age.ifPresent(a -> System.out.println("Age: " + a));
```

Using the Optional class helps handle the presence or absence of fields gracefully, avoiding null checks.

Transforming JSON

Functional transformations can be achieved using the Stream API. Suppose we have a list of JSON strings representing persons, and we want to transform them into a list of Person objects.

```
List<String> jsonStrings = Arrays.asList(
    "{\"name\":\"John Doe\",\"age\":30}",
    "{\"name\":\"Jane Smith\",\"age\":25}"
);

List<Person> persons = jsonStrings.stream()
    .map(json -> {
        try {
            JsonNode node = objectMapper.readTree(json);
            Person person = new Person();
            person.setName(node.get("name").asText());
            person.setAge(node.get("age").asInt());
            return person;
        } catch (IOException e) {
            throw new UncheckedIOException(e);
        }
    }).collect(Collectors.toList());

persons.forEach(p -> System.out.println("Person: " + p.getName() + ", Age: " + p.
    getAge()));
```

Utilizing streams simplifies the transformation and aggregation of JSON data, preserving readability and reducing boilerplate code.

Parsing XML

For XML, we use JAXB. JAXB (Java Architecture for XML Binding) allows mapping Java objects to XML representations.

```
String xmlString = "<person><name>John Doe</name><age>30</age></person>
    ";

JAXBContext jaxbContext = JAXBContext.newInstance(Person.class);
Unmarshaller unmarshaller = jaxbContext.createUnmarshaller();
StringReader reader = new StringReader(xmlString);
Person person = (Person) unmarshaller.unmarshal(reader);
```

The unmarshalling process converts the XML string into a Person object.

Transforming XML

Like JSON, we can use streams for transforming XML data. Assume we have a list of XML strings representing persons.

```
List<String> xmlStrings = Arrays.asList(
    "<person><name>John Doe</name><age>30</age></person>",
    "<person><name>Jane Smith</name><age>25</age></person>"
);

List<Person> persons = xmlStrings.stream()
    .map(xml -> {
        try {
            StringReader reader = new StringReader(xml);
            return (Person) unmarshaller.unmarshal(reader);
        } catch (JAXBException e) {
            throw new RuntimeException(e);
        }
    }).collect(Collectors.toList());

persons.forEach(p -> System.out.println("Person: " + p.getName() + ", Age: " + p.
    getAge()));
```

Functional programming techniques combined with powerful libraries like Jackson and JAXB enable efficient parsing and transformation of JSON and XML data. By applying lambdas and streams, we can create pipelines that are both expressive and concise, minimizing side effects and enhancing code maintainability.

10.11 Case Studies and Real-World Examples

Functional programming in Java offers numerous advantages, including easier reasoning about code, implicit parallelism, and stateless computation. To solidify your understanding, this section presents case studies and real-world examples that exemplify these benefits. We will explore practical scenarios in which functional programming has been effectively applied, showcasing its utility and efficiency in solving complex problems.

Case Study 1: Simplifying Data Processing Pipelines

One of the most compelling real-world applications of functional programming in Java is in the creation of data processing pipelines. In traditional imperative programming, managing sequences of data transformations can become convoluted, with state management and control flow intermingling. Functional programming decouples these concerns by focusing on transformations and data flow.

Consider a scenario where we need to process a list of customer transactions to generate a report of customers who have made high-value purchases. Using functional programming constructs like Stream, filter, map, and collect, we can achieve this concisely and readably.

```
// Define a Transaction class
class Transaction {
    private String customerId;
    private double amount;

    // constructors, getters, and setters omitted for brevity
}

// Define a Customer class
class Customer {
    private String id;
    private String name;

    // constructors, getters, and setters omitted for brevity
}

// Sample data
List<Transaction> transactions = Arrays.asList(
    new Transaction("C001", 1500.0),
    new Transaction("C002", 2300.0),
    new Transaction("C001", 1200.0),
    new Transaction("C003", 500.0)
);

List<Customer> customers = Arrays.asList(
    new Customer("C001", "John Doe"),
    new Customer("C002", "Jane Smith"),
    new Customer("C003", "Alice Johnson")
);

// Pipeline to process transactions and generate a report of high-value customers
List<String> highValueCustomers = transactions.stream()
    .filter(transaction -> transaction.getAmount() > 1000)
    .map(Transaction::getCustomerId)
    .distinct()
    .map(customerId -> customers.stream()
            .filter(customer -> customer.getId().equals(customerId))
            .findFirst()
            .orElseThrow(() -> new IllegalArgumentException("Customer Not Found"))
            .getName())
    .collect(Collectors.toList());

System.out.println(highValueCustomers);
```

Executing this code produces the following output:

```
[John Doe, Jane Smith]
```

This example demonstrates how functional programming facilitates creating a clear and intuitive data processing pipeline. The use of Stream operations allows us to abstract and simplify the data transformation process.

Case Study 2: Event-Driven Systems

Event-driven architecture (EDA) benefits immensely from functional programming. EDA often involves handling a series of events, where each event may trigger various actions. Implementing an event handler using functional programming can lead to more maintainable and scalable code.

Consider an example where we manage a system that processes orders. Each time an order is placed, we need to perform several actions, such as updating inventory, notifying the shipping department, and logging the order.

```
// Define Event and Order classes
class Event<T> {
    private String type;
    private T payload;

    // constructors, getters, and setters omitted for brevity
}

class Order {
    private String orderId;

    // constructors, getters, and setters omitted for brevity
}

// Sample event handlers
Consumer<Order> updateInventory = order -> {
    System.out.println("Inventory updated for order: " + order.getOrderId());
};

Consumer<Order> notifyShipping = order -> {
    System.out.println("Shipping notified for order: " + order.getOrderId());
};

Consumer<Order> logOrder = order -> {
    System.out.println("Order logged: " + order.getOrderId());
};

// Sample event
Event<Order> orderPlacedEvent = new Event<>("ORDER_PLACED", new Order("
    O123"));

// Event processing
List<Consumer<Order>> orderEventHandlers = Arrays.asList(updateInventory,
    notifyShipping, logOrder);
orderEventHandlers.forEach(handler -> handler.accept(orderPlacedEvent.getPayload())
    );
```

Executing this code produces the following output:

```
Inventory updated for order: O123
Shipping notified for order: O123
Order logged: O123
```

The use of Consumer<Order> interfaces and lambda expressions allows us to handle events in a clean and flexible manner. Each event handler is a separate functional unit, promoting code reusability and testability.

Case Study 3: Data Validation and Sanitization

Data validation and sanitization are critical in any application that processes user input. Functional programming can simplify these tasks by creating composable validators that transform and check inputs in a declarative style.

Consider an example where we need to validate and sanitize user registration data. We will use a series of functional validators to ensure the input meets certain criteria, such as a valid email format and a non-empty name.

```
import java.util.function.Function;

class User {
    private String name;
    private String email;

    // constructors, getters, and setters omitted for brevity
}

// Custom validator utility
class Validator<T> {
    private final Function<T, Boolean> validation;

    public Validator(Function<T, Boolean> validation) {
        this.validation = validation;
    }

    public boolean validate(T t) {
        return validation.apply(t);
    }

    public Validator<T> and(Validator<T> other) {
        return new Validator<>(t -> this.validate(t) && other.validate(t));
    }
}

// Validation functions
Function<User, Boolean> emailValidator = user -> user.getEmail().contains("@");
Function<User, Boolean> nameValidator = user -> !user.getName().isEmpty();

Validator<User> userValidator = new Validator<>(emailValidator).and(new Validator
    <>(nameValidator));

// Sample user
User user = new User("John Doe", "john.doe@example.com");
boolean isValid = userValidator.validate(user);

System.out.println("User valid: " + isValid);
```

Executing this code produces the following output:

```
User valid: true
```

This example demonstrates the power of functional programming in creating modular and reusable validation logic. The Validator class and the use of Function<T, Boolean> interfaces enable us to chain multiple validation criteria effortlessly.

Functional programming's ability to compose code, handle events declaratively, and create clear data processing pipelines exemplify its significance in real-world scenarios. The provided case studies underscore how functional programming can streamline complex tasks in Java applications.

Made in the USA
Monee, IL
05 November 2026

67911520R00177